Theology from Exile
Volume II

The Year of Matthew

COMMENTARY ON THE
REVISED COMMON LECTIONARY
FOR AN EMERGING CHRISTIANITY

Sea Raven, D.Min.

Cover design by Jinjer Stanton.
http://jinjerstanton.com/wp/design-services/

ISBN-13:
978-1491077320

Table of Contents

ABOUT THE AUTHOR

Sea Raven, D.Min., is an Associate of the Westar Institute (home of the Jesus Seminar), and a Worship Associate and member of the Unitarian Universalist Congregation of Frederick, Maryland. Her work as a freelance writer, musician, and worship leader is grounded in postmodern Christian scholarship, and focused on justice, peace, and the integrity of creation. Since 1992, Sea Raven has taught the concept of natural, creation-centered or earth-based ritual in worship services and life celebrations in various church settings, including retreats, pulpit supply, and religious education. Sea Raven's doctoral project, *The Wheel of the Year: A Worship Book for Creation Spirituality,* provides worship experiences that spring from pre-Christian Celtic spirituality, postmodern cosmology, and the theology and four-path principles of Creation Spirituality as developed by Rev. Dr. Matthew Fox. The project is published on her website along with a weekly blog (http://gaiarising.org).

ACKNOWLEDGMENTS

Thanks to the continuing awesome team: Jinjer Stanton, graphic artist extraordinaire; George Crossman, for initial editing and challenging theological questions; and Carol B. Singer for eagle-eyed copyediting. None of this would have even begun without the inspiration of Rev. Dr. Matthew Fox, and the scholars of the Jesus Seminar.

Introduction to Volume I
The Year of Luke

This book is the first in a series of commentaries on biblical scripture that follows the three-year cycle of Christian liturgical readings found in the *Revised Common Lectionary[1]* (RCL). Appendix One contains reimagined rituals of Holy Communion that reflect an invitation to commit to a new partnership with a non-theistic, "kenotic God"[2] in the ongoing salvation work of non-violent, distributive, justice-compassion. Appendix Two is a Bible study for Holy Week that explores in depth the meaning of *kenosis*. This project is grounded in the paradigm-shifting biblical scholarship of Karen Armstrong, Marcus J. Borg, John Dominic Crossan, Robert Funk, and Amy-Jill Levine, as well as the transformative work of Rev. Dr. Matthew Fox, whose theology of Creation Spirituality has reclaimed Catholic mysticism for post-modern cosmology.

Four Questions for the Apocalypse

The underlying framework for the commentaries is a series of four questions.

1)   What is the nature of God? Violent or nonviolent?
2)   What is the nature of Jesus's message? Inclusive or exclusive?
3)   What is faith? Literal belief, or trust in God's realm of distributive justice-compassion?
4)   What is deliverance? Salvation from hell or liberation from injustice?

These questions address what might be seen as apocalyptic times for humanity on Planet Earth. The twenty-first century – much like the first century – finds human social structures

---

[1] *Consultation on Common Texts, Revised Common Lectionary*, Nashville: Abingdon Press, 1992.

[2] Crossan and Reed, *In Search of Paul*, 288ff.

embroiled in political, social, spiritual, and theological issues that demand serious consideration of the answers to these questions. Unlike the first century, twenty-first century humanity is also confronted with the distinct possibility of a holocaust that is not confined to individuals, tribes, or nations, but threatens the very existence of planetary life as humanity has known it for 100,000 years.

Two possible choices arise from the answers to these four questions.

If the answers are: violent, exclusive, literal belief, and salvation from hell, then the context for personal, social, and political life is Empire, and the theology of Empire: piety, war, victory, peace.[3] "Empire" is normally defined in political and historical terms such as the Roman Empire, or the Persian Empire. John Dominic Crossan has developed the concept of Empire as a cultural framework – even a theology – that includes religious unity (piety); war (that defends or expands political power); victory (ensuring future security); and peace (the rule of imperial law and cultural hegemony). Further, Crossan suggests that Empire may be the inevitable outcome of normal human attempts at social organization (the "normalcy of civilization"). However, Crossan is quite clear that the "normalcy of civilization" is not due to human nature – hence the possibility (and continuing hope) for choosing different answers to the four questions proposed.

If the answers to the four questions are: nonviolent, inclusive, trust, and liberation, then the context for personal, social, and political life is participation in the ongoing work – the struggle – for distributive justice-compassion, in Covenant. *Distributive justice-compassion* is here defined as radical fairness, which is in direct opposition to the *retributive* "justice" of normal social systems. Instead of payback and revenge, distributive justice-compassion offers grace and radical fairness. The Covenant to participate in establishing such a paradigm is with a non-theistic, kenotic god, a force which – in John Dominic Crossan's words – "is the beating heart of the Universe, whose presence is justice and

---

[3]Ibid.

life, and whose absence is injustice and death."[4] The Covenant then reflects the inclusive peaceable kingdom described by the Old Testament prophets, in which "they will not hurt or destroy in all my holy mountain."[5]

Christianity has been in danger of diverting into false paths from the beginning. One of those false paths, which is all too easily found in John's Gospel, opposes Christian "enlightenment" to the "darkness" of Jewish tradition. Another is the path that leads to collaboration with political Empire. The Four Horsemen of the Apocalypse – War, Famine, Disease, and Death – galloping down the ages out of the Revelation of John – have brought humanity to the brink of extinction in the twenty-first century. We continue to terrorize ourselves with their seeming inevitability. Whether or not that metaphor is the one that prevails depends upon how humanity (not just Christians) ultimately answers the questions. The choice in these commentaries is clear.

John Shelby Spong has called for a profound change in the practice of Christianity that can carry us both back to its roots, and forward into a new Christianity relevant to life in the third millennium:

> I see in this moment of Christian history a new vocation . . . to legitimize the questions, the probings, and, in whatever form, the faith of the *believer in exile*. . . . [A] conversation and a dialogue must be opened with those who cannot any longer give their assent to those premodern theological concepts that continue to mark the life of our increasingly irrelevant ecclesiastical institution. . . . [T]he time has come for the Church to invite its people into a frightening journey into the mystery of God and to stop proclaiming that somehow the truth of God is still bound by either our literal scriptures or our literal creeds.[6]

This series, "Theology from Exile," applies Spong's concept to anyone who cannot accept orthodox Christian belief systems, yet is drawn to the social justice mandate found in such collections

---

[4]Ibid., 291.

[5]Isaiah 11:9a

[6]Spong, *Why Christianity Must Change*, 21.

of Jesus's teachings as the Sermon on the Mount. The commentaries are intended to address the "so what" question, implied by the continuing, ground-breaking work of the Westar Institute's Jesus Seminar scholars and others who are concerned with the role of Christianity, and religion in general, in the twenty-first century. Now that we have some sense of what the historical Jesus (a first-century Galilean Jew speaking to other Jews) actually said, taught, and did, so what? What does our Christian scriptural tradition mean now? Can we rely on the canon? What does this knowledge do to (or for) Christian liturgy – specifically, such defining rituals as Baptism and Holy Communion?

In his book, *Jesus: Uncovering the Life, Teachings, and Relevance of a Religious Revolutionary,* Marcus J. Borg contrasts doctrinal Christianity with an "emerging paradigm" that has been "the dominant understanding in divinity schools and seminaries of mainline churches" for most of the twentieth century. The problem is, that "emerging paradigm" has largely remained behind closed seminary classroom doors, and has not made it into the minds of the people occupying the pews in church on Sunday morning. These commentaries and accompanying liturgies are intended to provide courage to clergy and enlightenment to lay leadership in the sometimes "frightening journey" described by Spong, to integrate personal spirituality with twenty-first century cosmological realities. This series is a contribution to that dialogue for clergy, and a catalyst for progressive, lay-led Bible study groups.

Many of these commentaries contain a shorthand term that illustrates the frustration of worship leaders when confronted with the seeming unrelatedness of the liturgical readings proposed by the RCL. A clergy friend (now retired) describes the cherry-picking among the various portions of scripture as having been put together by "drunken elves." The RCL provides its own clues as to how and/or why certain passages from the Old Testament are paired with certain passages from the New. The most recent version (1992) certainly is its own testimony to the hard work of coming up with a three-year cycle of "common texts" that Catholics and mainline Protestants can use throughout the

Christian liturgical year of Sundays, Holy Days, Feast Days, and Seasons.

But as these commentaries point out, all too often the Old Testament readings are snipped out of context in order to support Christian messianic claims. This process functions to the detriment of Jewish wisdom, and it thereby robs Christianity of a rich source for understanding the message of Jesus himself. Worse, such selectivity legitimizes Christian hegemony, supersessionism, and ultimately antisemitism. While "the Elves" may seem to be subject to quite a bit of abuse here, no individual disrespect is intended. In addition, it is by no means an insult to the nobility of the Elven Race (as described by J.R.R. Tolkien) who long ago abandoned Middle Earth to its fate – a caution to those who use proof-texting to justify compliance with Empire.

Introduction to Volume II
The Year of Matthew

The answers to the four questions for the apocalypse introduced in The Year of Luke continue to frame the difference between the normalcy of civilization and its retributive systems of control, and participation in the ongoing program of restoring God's distributive justice-compassion, as taught by Jesus:

1) What is the nature of God? Violent or nonviolent?
2) What is the nature of Jesus's message? Inclusive or exclusive?
3) What is faith? Literal belief, or commitment to the great work of justice-compassion?
4) What is deliverance? Salvation from hell, or liberation from injustice?

The answers for the authoritarian right (Empire) are: violent, exclusive, literal belief, and salvation from hell in the next life. The answers for the countering partnership on the left (Covenant) are nonviolent, inclusive, commitment to the great work, and liberation from injustice in this life, here and now. These answers provide guideposts to the authentic teachings of Jesus, and to a faith that might swing the balance to sustainable, conscious life on Planet Earth.

The context for the above four questions is the postmodern era of the late twentieth and early twenty-first centuries. Generally, historians speak about time in terms of premodern, modern, and postmodern. Premodern refers to the time before the Enlightenment and Descartes. The modern era (post-Enlightenment) lasted for about 350 years. During that time, God was a separate being or entity who created the universe, and proclaimed humanity to be the fulfillment of God's creativity. The "postmodern" era might be argued to have actually begun with Charles Darwin. But regardless of the timing, "postmodern" means the time in which humanity began and continues to deal with the nature of the universe as science has described it. "God" as a separate being who intervenes in human life from "heaven" somewhere beyond Antares no longer makes intellectual sense.

This leads to another term that has migrated from postmodern science into postmodern spiritual and religious language. In common usage, "cosmology" means the science or theory of the universe. But the term as used by Rev. Dr. Matthew Fox in his ground-breaking theology of original blessing[7] goes beyond the scientific. Cosmology for Fox means humanity's intellectual understanding of the nature of the universe. "Cosmology," as Fox (and this writer, among others) uses the term, describes the mind-set of premodern, modern, and postmodern people, as each of these evolutions of human thought has understood our place in and our relationship to the universe and to God. If, as John Shelby Spong argues, Christianity is to have any relevance at all to postmodern spirituality, changes in focus and metaphor must be made.

As these essays have developed beginning with Year C, a slight modification to the third question has emerged: What is faith? Literal belief, or trust and commitment to the great work of justice-compassion? The postmodern meaning of faith is usually belief, regardless of the circumstances. The more basic meaning is trust – either in a person's (or God's) word, or actions, or in a process set in motion by a god, a prophet, or a leader. The Apostle Paul's letters make little or no sense to postmodern minds unless the distinction between faith as literal belief and faith as trust is clear. Further, as literal belief becomes untenable in the third millennium of the Common Era, Christian "faith" is increasingly confronted with John Shelby Spong's challenge to change or die. To the extent that Christian "faith" continues to mean "literal belief," the twenty-first century is a "post-Christian" era.

In addition to the four questions, a second theme that continues to determine these interpretations of the lectionary readings is the meaning of justice. Civilization defines justice as retribution – payback; an eye for an eye. But the deeper meaning of justice is distributive: the rain falls on the good, the bad, and the ugly without partiality. Civilization does not use that definition

---

[7]See, e.g., Fox, *Original Blessing*; *The Coming of the Cosmic Christ*.

except in cases where there is clearly injustice if partiality enters the picture. The classic example is that in the United States in the first quarter of the twenty-first century, if you are rich, white, and male your chances of serving jail time for possessing cocaine is an order of magnitude less than if you are poor, black, and female, charged with possessing marijuana. Occasionally there is a reversal of this pattern, as when an over-zealous North Carolina prosecutor trumped up a case of gang rape of a black stripper against a championship team of white lacrosse players. In either case, distributive justice is at work – although in a negative sense.

The positive understanding of distributive justice is contained in the term distributive justice-compassion. The normal development of civilizations has historically led to systems for assuring safety and security of citizens. But as any reader of Charles Dickens must be aware, those systems often exclude the poor, the uneducated, those who are presumed to have no economic or social power (women, minorities). Members of societies who are denied access to those powers often become ensnared in activities deemed anti-social or criminal in order to survive. Distributive justice-compassion would not demand payback or retribution for such activities, but would provide solutions: reeducation, rehabilitation, redress of grievances. Distributive justice-compassion holds sway in the Covenant relationship with the non-violent, inclusive, *kenotic* realm or kingdom of God. Justice as retribution/payback holds sway in the normal march of humanity into civilization. The short-hand term for the seemingly inevitable systems of injustice that are the result of that march is "Empire."

The Apostle Paul was convinced that Jesus's resurrection was the resurrection of a spiritual, mystical body, which was automatically part of the kingdom of God – and that we who are living today can also participate in that kingdom if we choose God's nonviolent distributive justice instead of the violent imperial theology of piety, war, victory. In God's kingdom of distributive justice, no one is judged by circumstance, but everyone is presumed to be transformed – or at least capable of transformation. The classic Biblical example is Luke's story of the Prodigal Son (Luke 15:1–32). Like it or not, the prodigal son's brother learned there is no place in his father's house for payback, for getting even, for locking people up and throwing away the key, for the death penalty. In God's realm of distributive justice the assumption is rehabilitation and hope; in God's realm of distributive justice the assumption is that everyone has access to power and the assurance of food, clothing, shelter, medical care, and peace regardless of who they are or where they come from. Paul writes in his second letter to the Corinthians that "there is a new creation: everything old has passed away; see, everything has become new!" John Dominic Crossan suggests "What better deserves the title of a new creation than the abnormalcy of a share-world replacing the normalcy of a greed-world?"[8] Because the coming of God's justice is ongoing – for upwards of two thousand years now – we are called to participate in a new creation– a new paradigm – a world based on letting go, and sharing (distributive justice-compassion), rather than keeping and greed.[9]

Third, in this series of commentaries "God" is understood as non-theistic and "kenotic."[10] *Kenosis* classically means "emptiness." As a Christian term it has been defined as in Philippians 2:6-7: "[A]lthough [the Anointed One] was born in the image of God, [he] did not regard 'being like God' as something to use for his own advantage, but rid himself of such vain pretension and accepted a servant's lot. . . . [H]e was born like all human beings. . . ."[11] In John Dominic Crossan's words, a *kenotic* god is "the beating heart of the Universe, whose presence is justice and life, and whose absence is injustice and death."[12] Here, kenosis includes the desire of a relational spirit for an exiled people to live in justice-compassion. The kenotic servant listens and continues to teach reconciliation with that spirit and distributive justice among the people. In these commentaries, kenotic "god" becomes

---

[8]Crossan and Reed, 176.

[9]*See* "Spring and the New Moon: Change the Paradigm V Fourth Sunday in Lent," Raven, 72.

[10]For a thorough exploration of the meaning of *kenosis* in the context of Holy Week, *see* Raven, Appendix Two.

[11]Dewey et al., 186.

[12]Crossan and Reed, 288-291.

interchangeable with kenotic "servant," as the creative force that both contains and is contained by the universe. In answer to the four questions, the nature of that force is nonviolent; Jesus's message is inclusive, faith is trust in an inclusive, non-violent universe, and deliverance is liberation from injustice. The context for human personal, social, and political life then becomes a Covenant with justice and life, and commitment to the ongoing struggle for liberation from injustice.

Finally, too much of Christian fundamentalism has become United States domestic and foreign policy. We can't counter it if we don't know what the facts are. While much of the history of the creation of the New Testament may be "old hat" to graduates of liberal Christian seminaries, lay folk must know something of the scholarship that is doing its best to lead Christianity out of the clutches of fundamentalism. Twentieth and twenty-first century scholarship agrees on at least the following two points about the writing of the Gospels in the Christian Bible. First, the Gospels were not written by the disciples of Jesus. They were not even written by people who knew Jesus. They were written down by people who knew the oral tradition about Jesus, and who also may well have had access to the letters written by the Apostle Paul to the non-Jewish Christian communities he founded outside Jerusalem around the Mediterranean Sea. Second, all of the Gospels were written after the Romans had sacked Jerusalem and had destroyed the Temple (66-70 C.E.). The Jewish people were in diaspora – essentially exiled, seemingly forever, from any political organization called "Israel." The first Gospel was Mark, written in about the year 65-70, a good thirty to forty years after the death of Jesus and ten or so years after the death of Paul. The Gospel of Matthew was written around the year 80 to 90; Luke was written around the year 90 to 95, and John, which is an entirely different kind of writing, was written after the first century had passed – possibly as late as 100 to 125 of our Common Era. Further, recent scholarship has raised the probability that Acts – written by the creator of the Gospel of Luke – was contemporaneous with the Gospel of John, early in the second century.[13]

The continued existence of a Christian "faith" as a religious system of belief is clearly under siege by twenty-first century Biblical scholarship as well as the continuing evolution of scientific knowledge. The question addressed by this series of commentaries is whether and how ancestral scriptures remain relevant and revelatory to twenty-first century cosmology.

---

[13]Levine and Brettler, 197.

Advent and Christmas

Guess Who's Coming Again
First Sunday in Advent

Isaiah 2:1-5: Psalm 122; Romans 13:11-14; Matthew 24:36-44

The first Sunday in Advent begins the Christian liturgical year, and the *Revised Common Lectionary* (RCL) starts again with Year A. The readings for the season are heavy with portent and hope, but these especially hint at the second coming of the Christ, and apocalypse. For literalists, the portion read from Matthew foretells the Rapture at the end of time. For Bible historians, these verses really belong toward the end of the story of Jesus's life. From the point of view of some scholars, apocalypticism was not part of Jesus's world view.[14] He rejected the apocalyptic ministry of John the Baptist early on, and never said or thought anything like Matthew (or Luke – both based on Mark) suggests.

If the purpose of liturgy is to celebrate the foundation myths of a people, it makes sense for the Christian liturgical year to begin with Advent – the Coming of the Messiah. We may well look into our Jewish heritage and reconnect with powerful metaphors that call for a return to a true homeland and to the restoration of God's distributive justice-compassion. Instead, Christianity got trapped into a kind of permanent state of alienation when the original community that knew Jesus died, and the major interpreter of the meaning of Jesus's life and teachings – Paul – and his followers and the members of the early Christian communities he founded also died, without seeing that restoration. The idea of a second coming and a final judgment at the end of time took hold, especially when the writer of Mark's Gospel saw the sacking of Jerusalem, the destruction of the Temple, and the disintegration of Jewish national identity. Clearly, God had no intention of acting to restore anything. But that kind of despair is not conducive to sustainable human life, and so Matthew borrowed from Mark

---

[14]*See* Robert J. Miller, ed., *The Apocalyptic Jesus – A Debate.*

13:33-36. "Keep awake," says Matthew's Jesus, " . . . for you do not know on what day your Lord is coming. . . . Blessed is that slave whom his master will find at work when he arrives"(Matthew 24:42-46). Spiritual leaders, searching for some hope to cling to, moved Matthew's words from the time leading up to Jesus's betrayal and death to the time leading up to Jesus's birth, and the prophesied intervention of God into human affairs. After a couple thousand years, Matthew's admonition became a pious maxim supporting a puritanical emphasis on morality, and the promise of reward for the chosen believers after the personal Armageddon of individual death, or the final Armageddon at the end of time.

The Psalm and Isaiah are all about foretelling, foreshadowing, getting ready for God to act, for the savior of the world to be born. Despite all our twenty-first century sophistication, postmodern humanity still projects salvation onto an interventionist, judgmental, parent-god. The bad news is, Jesus is dead – seriously dead. Perhaps that is the reason for revisiting Mark's Little Apocalypse in Matthew's retelling. The good news, as Paul reminds us, is that restoring God's realm of distributive justice-compassion – the life-supporting balance of the known universe – is up to us.

The portion of Paul's Letter to the Romans that is selected for this first Advent Sunday should be backed up to include verses 8-10: "Owe no one anything, except to love one another . . . love is the fulfilling of the law." What better time for postmodern Christians to recommit to partnership in the great work of restoring distributive justice-compassion? " . . . .[N]ow is the moment for you to wake from sleep," Paul writes. Now is indeed the time for changing consciousness, for transforming human society. Beat swords into plowshares, and spears into pruning hooks, as Isaiah says: "[N]ation shall not lift up sword against nation, neither shall they learn war any more."

We can "pray for the peace of Jerusalem" along with the Psalmist, but what is required to truly fulfill the law is to act with justice-compassion in radical abandonment of self-interest. Leaving our enemies out of the game while declaring victory assures the continuation of Empire, not the restoration of

Covenant. Suppose that instead of terrorizing ourselves with the Advent of violent judgment, we were to see this time leading up to the celebration of Jesus's birth as a celebration of the Advent of the Christ consciousness; instead of a Eucharist mourning the personal holocaust of Jesus's death, a Eucharist of Ordination, in which we recommit ourselves to the great work of distributive justice-compassion? Jesus is not coming again. We are.

Eucharist of Ordination Liturgy

Invitation to Participate in the Kingdom Community
Celebrant There is a story in the Gospel of Mark, Chapter 14, about when Jesus was at Bethany in the house of Simon the leper. As he sat at table, a woman came with an alabaster jar of very costly ointment of nard, and she broke open the jar and poured the ointment on his head. Jesus said, "Truly, I tell you, wherever the good news is proclaimed in the whole world, what she has done will be told in remembrance of her." And what was it that she did? Knowing she would probably not have the chance to do so if Jesus were executed by the Romans – which was highly likely – she anointed his body in advance for burial. So I invite us – in remembrance of her – to anoint one another as a symbol of our commitment to do what we can to live in a community of nonviolent justice-compassion, knowing that the struggle never ends.
     [Start the oil among the people]

Invitation to the Meal
Celebrant In Paul's first letter to the community in Corinth, he scolds them for falling out of the practice of justice-compassion, and getting side-tracked by the normalcy of injustice. He reminds the people that he received from the Lord what he also handed on to them. Jesus, on the night when he was betrayed by those who were trapped in the very same forces of injustice that affected the Corinthians, and all of us, took a loaf of

bread, and when he had given thanks, he broke it and said, "This is my body broken for you. Do this in remembrance of me." Participation in God's distributive justice means a radical denial of our own self-interest. As we share this bread, we share ourselves and make no distinction between them and us.

[Start the bread among the people]

Celebrant   Then Paul says, "In the same way he took the cup also, after supper, saying 'This cup is the new covenant written in my blood. Do this as often as you drink it, in remembrance of me.'" Again, in case we didn't get it when he broke the bread, Paul's Jesus says, the new Covenant – the new partnership with one another in God's Kingdom – is written in blood.

[Pour the wine and juice]

Celebrant   Whenever we eat this bread and share this cup, we proclaim our participation in God's ongoing, continuing work of justice-compassion until it is accomplished.

[Start the wine and juice among the people]

Thanksgiving

All   ***Eternal spirit of life,*** The gratitude from which the Eucharist derives its very name is not just our gratitude toward the Source of all things; it is also the gratitude of the universe for our presence and for our efforts at contributing, however imperfectly. The Eucharist is also our hearts expanding and responding generously: "Yes, we will." We will carry on the heart-work called compassion, the work of the cosmos itself.[15]

---

[15]Fox, *Sins of the Spirit,* 271.

The Dawning of the Age
Second Sunday in Advent

Isaiah 11:1-10; Psalm 72:1-7, 18-19; Romans 15:4-13;
Matthew 3:1-12

Suppose that the most obvious way for the evolutionary forces of the universe to assure the balance of power between human consciousness and the rest of the life forms on Planet Earth is to develop a psychology so prone to violence that it will kill itself off, with no need to be subject to any other predator. Whenever civilization reaches a level of erudition where the arts and priorities of the spirit are paramount, some barbarian horde comes sweeping across the desert or over the ocean or down the mountain or through the forest, valuing only what is essential to animal survival: land, females, and food. At the same time, humans seem to be genetically programmed to blame themselves for every adversity. Given these conditions, the archetypes of apocalyptic holocaust, interventionist tribal gods, and the savior king make ultimate psychological sense.

But consciousness evolves just as life forms do. Very early on, humans realized that the curse could be lifted, the prophesy could be confounded, if radically creative action was taken. The most recent rising of that kind of consciousness in the West brought cultural concepts such as "the dawning of the Age of Aquarius" borrowed from astrology, and the idea of "critical mass" borrowed from physics. These point us away from personal, interior concepts of intervening gods and heroes to aligning our energies with the powers that arise from postmodern understandings of the nature of the universe, leading beyond mere survival to flourishing abundance.

A brief digression for those who scoff at the "New Age": Some of that metaphor comes from the observation that the solar system of which Earth is a part travels its own path around the edge of the Milky Way Galaxy. Over vast amounts of time – ten thousand years or more – the star patterns seen from the Planet change. One theory about the cause of the rise of patriarchy is that the star patterns that governed the best times for planting and harvesting had gotten out of kilter with the prevailing seasonal and weather conditions on earth, and the women who had read those patterns lost credibility. This has nothing to do with superstitions about whether the stars predict destiny, and everything to do with an inability on the part of ancient leaders (women or men) to realize that the planetary position had changed relative to the stars, and that other conditions should be considered. A similar problem resulted in calendar changes in the West from Julian to Gregorian. The current rate of climate change has had this same effect on those tribal people who still rely on the old ways. Because the stars in the sky no longer correspond with expected weather patterns, people don't know what to do. In the twenty-first century, our solar system has traveled far enough around the Milky Way to begin to bring us out of the star patterns in the Zodiac that comprise Pisces, and into Aquarius. Because the Age of Pisces brought the Axial Age that produced the great religious and spiritual ideas ranging from the Tao to Buddhism in the East and monotheistic Judaism and early Christianity in the West, people who see patterns in human spiritual development are finding hope for a "second axial age" as the star patterns of Aquarius begin to fill the horizon.

The problem with the readings in the RCL for this Second Sunday in Advent is that they are stuck in the muck of personal blame, shame, and guilt for the human condition, and look – in vain – for a savior hero to roar in on Santa Ana winds and burn with unquenchable fire the useless and evil chaff winnowed out of the whole grain on the threshing floor. Isaiah looks for a descendent of the great King David to restore the political power and might of ancient Israel. The Psalm is a coronation anthem, calling down the tribal god's spirit of justice on the ordained ruler. In the cherry-picked portion of the letter to his community in Rome, Paul calls for everyone to live in harmony, because the Christ who brought God's truth to the Jews did it in order to also "rule the Gentiles," as foretold by the prophets.

Clearly, Paul was not above a little cherry-picked proof-texting himself. But Paul was not writing after the cataclysmic sacking of Jerusalem and the destruction of the Temple in 70 C.E. Paul was not writing after the political settlement of theological debate by the Council of Nicea, convened by the Emperor Constantine in the fourth century. Paul was not writing after three millennia of Christian dogma had appropriated the agricultural metaphors of Celtic Europe into a liturgical year whose purpose is to convince the people of their unpardonable original sin, and – in the spirit of every barbarian horde since the beginning of human time – to control the most intimate and important aspect of human survival after food: women and sexual behavior.

The precursor to the metaphor of "critical mass" that leads to cataclysmic transformation at the atomic and sub-atomic levels may be Victor Hugo's pronouncement in the nineteenth century that "nothing is so powerful as an idea whose time has come." The work of the Westar Institute's Jesus Seminar, and specific scholars such as Karen Armstrong, Marcus J. Borg, John Dominic Crossan, Matthew Fox, and John Shelby Spong, may be the pivotal work that launches such an idea in the twenty-first century. Bishop Spong has said that Christianity must change or die. Hopefully that death will not mean the death by fundamentalist terrorists – from whatever religion – of the current experiment in self-consciousness launched some one hundred thousand years ago by the known universe. Karen Armstrong has constructed a history of God in the West that includes all three religions of the Book, while Borg, Crossan, and others have done the historical research that is beginning to remove the veils of premodern misunderstanding of who Jesus was, where he came from, and what his message meant. Matthew Fox, in alignment with visionary mystics such as Thomas Berry, Brian Swimme, and Starhawk (among others), works to create the foundational myths that can inform and shape spiritual life in a postmodern cosmology that speaks to all exiles from premodern religions. With such enormous enlightened minds engaged in such an endeavor, how can "progressive" Christianity continue to insist on teaching and preaching traditional orthodoxy?

It is patently unfair to the unfailing commitment of the Apostle Paul to the great work of restoring God's realm of justice-compassion through his interpretation of Jesus's life, ministry, and death, to continue to solidify Christian dogma by cherry-picking and proof-texting Paul's authentic letters to the communities he founded in Rome, Corinth, Galatia, Philippi, Thessalonika (the first letter), and to Philemon, the leader of one of those communities. Letters attributed to Paul that are clearly not Paul require some careful homework before they are incorporated as definitive guidelines for postmodern Christianity. If Christian worship leaders are going to preach on passages from Paul's letters (authentic or not), that should be done in the context of the entire letter and the political and social conditions of the first century, and how those principles that Paul spells out apply to Christian (and other) corporate and secular life in the twenty-first century – if they do. The same admonition applies to the rest of the canon, and perhaps most strongly to the books of the ancient Hebrew prophets.

So what do we do with the voice crying in the wilderness: "Change your ways, because God's realm of distributive justice-compassion is closer than you think!! Prepare the way of the Lord! Make that path straight!" Use it, not to terrify and condemn, but to ignite the flame – the fire in the belly – that inspires Covenant, nonviolence, distributive justice, and peace – which was the intent of the liturgist who wrote Matthew's Gospel in the flickering light of torched Jerusalem. Then review all of Paul's Letter to the Romans, and remind readers and listeners that nothing can separate us from the love of God as Jesus experienced it and taught it. Nothing. The Covenant is there. All we have to do is choose to participate. Then perhaps the legacy of that "shoot from the stump of Jesse" might be realized: "They will not hurt or destroy on all my holy mountain; for the earth will be full of the knowledge of the Lord as the waters cover the sea."

The Emperor's Soft Clothes
Third Sunday in Advent

Isaiah 35:1-10; Psalm 146:5-10; Luke 1:47-55; James 5:7-10; Matthew 11:2-11; Thomas 78.

The third Sunday in Advent is full of familiar themes: John the Baptist, acknowledged by Jesus himself as the messenger who prepares the way for the coming of the Messiah; Mary's *Magnificat*, put into exquisite musical format by C.P.E. Bach: "My soul does magnify the Lord for he has done great things for me" – chosen to be the Mother of the Messiah; Isaiah promises, "Here is your God. He will come with vengeance, with terrible recompense, He will come and save you. Then the eyes of the blind shall be opened, and the ears of the deaf unstopped . . . "; and James reminds us to "be patient, . . . for the coming of the Lord is near. . . . See, the Judge is standing at the doors!" Here is the entire Christian belief system laid out at once: The Old Testament prophecies are fulfilled; the blind see, the lame walk, lepers are cleansed, the deaf hear, the dead are raised, and the poor have good news; Mary, the blessed Virgin mother; the judgment of God against those who do not believe in Jesus, and the judgment of Jesus himself against those who "grumble against one another."

Only one item is missing from the list: distributive justice. There is plenty of *retributive* justice – judgment – found in Isaiah and hinted at in James's letter to the church in Jerusalem. But *distributive* justice – the kind that Jesus was talking about, which has nothing to do with payback and everything to do with radical abandonment of self-interest – is easily missed. Perhaps it is there, behind the "good news" preached to the poor; perhaps it is more evident in Mary's song of praise: " . . . he has filled the hungry with good things, and sent the rich away empty." "Justice" is assumed to be automatic once Jesus has arrived on the scene. All we have to do – according to James's letter – is to have patience and stop grumbling.

Matthew's Jesus is already well advanced in his ministry by the time Chapter 11 rolls around. John has sent him a message, demanding to know if he is "the One," or " . . . are we to wait for another?" Jesus tells John's disciples to go and tell John what they have seen and heard, as evidence, and says further that those who don't take offense at his (Jesus's) teaching are to be congratulated. Maybe Jesus was thanking John and his disciples for taking him seriously. After they leave, according to Matthew's story, Jesus turns to the watching crowd and says, in effect, "What did you come out here into the boonies to see? Somebody with no conviction? Some rich bigot slumming?" In Matthew's story, Jesus is talking about John the Baptist. But in the sayings Gospel of Thomas, the same words appear with no context: "Why have you come out to the countryside? To see a reed shaken by the wind? And to see a person dressed in soft clothes [like your] rulers and your powerful ones?" Jesus may be talking about himself, challenging the people who came out to see him, not John. If you came out expecting a pious show, forget it.

In Isaiah 35, the exiles – redeemed – return to Zion. They are redeemed because they return to the ways of the Lord. And what are those ways? Psalm 146 spells them out: "Do not put your trust in princes, in mortals, in whom there is no help . . . . Happy are those whose help is the God of Jacob, who keeps faith forever, who executes justice for the oppressed, who gives food to the hungry. . . . The Lord . . . upholds the orphan and the widow, but the way of the wicked he brings to ruin." That's distributive justice. Mary also sings about distributive justice: "He has put the arrogant to rout along with their private schemes; he has pulled the mighty down from their thrones and exalted the lowly; he has filled the hungry with good things, and sent the rich away empty. . . . "[16] Jesus challenges people who come out into the countryside expecting to see the usual rulers and collaborators with injustice, who wear soft "rich" clothing. Neither Jesus nor the Messiah foretold of old fit that expectation.

The favorite theme of the prophets, and especially those who wrote from Babylonian exile (Jeremiah and the writer of portions

---

[16]Miller, *The Complete Gospels*, 127 (Scholars Version). New Testament quotations use this translation unless stated otherwise.

of the Book of Isaiah), is reconciliation with the Hebrew God by returning to a way of life that restores God's justice. God metes out *retributive* justice to anyone who does not participate in the *distributive* justice required in order to survive and thrive in God's community. In other words, if you don't take care of the poor, and protect the "widow and orphan" – read, unmarried women and fatherless children – God will get you. But if you do, then "A highway shall be there, and it shall be called the Holy Way; the unclean shall not travel on it, but it shall be for God's people; no traveler, not even fools, shall go astray."

Isaiah is metaphor, not to be taken literally. Using the metaphor of exile from God as illustrating those who ignore justice, who are the exiles today? Maybe the ones who are collaborating with Empire? What is "collaboration with Empire" today if not predatory bank and credit card practices that ensnare the poor and naive? What is "collaboration with Empire today" if not protecting corporate profits at all costs? Structuring a world economy so that poor nations are required to decimate their rain forests in order to feed their people? Forbidding free access to medical care? Disenfranchising women – who are more than half of the human population? These – and other injustices, economic, political, social, environmental – are an exile of the spirit into mind, ego-driven, power-mad, and unable to see that the Emperor's fine clothes and pious talk are an illusion. Political leaders in the U.S.[17] are so intimidated by the self-righteous posturing of the religious right that Congress has been unable to control the conduct of war, devise a sustainable energy policy, remedy the increasingly unfair federal tax code, protect the Constitutionally-mandated civil rights of the people, or quell the alarm among European allies raised by unilateral policies that ignore hard-won international customs respecting human rights and mutual cooperation.

The writer of James's letter and institutional Christian church leadership since the second century have missed the point. The Messiah's coming, or "return" is not about putting a stop to petty "grumbling" among privileged members of society over who pays

---

[17]Including a former president, who believed the interventionist, tribal God of ancient Israel put him in the White House.

the most taxes, or arguing about whether or not the Planet is in the midst of human-caused environmental disaster. These are the soft clothes and easy piety of Empire. The Messiah comes and the redeemed return when the exiles abandon self-interest and start working for distributive justice-compassion.

Light Beings
Fourth Sunday in Advent

Isaiah 7:10-16; Psalm 80:1-7, 17-19; Romans 1:1-7;
Matthew 1:18-25; Isaiah 52:7-10; Psalm 98; Hebrews 1:1-12;
John 1:1-14

The readings for this fourth Sunday in Advent for Year A simply present Matthew's version of Jesus's birth, backed up by the familiar prophecy from Isaiah, along with a prayer for deliverance, and the Apostle Paul's greeting to his community in Rome. The fourth Sunday and Christmas Eve allow plenty of opportunity to read both of the Gospel versions of the birth stories, and compare them – if desired. Sure enough, they don't agree – that's because the Gospel writers had different agendas for their stories. Matthew's agenda was to show that this Jesus was the long looked-for Messiah, who would bring deliverance to the oppressed and despairing people in occupied Palestine and sacked Jerusalem in the 60s to 70s, C.E. Luke's agenda, twenty years or so later, was to convince the communities in the diaspora that had made their peace with the Roman empire that Jesus was the embodiment of the mythical hero that would show them the way into the kingdom of heaven by righteous living – most especially caring for the poor. Arguing about whether any of the stories are literally true misses the point. At Christmas, there is hope for deliverance and opportunity for repentance. So listen to the stories, sing the carols, exchange the gifts – but don't check your mind at the church door. Palestine is still occupied, Jerusalem is divided, and Christianity is almost completely aligned with Empire – ecclesiastical and secular.

There are three sets of "Propers" and four other sets of readings to choose from during the twelve days between Christmas Eve and Epiphany. The creators of the RCL direct that "If Proper III is not used on Christmas Day, it should be used at some service during the Christmas cycle because of the significance of John's prologue." Proper III it is.

John's prologue is significant on many levels. First (in terms of the development of Christian dogma) it is important because it is a hymn to the mysterious presence from the beginning of God's "word," or "wisdom," conventionally interpreted to be the Christ. Second, John's mystical language defies literal interpretation. Even if belief goes so far as to insist that Jesus physically existed somewhere in the "sky" from the beginning of time along with the proverbial Grandfather Almighty, John still confounds even the least developed imagination with metaphor: "In him was life; and the life was the light of men. And the light shineth in darkness; and the darkness comprehended it not" (John 1:4-5, KJV). Third, for postmodern, post-theistic minds, John's prologue is poetry that speaks to the mystic and spiritual realms of human understanding, even when those realms are informed by the more esoteric discoveries of postmodern physics. Here is the translation developed by the scholars of the Westar Institute's Jesus Seminar:

In the beginning there was the divine word and wisdom. The divine word and wisdom was there with God, and it was what God was. It was there with God from the beginning. Everything came to be by means of it; nothing that exists came to be without its agency. In it was life, and this life was the light of humanity. Light was shining in darkness, and darkness did not master it.[18]

The "divine word and wisdom" combines masculine logos with feminine mythos – personified in the Greek pantheon by the Goddess Sophia. Wisdom then segues into Life and Light. After nearly two hundred years of the study of physics, the nature of light, and the origins of the universe, John's metaphor continues to resonate. We now know that the universe is made up of light, and that we ourselves are also made up of that same light.[19] We

---

[18]Funk, et al., 401

[19]Editor's Note: (for physicists for whom the light metaphor is problematic). We are, in fact, made of little "fuzz balls" of energy which, under certain conditions, emit radiation. When that radiation falls within the proper range of the radiation spectrum, it will appear as visible light. Otherwise it is not really "light" but X-rays, or cosmic rays, or electrons, or protons, or a dozen other kinds of wave/particles. We are made of the same material as light, but we are not "made of light" – GC.

cannot survive without it. "Being" the light is not something we can opt into or out of, so "believing" in the light is about as useful as "believing" in air. John claims that the darkness did not master this genuine light, because Jesus rose from the dead, and will come again. Yet despite John's certainty, humanity continues to live in darkness: continues to deny that human rights are the foundation for human security; continues to insist that security resides in the suspension of disbelief in an interventionist god, or the reliance on raw, secular, imperial militarism masquerading as that god.

After the prologue, John begins to tell his version of the story of Jesus:

> There appeared a man sent from God named John. He came to testify – to testify to the light – so everyone would believe through him. He was not the light; he came only to attest to the light.

So that no one (hopefully) will misunderstand, the writer explains what he means by "the light": "Genuine light – the kind that provides light for everyone – was coming into the world." Appropriating John's metaphor to postmodern mythological experience, if we embrace Jesus as the bringer of spiritual light to the world and we take into ourselves Jesus's radical, nonviolent abandonment of self-interest (love), then we also become bringers of the light. We also participate as word and wisdom in the realm of distributive justice-compassion.

Forget the talk of "victory" in Psalm 98, and the triumphalism of the sermon found in Hebrews 1:1-12. Genuine light, says John, provides light for everyone. No room here for "my Messiah is higher than your angels" (Hebrews 1:3b-4). We continue to ignore the fact that like the rest of the beings in the universe, we are light beings. If we realize that we are made of light, how can we continue to deny the light that flames in the very DNA of all earthly beings whether animal or plant? Jesus was not the only light being who taught justice-compassion as the way. But of course, anyone who has lived into adulthood on Planet Earth knows that you can lead a horse to water, but you can't make him drink.

> Although [the light] was in the world, and the world
> came about through its agency, the world did not
> recognize it. It came to its own place, but its own people
> were not receptive to it.

In the midst of a universe made of light are black holes in the
center of collapsing galaxies with energies so great that light
cannot escape. Fear is the black hole in human spirituality that
swallows up trust. It is born of belief in a capricious,
interventionist god, and evil is the result.

> But to all who did embrace [the light], to those who
> believed in it, it gave the right to become children of
> God. They were not born from sexual union, not from
> physical desire, and not from male willfulness; they were
> born of God.

John's theology might have been informed by the theology
developed forty to fifty years earlier by the Apostle Paul, but
John's Gospel has to be read with care. Taken literally and without
a sense of the context in which it was written, the fourth Gospel
has led to some of the worst excesses of Christian imperialism.
"Believing" in the light is not a prerequisite for becoming children
of God. As Paul argues in Romans 8, nothing can separate us from
the love of God – not powers nor principalities, nor heights nor
depths. A postmodern experience of a kenotic god, whose
presence is justice and life, but whose absence is injustice and
death,[20] leaves no opportunity for patriarchal "male willfulness" to
exclude anyone from the realm of distributive justice-compassion.

> The divine word and wisdom became human and made
> itself at home among us. We have seen its majesty,
> majesty appropriate to a Father's only son, brimming
> with generosity and truth.

The Jesus Seminar scholars' translation is inclusive of the
masculine logos (word) and feminine wisdom (Sophia), and so is
the interpretation of the Apostle Paul in 1 Corinthians 1:22-30,
who argues that Jesus the Christ is (for Christians) the Wisdom
(Sophia) from God, and in Galatians 3:28, "There is no longer Jew

---

[20]Crossan and Reed, 288.

or Greek, there is no longer slave or free, there is no longer male and female; for all of you are one in Christ Jesus."

It is no accident that the birth of the light has been celebrated from the beginning of human time during the darkest times of the year, from the winter solstice (December 21-22 in the Northern Hemisphere) through the first cross-quarter day six weeks later (Imbolc/Candlemas – February 2). In the darkness of mid-winter, in the black hole of human spiritual despair, it is easy to begin to feel as though the light has been extinguished, and there is no escape. But we have learned that the universe continues its unfinished story. God's Covenant with humanity remains: the Earth's poles tilt back toward the Sun as the Earth continues its eternal rounds; the Sun returns, and light is reborn. Even though we are made of light, the only way to experience being that light is to actively, consciously choose to live in the light. Then we can realize that we are not only partners in the Covenant, we are co-creators.

Heirs and Children of God
First Sunday after Christmas

Isaiah 63:7-9; Psalm 148; Matthew 2:13-23; Galatians 4:4-7;
Philippians 2:5-11; Matthew 2:13-23

The RCL actually suggests Hebrews 2:10-18 for this first Sunday after Christmas, but there are also two sets of readings for January 1. The choice depends on whether the church community wants to celebrate January 1 as honoring Mary, the Mother of God, or to observe New Year's Day. The choice may also depend on whether the readings offer a coherent message, and whether that coherent message speaks to the realities of postmodern life in the twenty-first century. The reading from the letter to the Hebrews is attributed to Paul but not actually written by him; so coherence may be more easily found in the passages from Galatians and Philippians, which are the authentic writings of Paul himself. The Galatians passage also appears in Romans 8:14-17, allowing for a triple dose of Paul.

Matthew's story about the escape to Egypt, the massacre of the infants, and the return to Nazareth is wonderful and familiar. None of this is historical fact, but that doesn't mean it isn't true. Story-tellers know that all stories are true, but the truth of a story is different from the truth of day-to-day happenings. A criminal investigation establishes precisely what happened, when, and where, but – as we all know – *why* something happened is seldom answered. On the other hand, a story or novel that simply records the mundane goings on of daily life is not only boring, it is meaningless – and there is the clue to how it is that all stories are true. They are true because they illustrate the meaning that lies beneath ordinary existence. So when Matthew tells his story about dramatic events that surrounded the birth and the early infancy of Jesus, he is not recording facts. No one knows exactly when or even precisely where Jesus was born. But that doesn't matter, because what Matthew – and Luke – were doing was showing the people in the first Christian communities what the birth of this

Jesus meant. Matthew shows how Jesus was the fulfillment of the prophecy – the promise to the people of Israel – that God would act in the world to restore God's realm of distributive justice-compassion.

Jesus was born during the *Roman* occupation of Palestine, under the rule of Caesar Augustus, somewhere between the years of 4 B.C.E. and 4 C.E. It was a time of repression, oppression, extreme poverty, and constant rebellion against Roman rule. The Jewish people had a long history of wars and occupations. Nevertheless, they believed that God is just, and the world belongs to God. So whenever they experienced injustice and political turmoil, they knew that God would act to restore God's justice to the world. Otherwise, God would not be God. Matthew's story shows that Jesus is the one sent by God to set things right. God has acted, through the life, teachings, death, and resurrection of Jesus.

In Paul's letters to the non-Jewish Christian communities he founded outside Jerusalem, all around the shores of the Mediterranean Sea, he says that God continues to act in the world when we use Jesus's example as a pattern for justice-compassion in our own lives. This makes us adopted by God as brothers and sisters of Jesus, and heirs to the kingdom of God. The problem lies in what it all means.

Paul's words have traditionally been interpreted to mean the supremacy, the hegemony, the over-lordship, the exclusivity of Jesus's message: "God . . . gave him the name that is above every name, so that at the name of Jesus every knee should bend, in heaven and on earth and under the earth, and every tongue should confess that Jesus Christ is Lord, to the glory of God the Father." These words have been used to justify the eradication of entire civilizations from the Asian Pacific Islands to North, Central, and South America.. These words were behind the Crusades of the fourteenth century, the heresy trials of the Inquisition, and today these words are the grounding for fundamentalist Christian Zionism, which has informed the foreign policy of more than one occupant of the White House. In the words of the late Jesus Seminar Scholar Robert Funk, the Spanish invaders came with a Bible in one hand and a gun in the other. "Convert or else!"

But that is not what Paul meant. Before he gets to that ecstatic declaration of who Jesus is – the counter to Empire in every time and place – Paul uses the most humiliating imagery he can think of to hammer away at the point that being a Christian does not mean we are lords and masters of all we can conquer in Jesus's name. Instead, Paul says, we are slaves. Slavery – human trafficking – possibly the worst crime against Divinity that humanity can devise – is the metaphor Paul uses to describe the powerlessness of true Christians who follow Jesus's Way. This is not an easy path to follow. It means giving up power as power is usually perceived: So forget about taking over the local neighborhood association so you can keep the immigrants out; forget about becoming the name partner in the biggest law firm in Washington, D.C. so you can represent the richest corporation on the Planet and have all the things that money can buy; forget about running for President of the United States. Slaves cannot do any of those things.

Power as it is usually defined by normal civilization is power over everything that is a challenge to human survival: power over the land and its natural resources, so that the harvest will be sufficient, and an economic basis can be assured; power over outsiders – enemies – so that the people can live in security; power over the everyday conduct of life within the civilization so that order can be maintained, and the civilization can grow and prosper.

Because of the inevitable structures that normal civilization creates to sustain itself, people who are not part of the mainstream become marginalized – single women with children, and others who do not fit the accepted description of family; people with physical or psychological abnormalities, orphans; people who for whatever reason are unable to participate in the usual ways that make an economic or social contribution. Such people are easy to oppress because they are denied access to the usual political and social and economic power that enables participation and success in normal society: health care, housing, education, nutritious food. This is especially true in societies where the distribution of wealth is confined to those who hold the power over health care, housing, education, nutritious food. Injustice becomes inevitable, as access to the basic necessities of life becomes dependent upon the ability to pay. Add in the normal human proclivity to insist upon payback and retribution instead of fair sharing, and injustice becomes the norm.

Christians believe that Jesus came to overthrow that kind of injustice. But that's not what Jesus did. Jesus was himself a victim of the injustice of normal civilization. He died at the hands of the oppressors. Thirty years after his death, the Romans sacked Jerusalem. Twenty years after the death of the Apostle Paul, disillusioned Christians began to believe that Jesus will come again to bring a violent end to all injustice, and establish his kingdom once and for all – we just don't know when that will happen, so we need to be ready. Most Christians today persist in that belief.

What's going on here? Is the Jesus story true or not?

Look at what Paul is saying in the passages from Philippians: " . . . though he was in the form of God, [Jesus] did not regard equality with God as something to be exploited, but emptied himself, taking the form of a slave, being born in human likeness. And being found in human form, he humbled himself and became obedient to the point of death. . . ." Jesus gave up all the usual forms of power instead of taking advantage of them or seizing them for himself. Surely he had plenty of opportunity to join the resistance – the Zealots – and others who carried out a constant guerilla war against the Roman occupation. Quite possibly, some of his followers were members of those groups. They are called "terrorists" today.

But Jesus did not do that. Jesus came up with a very different definition of power. "Look around you at the lilies in the field and the birds in the air," he said. "God takes care of them, doesn't he? Why wouldn't God take care of you?" When Jesus says "God," he is not talking about the Roman emperor or those who acted in the name of the emperor to control the power over the occupied people of Palestine. He is talking about the God of Abraham, Isaac, and Jacob, who owns the world. By doing that, by letting go of the usual expectations and definitions of power, Jesus became such a threat to the Roman empire that he had to be killed. And what was that threat? It was to say to the emperor that the emperor is not God. It was to advise that when the Roman soldier or his representative demanded that you carry his gear for a mile, carry it two miles – thereby forcing the Roman to break his own law. The threat to Empire lies in the subversion of law that happens when people refuse to act in their own self interest. When James Loney[21] and the Christian Peacemaker Teams refused to testify against their Iraqi captors, those people were set free – which effectively negated everything the United States government hoped to accomplish in Iraq. From the point of view of Empire, to refuse to testify lends aid and comfort to the enemy. But Jesus taught that we are to love our enemies. Loving our enemies is probably the most compelling illustration of the willing sacrifice of our own self-interest. When the people love their enemies, what happens to the need for imperial war? Jesus had to die. He was a greater threat to the normal course of civilization than the terrorists making raids on supply caravans making their way through the Judean hills.

This is all very romantic and dramatic. But the truth is, who wants to put their life in danger? Paul is not demanding that I put my life in danger. If we back up to the beginning of Chapter 2 of the Philippians reading, we find the secret: "If then there is any encouragement in Christ, any consolation from love, any sharing in the Spirit, any compassion and sympathy, make my joy complete: . . ." [in other words, Paul is saying "Please! Make my day!"] ". . . be of the same mind, having the same love, being in full accord and of one mind. Do nothing from selfish ambition or conceit, but in humility regard others as better than yourselves. Let each of you look not to your own interests, but to the interests of others."

When we do that, we inherit the legacy that Jesus left us: the kingdom of God – or in postmodern, non-theistic language, when we abandon self-interest, we step into the parallel universe where distributive justice-compassion rules, because if I do not demand retribution, but insist upon the kind of radical fairness that preserves the well-being of my enemy – if I allow my enemy to win – I give up even the justice that should rightfully to given to

---

[21]Loney, "118 Days."

me and I subvert the whole system. Paul spells this out in Romans 8:12-17. Paul's language is first century language. It is mystical language, and it is language that has been translated and re-translated, and interpreted through the lenses of people who read Paul's words and applied them to the developing theology of the organized Church. When Paul says, in verse 13, ". . . if you live according to the flesh you will die; but if by the Spirit you put to death the deeds of the body, you will live," he is not talking about sexual morality and going to hell if you shack up with your boyfriend for the weekend.

He is talking about living according to the normalcy of civilization, which demands retribution and payback, not justice-compassion. If I live in the demand and expectation of retribution and payback, I live in bondage to fear, and I am dead to the possibility of inclusive love. I am always afraid of what somebody is going to do to me in payback for what I did to them first. But, Paul says, in verse 15: "For you did not receive a spirit of slavery [so that you would] fall back into fear, but you have received a spirit of adoption." Again, first century Paul has to use theistic language, God-language, because there is no other way to express the unity of spirit that Paul – and we – can experience in that moment of giving up self-interest. So Paul says, "When we cry, 'Abba! Father!' it is that very spirit bearing witness with our spirit that we are children of God, and if children, then heirs, heirs of God and joint heirs with Christ – IF, in fact, we suffer with him. . . ." IF, in fact, we abandon the whole idea of looking out for ourselves first. A radical abandonment of self-interest applies individually, socially, corporately, nationally, internationally. Is this easy? Of course not. Who wants to die? In a custody battle with your hostile spouse, can you really abandon your own self-interest? What about the children's welfare? Maybe they would be better off with the other parent. If somebody runs a red light and totals your car, do you really want to forego the justifiable financial windfall you will receive if you take that person to court? What would have happened at the Bali conference[22] if the United States had not tried to insist that developing countries adhere to

---

[22]http://unfccc.int/meetings/bali_dec_2007/meeting/6319.php

the same level of reductions in greenhouse gases as the industrialized nations? Suppose the United States had agreed to a real number – as the entire Planet wanted to do? Would that not have empowered all nations to make a difference in the speed at which the climate is changing?

Are these questions naive?

Slaves for Christ are adopted by God – the Great Spirit, the Creative Force for abundant life in the universe – and thereby are empowered to enter into an unbreakable covenant that has nothing to do with any of the things that normal civilization associates with power. Jesus was born two thousand years ago, and for Christians, he is the one who started the restoration of distributive justice, as Isaiah foretold: "For he said, 'Surely they are my people, children who will not deal falsely'; and he became their savior in all their distress." But slaves for Christ are not just believers in the Christian religion. Anyone who participates in that Covenant inherits the kingdom. Anyone who participates in that Covenant steps into the alternative universe. Anyone who participates in that Covenant becomes a partner with Jesus in the ongoing, great work of justice-compassion.

Jesus is not coming back. He is wherever the great work is done, wherever the Covenant is joined. In the words of the beloved Christmas hymn, "O Holy Child of Bethlehem, descend to us we pray, cast out our sin and enter in, be born in us today."

The stories are true. But we are the ones we are waiting for.

Epiphany

Epiphany: It's Not What You Think

Isaiah 60:1-6; Psalm 72:1-14; Matthew 2

An "epiphany" is a manifestation of a god. A god (or goddess) appears and is recognized – made manifest – among ordinary people. The word "epiphany," like a lot of other things, has been almost completely appropriated by the Christian meaning: the manifestation of the Christ to the Magi (the three kings), and the festival commemorating this event. The festival date is January 6 – which is the Orthodox Christmas day. Sometime in the Middle Ages, that stretch of time between December 24 and January 6 began to be celebrated as the Twelve Days of Christmas. Twelfth Night – January 6 – marks the end of the festivities. In postmodern language usage, an "epiphany" has come to also mean a revelation of a truth about one's self. In a recent interview, Alan Greenspan, the former director of the Federal Reserve – said that when he was a young man he at first thought he would be a jazz musician. Then one time he was playing backup for Lionel Hampton, and had an "epiphany." He would never be a full-time, famous jazz musician because –as opposed to Mr. Hampton – in Greenspan's spare time, he was reading economics books. In premodern times – before Galileo and Copernicus and the dawning of the Enlightenment – gods and goddesses visited earth fairly often, so we should not be surprised to discover that when the Gospel of Matthew was created, that writer would do his best to associate Jesus with the god-like qualities the oppressed people of the land of Judah were longing for – a manifestation of God – an "epiphany."

The writer of Matthew may well have been a liturgist – a worship leader in the Jewish community – who was writing for Jewish people who were accustomed to hearing readings from the Torah in Synagogue. So he followed a format that would be familiar to people honoring the Jewish Sabbath who also knew the stories about Jesus. The two great foundational myths in the Jewish tradition are the exodus from Egypt, and the exile to Babylon and the subsequent return to Judah during the sixth century before the Common Era. Matthew interpreted the birth of Jesus to be the new symbol for the Exodus of the Hebrew people from Egypt, and he claimed that Jesus was the Messiah prophesied by Isaiah and Jeremiah, who would liberate the people from exile. The technical term for this kind of exercise is "midrash." It means retelling a sacred story in a way that has special meaning for the current time, to fit a new occasion, and a different context, and from a different point of view.

Midrash is an argument that plays a serious game of one-upmanship –"top this." So Matthew says, Moses led the Hebrew people out of bondage in Egypt? Well – get this: Jesus came from Egypt to lead the people out of bondage to Roman imperial injustice – and not just the Hebrew people, but everyone who follows Jesus's way – gentile or not. And not only that, Jesus is the Messiah prophesied by Isaiah and Jeremiah. Those prophets proclaimed that if the people follow the way of justice-compassion, as written in the law of Moses, then Judah would rise again to reach the same greatness it enjoyed during the reign of King Solomon.

In Isaiah 60:1-6, one of the traditional readings for this Epiphany Sunday, the camel caravans will bring riches: gold and frankincense, and the whole known world will recognize the power of Israel's God. In Matthew's midrash, three wizards, or holy men – sages, wise men from the East, bringing their symbolic royal gifts of gold and frankincense honor Jesus as the Messiah who would bring God's justice-compassion to the entire world. Matthew says they also brought myrrh – an embalming herb – "A bitter perfume," as the carol of the Three Kings says. Christians have associated that reference with the death of Jesus, and in Matthew's midrash, a foreshadowing of the bitter injustice of Jesus's death, and the mystery of the meaning of the resurrection story.

These are powerful metaphors that have unfortunately fed the triumphalist Christology that has collaborated with political Empire since about the fourth century. They must not be taken literally. Nothing in the story is based on fact. This is not history remembered. It is a powerful foundational myth, created to bring hope to a hopeless situation in the first century. Once again, the temple had been destroyed and the people dispersed – this time by the Romans.

The question is, does it have any meaning for twenty-first century, sophisticated, postmodern, post-Christian people? One of the challenges faced by postmodern folk is that such myths are no longer accepted as foundational. We think that *myth* means something that isn't true. Most of us no longer take our dreams seriously. When was the last time an angel was actually documented appearing to anyone? These stories are fodder for jokes. But under our sophisticated knowledge about the nature of the universe and our scientific understanding of how the brain functions, are ideas common to all of humankind – regardless of culture. Those ideas are called archetypes. They often make up the content of the dreams we remember. They are symbols that represent life experience that is shared by all human beings everywhere, from illiterate Afghan tribal leaders to physicists from MIT, hotel maids, and engineers at the Jet Propulsion Laboratories.

One of those archetypes is the Divine Child. This archetype gets associated with great leaders, whether spiritual or political. Anyone who has an extraordinary impact on human history or thought is at risk of being accused of having been born as a Divine Child. Even today, there are stories about extraordinary children who are somehow smarter, more spiritually aware than usual. They are called "Indigo Children." One of them was the poet Mattie Stepanek, who died of cancer a few years ago at the young age of 14. Before he died, he published a book of poetry. He was on all the talk shows, and traveled from coast to coast, raising money for other children with terminal cancer. There is your manifestation of a god in the twenty-first century. The archetype is alive and well, and living next door.

We project onto others the power we think we ourselves do not possess. Jeremy Taylor, who is an expert in Jungian archetypes that appear in our dreams, calls this projection of the best of our own hopes *the bright shadow*. It is the wondrous, positive, powerful aspect of ourselves that we do not recognize. Sometimes we elect those people to office. Sometimes we join their megachurches. Sometimes we expect far more of those people than they could ever deliver. Sometimes we call them "Messiah."

But there is more to the Divine Child than this kind of outward projection of specialness onto someone other than ourselves. The Divine Child also lives within. The Divine Child is the one who brings something new into the world. The Divine Child challenges the way things are. The Divine Child overturns the kind of injustice that results from the mindless indifference of social systems. The Divine Child overturns everything we think we know about what makes life safe and secure and predictable and under our control. The Divine Child puts us in touch with what we don't want to be in touch with. The Divine Child is the wild part of ourselves that isn't constrained by rules about what's proper or possible or practical. That wildness is rooted in passionate, radical, inclusive, nonviolent, self-denying justice.

That's why the Divine Child is dangerous, and that is why Herod has to kill them all.

Who is Herod? Herod is the ego that likes things to be predictable and normal. Herod is the ego that wants things to be a certain way. Herod will do anything to assure that control is maintained. Herod kills creativity, suppresses change, prevents life. At the personal level, Herod is the part of us that says, "Oh, I'm not creative. I could never paint, write, sing, design a sustainable urban community, start a non-profit . . . I could never divorce my husband, come out of the closet, move to Canada, adopt a child . . . I don't make a difference." At the collective level of human civilization, Herod is the imperial force of oppression and injustice, and we collaborate with that imperial, collective Herod whenever we prevent ourselves from taking a step that will personally liberate us.

The first century followers of Jesus's Way saw Jesus as an extraordinary example of how to live life so that the world can be reclaimed as God's world. The psalmists and the prophets all taught that God's realm – God's kingdom – is a realm of justice-compassion. Jesus taught that God is just, and the world belongs to God, not to the Emperor, and not to the social and religious establishment.

Some of those early followers knew Jesus personally, but the vast majority did not – especially as time wore on, and the story was shared outside the Jewish tradition, and outside Jerusalem. It made psychic sense to see the infant Jesus as the Divine Child, who resacralizes the world. If the world belongs to God, but humanity has appropriated it for imperial interests – or economic exploitation – The Divine Child reclaims the world for justice-compassion.

The liberal, progressive Christian message from the Christian readings for today is that if we allow our Divine Child to rule in our hearts, then our deepest and most meaningful creativity can shine forth like the moon and the stars, and those normal, conventional structures of our advanced civilization that result in injustice can be overturned at last.

Baptism-Schmaptism: Jesus Is Lord
First Sunday after the Epiphany

Isaiah 42:1-9; Psalm 29; Acts 10:34-43; Matthew 3:13-17

The creators of the RCL provide a progression of the Jesus story from birth, to the revelation of the meaning of the birth, and now the baptism. It is a somewhat dizzying bounce from newborn infant to a 2-year old, then to the adult Jesus coming to do what is proper and to fulfill the law (see Matthew 5:17-20). But Matthew isn't interested in Jesus's early life. Matthew is most interested in confirming the legitimacy of Jesus as God's chosen Messiah.

The lectionary readings begin with one of the four "Servant Songs" from Isaiah. The writer is referring to the land and people of Israel as the servant of God who establishes justice in the earth. The coastlands – the boundaries of the known world – wait for that teaching. God says to the servant Israel, "I have given you as a covenant to the people, a light to the nations, to open the eyes that are blind, to bring out the prisoners from the dungeon. . . ." The covenant people – those who contract with God to establish justice on the earth – are the people of Israel. From that covenant, all the nations of the earth will benefit from God's justice-compassion.

Matthew's story of Jesus is classic midrash. With his extraordinary addition to Mark's story about Jesus seeking out baptism by the itinerant, crazed, John – who is out on the fringes of propriety (Mark 1:6-11) – Matthew transforms Isaiah's servant Israel into the servant Jesus. John wants to know how it is that one so much greater than he should come to him for baptism. "Don't worry about it," Matthew's Jesus says, "It is proper for us in this way to fulfill God's will, as revealed in scripture." Then the heavens open, and God's dove descends – just as it had after the great flood – and God's voice says, "This is my favored son – I fully approve of him!" What more proof is needed that the known world has been rearranged, just as it had been in the time of Noah. But this time, instead of destroying the world in storm and flood, God covenants to save the world through the servant Jesus.

Matthew is the only writer that finds the conundrum of the baptism of Jesus by the spiritually inferior John to be significant enough to add that conundrum to Mark's original story. Some of the early Christian communities had major problems with the idea that one who was supposed to be perfect and free of sin would need to be cleansed of sin. "The fact that Jesus had been baptized at all by John and that John was his mentor for a time was an embarrassment for the Christian community that wanted to distance itself from both the baptist movement and rabbinic Judaism, so it developed various apologetic ploys to explain those earlier connections to John and to Judean religion."[23]

So it was and is that Jesus's overturning of the conventional understanding of power is watered down, denied, and forgotten.

Some consensus is developing among scholars researching the origins of the book of Acts that Acts was written "early in the second century to respond to issues in its own day . . . The discussion . . . provided an occasion to grapple with the implications of dating for the interpretation of Acts."[24] Acts is not the record of historical events, but is most likely one of the pieces of thought that went into the formation of early Christian theology/Christology. Peter's sermon at Caesarea affirms the inclusiveness of the Christian Way: "God shows no partiality, but in every nation anyone who fears him and does what is right is acceptable to him." This is hardly news (see Deuteronomy 10:17-18; 2 Kings 5; Romans 2:11), but in the context of the entire story (which is of course left out by the Elves – see Acts 10 in total) gentiles are not only carrying the message without regard to social barriers, they receive the Holy Spirit in the same way as the apostles did at Pentecost (Acts 2:17-18).

But whether or not the stories told in Acts were written late in the first century or early in the second century, and whether or not they were written by whoever wrote the Gospel of Luke, the language tells us that the bodily resurrection of Jesus is the whole point of the story of Jesus, and that belief is what saves people

---

[23]Funk, et al., 133.

[24]Dennis R. Smith, "Report on the Acts Seminar," *The 4th R,* January-February 2008, 19.

from sin. "[Jesus] commanded us to preach to the people and to testify that he is the one ordained by God as judge of the living and the dead. All the prophets testify about him that everyone who believes in him receives forgiveness of sins through his name" (Acts 10:42-43).

The extraordinary overturning of conventional understanding of true power is not even on the radar. Isaiah's servant, whom Matthew does his level best to illustrate has to be Jesus, who will "bring forth justice to the nations [and who] will not cry or lift up his voice, or make it heard in the street; a bruised reed he will not break, and a dimly burning wick he will not quench," and who subordinates himself for purification to the rabble-rousing crazy at the edge of town, is buried under the concern for individual salvation from hell.

Personal piety has supplanted Jesus's kenotic disregard for self-interest, and it's only been a couple of generations.

Humanity has always been confronted with the four questions for the apocalypse:

1)   What is the nature of God? Violent or nonviolent?
2)   What is the nature of Jesus's message? Inclusive or exclusive?
3)   What is faith? Literal belief (suspension of disbelief) or trust in God?
4)   What is deliverance? Salvation from hell, or liberation from injustice?

For some reason known only to the forces of the evolution of consciousness, human history seems to be defined by answering: violent, exclusive, belief (piety), and salvation from hell. The struggle continues as we attempt to throw off injustice while maintaining our own survival through violence, exclusivity, and belief. For those who nit-pick and want to know "what about the problem of evil?" consider the idea that evil is the perpetuation of injustice because of a concentration on salvation from hell based on violence, exclusiveness, and belief (piety), or in postmodern times, suspension of disbelief in a triple decker, earth-centered cosmology, controlled by an interventionst, personalized god.

Who knows why Jesus went for baptism by John – if he did. But in his careful midrash, changing the metaphor of the servant people Israel to the servant Messiah Jesus, Matthew answers the question, and points toward a god of nonviolence, a message that is inclusive, and trust in a kenotic, non-theistic process of creation, all of which results in deliverance: liberation through the great work of justice-compassion.

The readings reinforce the view that Jesus is the manifestation of God's direct action to save the entire world from sin. Psalm 29 tells us clearly that God's voice is like the incredible power of a tornado or hurricane – a storm that arises and rearranges the known world in a heartbeat. But that rearrangement is not about instantaneous salvation from sin and escape from hell for Jew and gentile alike. Jesus rearranges the order of the universe by reversing the normal polarities of power from strength to weakness, from hysterical rant to quiet consciousness; from violence to nonviolence.

The Priesthood of All
Second Sunday in Epiphany

Isaiah 49:1-7; Psalm 40:1-11; 1 Corinthians 1:1-9; John 1:29-42

The second Sunday in the season of Epiphany is occasionally the prologue to a foreshortened liturgical year. The movable feast of Easter often allows only three Sundays before the Transfiguration, and Ash Wednesday when Lent begins. Because the foreshortened Year A concentrates on orthodox mysticism and belief in the early church by studying the Gospel of John throughout Lent, Holy Week, and Easter, Matthew 5, 6, and most of 7 are sometimes not considered. Readings from Matthew then continue in the sason after Pentecost, and "ordinary time" in May.

Perhaps it is good to have a long dose of orthodox mysticism. It gives believers a break from all that guilt about distributive justice-compassion.

Now Matthew's midrash is abandoned in order to consider John's declaration that Jesus is " the lamb of god that does away with the sins of the world." The creators of the RCL also get started on 1 Corinthians, which is the orthodox template for church organization from Paul, but they don't get past the first chapter. The subject matter is the establishment of the early church. In John's version of the Jesus story, the brothers Simon and Andrew are disciples of John the Baptist. When Jesus comes to be baptized, and John declares that Jesus is the lamb of god that does away with the sins of the world, Andrew takes note, and tells his brother Simon that Jesus is the Messiah, and they had better leave the Baptist and join him. Jesus declares Simon to be "the rock." Psalm 40 is a hymn of thanksgiving to God, who "drew me up . . . out of the miry bog, and set my feet upon a rock. . . ." It is only in Matthew 16:18 that Jesus is made to say that "upon this Rock I will build my church." The Elves don't mention that at this time, but we all know it already anyway. The second Servant Song from Isaiah can be read to confirm the establishment of the church as "the light to the nations, that my salvation may reach to the end of the earth." Paul's greeting to the church in Corinth reminds us that God is faithful, and we are called by God into fellowship with his Son.

What are post-Christian exiles supposed to do with this? Perhaps treat it as how not to start an institution, because institutions, like civilizations, inevitably fall into the trap entitled Piety, War (violence), Victory, Peace.[25] Institutions, like civilizations, are prone to act in their own self-interest. However, John Dominic Crossan is careful to point out that this is not an indictment of human nature. In other words, our self-governing organizations do not fall into the imperial pattern because humans are basically evil or selfish. Instead, when individuals band together for collective security – whether economic, intellectual, spiritual, or physical – the rules devised for peaceful prosperous community slide easily into control, hierarchy, consequences for divergence, retribution, sin, and salvation.

What the three-year span of the RCL seems to be setting up is a confrontation between those who – like Jesus – experience a seamless relationship between humanity and the rest of creation (Covenant) and those who insist that God and God's kingdom are inaccessible except through an intermediary: Jesus and his representatives – the priest, the bishop, the pope. Starting with Epiphany, Jesus is revealed as the Messiah first by kings, then by John the Baptist, then revealed to Simon by his brother Andrew. Apparently even the great Peter can't recognize the Lord on his own – perhaps confirming his inability at a later time to recognize the Lord while waiting in Pilate's courtyard.

Hierarchy, a vertical relationship, most commonly seen in imperial systems that lead inevitably to inequality and injustice, is implied as the norm in these readings. The opening to Paul's first letter to the Corinthians is used to bolster that normalcy of power-over others in the early Christian community. But contemporary scholarship is suggesting that was not Paul's intention. Paul was arguing for horizontal equality of relationships in the Christian community, and Covenant with God's kingdom of justice-compassion as taught and modeled by the life of Jesus. Paul insists

---

[25]Crossan and Reed, *passim.*

on a kenotic community that, while diverse, uses its many talents for the common good – a radical abandonment of self-interest that results in Covenant, nonviolence, distributive justice, and peace.

Nor is the reading from the second Servant Song in Isaiah to be interpreted as the Church triumphant. God tells the servant (the nation of Israel) that Israel is given as the light to the nations – the example of how to live in God's justice – so that God's salvation (liberation from injustice) may reach to the "ends" of the earth. This is Covenant, not imperial theology, and it is counter to the demand for apostolic succession being cultivated by the writer of John's Gospel, and implied as settled orthodoxy. Jesus's great Sermon on the Mount, preaching Covenant, nonviolence, distributive justice, and peace, is left out of the readings selected from Matthew's Gospel, and Paul's passionate argument for kenotic community is ignored because the Roman church won the fight over how the timing of the celebration of Easter is calculated.

The Covenant is universal. The servant says that while s/he realizes the original purpose may have been to reconcile the people of Israel with their God, that is not enough. Certainly it is true today that "saving" one particular nation or way of life is not enough. Earth is in the midst of one of the greatest extinctions of life forms since the beginning of its existence. The loss of diversity means the loss of flexibility in evolution that creates niches for survival among all the beings in the universe, not just the Planet.

If the unique contribution that humanity has to make is consciousness, then we cannot remain unconscious – unaware – of the impact of the human life form on the others. God says, "It is too light a thing [not enough] that you should be my servant to raise up the tribes of Jacob and to restore the survivors of Israel. . . ." The very survival of the planetary biosphere and the thousands of ecosystems that live within it appears to be at stake. The time for intermediaries is past. There is still mystery and wonder to be enjoyed, explored, explained, and experienced, but we no longer need priests or shamans to tell us what to do in order to be in covenant relationship with that mystery. All we have to do, says Jesus, in the portions of Matthew we are not supposed to read in a foreshortened year, is open our eyes, and look, and listen.

Last Chance for Justice
Third Sunday in Epiphany

Isaiah 9:1-4; Psalm 27:1, 4-9; 1 Corinthians 1:10-18;
Matthew 4:12-23

The creators of the RCL return to Matthew's midrash of Isaiah's prophecy, this time recording that after the arrest of John the Baptist, Jesus left Nazareth and settled in Capernaum by the sea of Gallilee, just as the prophet Isaiah predicts. In Isaiah's blessing oracle of coronation for a Judean king, the new king liberates the land surrounding Galilee that had been subjected to enemy rule. In Matthew's midrash, Jesus tours all over Galilee, teaching in the synagogues, curing all kinds of diseases, and proclaiming that God's kingdom has come. These verses in chapter 4 are the preface to Matthew 5:1 through 7:29, the great Sermon on the Mount. But with Roman Easter tied to the Northern European Spring Equinox, except for a couple of carefully cherry-picked verses during Lent, Matthew's liturgical setting for the heart of Jesus's life and teaching can get edited out of the RCL, leaving no time for justice.

But before following the Elves into the easy piety of petty sin and salvation, consider what Matthew and the Apostle Paul are really talking about. Matthew may have been suggesting that his five-part treatise on the life and teachings of Jesus was a "new Torah," to be read in place of the Pentateuch in Jewish-Christian synagogues. Instead of the law of Moses, Matthew lays out the new covenant with the Anointed One, beginning with the Sermon on the Mount, and continuing with instructions for the disciples, the parables Jesus told, regulations for community organization, and judgment for those who decline to comply. Beneath it all is the declaration that the kingdom of God (God's imperial rule) is now in force, not Roman rule. The new day foretold by the prophets and the martyred John the Baptist has dawned. Moses and the Exodus have been superseded.

Jesus walks by the Sea of Galilee, and invites his disciples to leave their nets and become "fishers for people." This is usually interpreted to mean saving souls from hell. But John Dominic Crossan points out that Jesus could have brought his message of liberation anywhere in Roman occupied Judea. Why Galilee? Why Capernaum? Perhaps because Herod Antipas had built a commercial fishing operation on the shores of the lake, in direct competition with the local fishermen such as Peter, Andrew, James, John, and the others. The injustice of the Roman imperial foreign policy, "Romanization by urbanization for commercialization,"[26] has predictable results: namely rampant unemployment, poverty, and deprivation. What used to be freely fished from the lake now is only available at high prices from the markets. Fishing boats that had been in fishing families for generations now were taxed as franchises. Perhaps the phrase survives in the tradition because Jesus said it as a bitter joke."People" are the only things left to be fished for.

This all sounds very familiar in the twenty-first century. Instead of "Romanization by urbanization for commercialization" we have Americanization (masquerading as democratization) by militarization for economic exploitation. But while in the first century one could escape the Roman world if one were willing to walk, ride a pack-horse, or sail long enough and far enough, in the twenty-first century the last frontier lies off-Planet, and out of practical reach. In the past, one super-power's economic stumbles could threaten global economic collapse; but now, it is the unjust imperial systems of all of the developed and developing nations that force plundering the world's resources in order to survive economically and politically. As in the first century, what used to be freely fished from the lakes and the oceans now is only available at high prices from the markets. Fishing boats that had been in fishing families for generations now are taxed as franchises or prohibited from the trade because either the fishing stocks are gone, or because of belated environmental regulations – which often benefit those who are able to pay their way around them.

---

[26]Crossan, *God and Empire,* 102.

Truly, "people" are the only life forms left to be fished for. But it is tough going, convincing the people that it is when they lose their life and livelihood that they will truly find it. That teaching has been reduced to a New Age self-help mantra ("follow your bliss"), often masquerading as Christian piety: "God has a plan for you."

In the first century, the Apostle Paul read the riot act to the hapless Corinthian house church, which had fallen into the usual factions and disagreements that every organization falls into. Paul's sarcasm is scathing: "I thank God that I baptized none of you except Crispus and Gaius, so that no one can say that you were baptized in my name." They have apparently forgotten what Paul taught them about the saving grace of the risen Christ. They have reverted to the hierarchical Roman social system of patronage, and are fighting over who owes what to whom and why, and who deserves to sit at the head table, and who will get the best food. Some of them have even begun eating their meal before coming to participate in the sacramental communal meal because they don't want to associate with people who are beneath them in the Roman social hierarchy. Piety in the form of proper behavior is clearly the order of the day.

But is that what Paul means? Cherry-picking the opening is patently unfair to the rest of the Christian theology that Paul sends to the Corinthians over the course of several letters. Still, he says, in 1 Corinthians 1:17, he was not sent to baptize people, but to proclaim the Gospel so that "the cross of Christ might not be emptied of its power." The power of the cross is not saving people from hell. The power of the cross is in the radical denial of self-interest that overthrows social systems whether of patronage or conventional access to the means of survival: food, clothing, shelter, and the work required to earn them. In the twenty-first century, we have to add planetary ecosystems to the list because we have strayed so far from Jesus's experience of God's kingdom as a seamless fabric that supports and sustains all of life.

Jesus's first words in the version of the Sermon on the Mount from the Gospel of Thomas are, "Congratulations to the poor, for to you belongs Heaven's domain." Thomas is largely assumed to be without the gloss of late first-century Christian interpretation.

The poor, who have nothing that the conventional, imperial world deems of value, own the kingdom of God – just as the lilies of the field and the birds of the air. In the twenty-first century, the earth that the poor and disenfranchised have inherited has become a commodity to be exploited. In the words of Joni Mitchell, "They paved Paradise, and put up a parking lot."

In order to save life as we have known it, we must be willing to let go of conventional ideas about survival of the fittest, the richest, the smartest. The first century Corinthians had decided that the message of the cross is foolishness. Paul says it's only foolishness to those who are not being saved.

Creating the Kingdom Part I:
Who Can Live in God's Tent?
Fourth Sunday in Epiphany

Matthew 5:1-12; 1 Corinthians 1:18-31; Micah 6:1-6; Psalm 15

Rarely are all eight Sundays in Epiphany observed before the Transfiguration intervenes and impels followers of the RCL to abandon pragmatism for mysticism in preparation for the long season of fasting and repentance, which is Lent. The five remaining Sundays in Epiphany for Year A are dedicated to creating the kingdom of God here and now, on earth as in "heaven."

If the scripture selections for the fourth Sunday are read in the usual liturgical order from the KJV or the NRSV, they seem unrelated. Matthew's Jesus begins his first discourse with the familiar "Beatitudes," memorized by Sunday School children and confirmands who puzzle over the meaning of "poor in spirit," and "persecuted for righteousness' sake." The Apostle Paul rants on about how "we proclaim Christ crucified, a stumbling block for Jews," which prompts assurances from preachers that antisemitism is not what he meant. The prophet Micah declares that God "has a controversy with his people and he will contend with Israel," which seems to feed the antisemitism implied for the unwary in 1 Cointhians 1:23. Finally, Psalm 15 is clear about who will be allowed to live in God's tent: "Those who walk blamelessly and do what is right," which seems to circle back to the description of who is blessed in Jesus's opening salvo.

The easiest action to take is to simply pick one reading for sermon material and just have the lay leader read the rest. But if the cause of Biblical literacy is to be advanced, three steps are necessary. First, reverse the order of the readings, which gives a rough historical time line for when they were written. Second, use alternative translations by the Westar Institute scholars for

Corinthians (*The Authentic Letters of Paul*[27]) and Matthew (*The Complete Gospels*).[28] Third, note that the word "heaven" as used by the writer of Matthew's Gospel is a synonym for "God," or God's realm or rule, not a place in the sky. The readings then begin to inform one another from antiquity about how to live in a Covenant community.

The Psalmist asks, "Who has the right to enter your tent, Adonai, or to live on your holy mountain?" The answer is, "Those who conduct themselves with integrity, and work for justice."[29] The reading from the prophet Micah is not so straight-forward because the Elves have left out the heart of the matter. Micah says that "the Lord has a controversy with his people." He goes on to spell out exactly what that controversy is. God is perplexed about what God might have done to cause God's people to cheat one another and act with violence against one another after God brought the people out of bondage and gave them leaders on the order of Moses, Aaron, and Miriam. God has kept the Covenant; it is the people who have not. The prophet reminds the people, "[God] has told you, O mortal, what is good; and what does the Lord require of you but to do justice, and to love kindness, and to walk humbly with your God?" Without this reminder (never read, if the RCL is followed), the psalm is simply a rant against "Israel." The reading from Paul's first letter to the community he founded in Corinth can now be seen to expand the ancient formula for living in Covenant with God in light of the life, death, and resurrection of Jesus. Finally, in the introduction to Jesus's Sermon on the Mount, the writer of Matthew's Gospel clarifies even further what Paul was trying to get the Corinthians to understand.

In *The Authentic Letters of Paul* (Scholars Version [SV]), 1 Corinthians 1:18-24 is translated as follows:

> The message about the cross is utter nonsense to those who are heading for ruin, but to us who are bound for salvation it is the effective power of God . . . . Since in

---

[27]Dewey, et al.

[28]Miller, ed.

[29]Priests for Equality, 15.

the larger scheme of God's wisdom the world did not come to acknowledge God through its own wisdom, God decided to save those who embrace God's world-transforming news through the "nonsense" that we preach. At a time when Jews expect a miracle and Greeks seek enlightenment, we speak about God's Anointed *crucified*! This is an offense to Jews, nonsense to the nations; but to those who have heard God's call, both Jews and Greeks, the Anointed represents God's power and God's wisdom . . . .[30]

Jesus's execution as a common criminal at the hands of the Romans flies in the face of conventional expectation and understanding of one considered to be anointed by God as a savior, or even more outrageous, as a son of God. After two thousand years of hearing the story, Christians and others have lost touch with just how outrageous such a claim was and still is. Paul then goes on to explain to the people listening to the letter being read that not many of them were considered wise or people of power and influence (although by implication, some were – which probably was part of the problem with the community). Paul says,

God has chosen people the world regards as fools to expose the pretensions of those who think they know it all, and God has chosen people the world regards as weak to expose the pretensions of those who are in power. God has chosen people who have no status in the world and even those who are held in contempt, people who count for nothing, in order to bring to nothing those who are thought to be really something . . . . It is God's doing that you belong to the people of the Anointed Jesus. God has made him our wisdom and the source of our goodness and integrity and liberation. So, as scripture says, "If you have to take pride in something, take pride in what God has done."

Paul's words recall Micah's reminder of what God had done in Covenant with the Israelites, and what is expected of the people

---

[30]Dewey, et al., 79 (emphasis in original).

in return, and sets up Matthew's opening words for the collection of teachings that begins,

> Congratulations to the poor in spirit! The empire of heaven belongs to them.
>
> Congratulations to those who grieve! They will be consoled.
>
> Congratulations to the gentle! They will inherit the earth.
>
> Congratulations to those who hunger and thirst for justice! They will have a feast.
>
> Congratulations to the merciful! They will receive mercy.
>
> Congratulations to those whose motives are pure! They will see God.
>
> Congratulations to those who work for peace! They will be called God's children.
>
> Congratulations to those who have suffered persecution for the sake of justice! The empire of Heaven belongs to them.

Neither Paul nor Matthew is talking about easy piety. They are talking about the hard work of living in Covenant with God's realm of distributive justice-compassion. Paul is developing his argument to the community in Corinth that the power of the cross is in the radical denial of self-interest that overthrows social systems. Matthew's Jesus confirms that. "Congratulations!" he says. "Rejoice and be glad" when you are denounced and persecuted for refusing to participate in society's unjust conventions because in God's realm, under God's rule, you will be more than rewarded. You will inherit the earth; receive mercy; see God; be called God's children – in this life here and now.

Full circle, back to the psalmist: "O Lord, who may abide in your tent? Who may dwell on your holy hill? Those who walk blamelessly, and do what is right, and speak the truth from their heart."

Creating the Kingdom Part II:
Living the Wisdom of God
Fifth Sunday in Epiphany

Matthew 5:13-20; 1 Corinthians 2:1-12 (13-16); Isaiah 58:1-9a (9b-12); Psalm 112:1-9 (10

When taken at face value, in the context of orthodox interpretation, the readings for this fifth Sunday in Epiphany seem most concerned with "righteousness." The Psalm celebrates the blessings of the righteous: "Wealth and riches are in their houses . . . . They arise in darkness as a light for the upright . . . ." Matthew's Jesus continues his introductory remarks, encouraging the listeners on the mountainside to stand up and be counted among those who work to carry out God's law. The metaphors are familiar: salt that has lost its savor (saltiness) is to be thrown out and stomped into the ground; a city on a hill cannot be hidden; let your light shine so that people can see your good works and praise God. In case any of the people in Matthew's community were uncomfortable with what they may have heard about Jesus's radical ideas, Matthew is careful to reassure everyone that Jesus has no intention of abolishing Torah. Anyone who does will be called "least in the kingdom of heaven; but whoever . . . teaches them will be called great . . . ." This portion ends with the warning that "unless your righteousness exceeds that of the scribes and Pharisees, you will never enter the kingdom of heaven" (NRSV).

"Righteousness" usually means "justice." Calling for a righteousness that exceeds the leaders of Matthew's religious establishment implies that the religious authorities were among those breaking the law and encouraging others to do the same. Jesus's warning fits the admonition in Isaiah 58 and the congratulatory tone of Psalm 115 when the Scholar's Version is used to translate "righteousness" as "religion": "Unless you live your religion more fully than the scholars and Pharisees, you won't set foot in the empire of Heaven."[31] Isaiah 58 and Psalm 112 clarify how religion that is practiced with integrity fulfills humanity's part of the Covenant:

> Is this not the fast that I choose: to loose the bonds of injustice, to undo the thongs of the yoke, to let the oppressed go free, and to break every yoke? Is it not to share your bread with the hungry, and bring the homeless poor into your house; when you see the naked to clothe them, and not to hide yourself from your own kin? Then your light shall break forth like the dawn and your healing shall spring up quickly; your vindicator shall go before you, the glory of the Lord shall be your rear guard. Then you shall call, and the Lord will answer; you shall cry for help, and he will say, Here I am (Is. 58: 6-9).

> Happy are those who fear the Lord, ... They have distributed freely, they have given to the poor; their righteousness endures forever . . . . The wicked see it and are angry; they gnash their teeth and melt away; the desire of the wicked comes to nothing (Psalm 112:1b, 9-10).

The traditional interpretation of the next selected portion of Paul's first letter to the Corinthians seems at first to reflect the attitude of Matthew's Jesus's toward the scribes and Pharisees, although Paul at first seems embarrassingly humble. "I did not come proclaiming the mystery of God to you in lofty words or wisdom. For I decided to know nothing among you except Jesus Christ and him crucified." Scribes and Pharisees rejected Jesus's message, according to orthodox interpretation of Matthew and Luke, and 1 Corinthians 2:6-8 seems to concur:

> Yet among the mature we do speak wisdom, though it is not a wisdom of this age or of the rulers of this age, who are doomed to perish. But we speak of God's wisdom, secret and hidden, which God decreed before the ages for our glory. None of the rulers of this age understood this; for if they had, they would not have crucified the Lord of glory (NRSV).

---

[31]Miller, *The Complete Gospels*, 72.

Paul then explains that God reveals God's wisdom and truth through the spirit of God to "those who are spiritual." Those who are "unspiritual" can't understand God's wisdom. Believers in the crucified Christ, Paul seems to be saying, are the only ones who can know the mind of God because "we have the mind of Christ," which presumably results in a convenient spirituality. Orthodox understanding of Paul's carefully crafted argument to the confused people in Corinth can and has resulted in the very imperial hubris that Paul is trying to get his readers to avoid. Much of the problem lies in translation. The Scholars Version provides a more inclusive illumination of Paul's point:

> Who knows the things that constitute human life except by the capacity to comprehend what is hidden within a human being? So also, no one knows the things that God intends except the hidden wisdom of God. We have not received as a special gift the capacity to understand the nature of this world, but the capacity to comprehend the things that God has generously given to us. And we speak about these things not in terms derived from the instruction of human wisdom, but by the instruction of God's presence and power, interpreting the hidden wisdom of God for those who can comprehend it. People who are concerned only with worldly affairs do not respond to the hidden wisdom of God. It makes no sense to them. They are unable to comprehend such things, because the hidden wisdom of God is discerned only by people who can recognize it . . . . But we have the mind of the Anointed (1 Corinthians 2:11-16).[32]

A second part of the problem is that Paul's theology has seldom been interpreted from the point of view (to the extent possible) of Paul's own time (first century), culture (Greek/Roman), and religion (Jewish). Paul writes in 1 Corinthians 2:7-8 (NRSV), "But we speak God's wisdom, secret and hidden, which God decreed before the ages *for our glory*. None of the rulers of this age understood this; for if they had, they would not have crucified the *Lord of glory* (emphasis mine)." This

---

[32]Dewey, et al., 81.

is gobbledegook to most folks in the pews of a Sunday morning. "Our Glory" often means "going to heaven"; and the "Lord of glory" is of course Jesus, who died so that we can indeed go to heaven. But the scholar's translation sheds light not only on the passage selected by the RCL, it also refers to Paul's apocalyptic understanding of who Jesus was:

> I am talking about a hidden and mysterious wisdom of
> God which God intended before time began: to raise us
> to the glory of God's presence. None of the rulers of this
> age knew anything about this. If they had known, they
> would not have crucified the one who has become our
> exalted lord.

Paul subscribed to the Jewish apocalyptic legend set forth in the book of Daniel. In this legend, God will act to restore God's justice in the world by first sending a savior, who will then be raised up to remain with God until the world complies with God's intended realm of justice-compassion. This is the "hidden wisdom" that the rulers of Paul's age (*i.e.,* the Romans) did not know anything about. Paul was convinced through his own insight that Jesus was this Anointed one who would be raised up (exalted) from the subterranean world of the dead to God's realm above the firmament. The rest of the legend is that once this has happened, all the rest of the dead *and the living* would also be raised to be with God. It was not essential that the savior – or anyone else – be dead first. At the moment the Anointed was raised up, dead or alive (remember Elijah), the world would be transformed.

This is also gobbledegook to most folks of a Sunday, whether progressive or traditional followers of Jesus's Way. But it is important to know about Paul's point of view, even as – in the time-honored activity of midrash – we glean what meaning we may of Paul's words for our time, culture, and religion. Then – in the spirit of Matthew's Jesus – we may indeed live our faith far more fully than the scholars and Pharisees.

Creating the Kingdom Part III:
Freedom of Choice: Life or Death
Sixth Sunday in Epiphany

Matthew 5:21-37; 1 Corinthians 3:1-9; Deuteronomy 30:15-20; Sirach 15:15-20; Psalm 119

As Paul pointed out in the reading for last week, "the hidden wisdom of God is discerned only by people who can recognize it" (Scholars Verson). Or, as the NRSV puts it, the "unspiritual" are unable to understand because they do not have the "mind of Christ." Paul continues to explain that so long as the Corinthians are preoccupied with "mundane interests," they will be unable to hear God's world-transforming message. That message was that God had acted in real time to raise up what the Roman world called a common criminal into the very presence of God, and that therefore whoever took on that same mind that the Anointed One had would also be brought into God's realm. Paul may have been referring to his own profound insight that Jesus was the savior sent by God as described in the apocalyptic legend of Daniel. While such theology would have made sense to first century Jews, Paul's lengthy complicated plea illustrates the challenge to making it relevant to first century Greeks. Over time the legend morphed into theories of atonement (Jesus died to save us from hell in the next life) and belief in a resuscitated corpse that somehow got sucked up into the sky, promising to return on clouds of fire to rapture the saved and leave the unbelievers behind. In a twenty-first century, postmodern context, this is meaningless. What can and does speak is Paul's counter-intuitive realization that what is deemed weakness or powerlessness in conventional society actually possesses the greatest power.

Paul is dealing with rival factions among the people in the community in Corinth. His point is that so long as people are mired in mundane politics, they cannot discern the spirit of God that contains that truth. The wisdom of God that reverses the world's wisdom is invisible to them. The Corinthians are called to abandon the ways of Rome and agree to the Covenant – sign on to the program that will result in the transformation of human life. "We [Apollos and I] are co-workers for God," Paul says, "You are God's field, God's building project." Petty political rivalries don't matter. What matters is the growth of the community in God's Covenant for distributive justice-compassion, which lies far outside the boundaries of the normalcy of everyday civilization.

Paul sounds almost gentle in this early portion of his letter to his Corinthian friends. The writer of Matthew apparently had a much larger problem on his hands. Some of the "antitheses" in Matthew 5:21-48 are more like "intensifications" than either-or contrasts. Aaron M. Gale suggests they are comparable to "making a fence around the Torah,"[33] which is a "principle of supreme importance in Judaism":

> There are many laws that are not strictly obligatory upon a person from the Torah, but rather were instituted by the Rabbis to prevent a Jew from transgressing a Torah law. An example is the use of money on Shabbat. The Torah itself does not prohibit using money on Shabbat. However, the Rabbis said one should not do so, lest one write, which is prohibited by the Torah (at least the midrashic understanding of the Torah).[34]

In that spirit, Matthew's Jesus raises piety to an art form. Scribes or scholars and Pharisees may preach "do not kill," but anyone who is merely angry, or who calls somebody an "idiot" has essentially violated the commandment. "You have heard that it was said, 'You shall not commit adultery.' But I say to you that everyone who looks at a woman with lust has already committed adultery with her in his heart." He says it is better to lose a part of your body than have your whole body thrown into hell.

The Psalm extols the law of God; Matthew's Jesus demonstrates how to go beyond even the spirit of the law in righteous living. But Deuteronomy and Sirach suggest a cosmic

---

[33]Levine and Brettler, 9, n5:21-48.

[34]Avoth, Chapter One, Mishna http://www.uscj.org/ LearningandTeaching/ DailyStudyMaterials/ MishnahYomit/

joke: Covenant does not just happen; people do have freedom of choice. The punch line is the fine print in God's Covenant: it is not God's fault if anyone chooses not to follow God's law. John Dominic Crossan's concept of a kenotic[35] God now comes into sharper focus and the battle over the "problem of evil" is joined. Crossan suggests that a kenotic God is a God whose presence is justice and life, and whose absence is injustice and death.[36] Deuteronomy 30:15-20 lays out the choice before the Israelite people waiting to cross the Jordan and claim the promised land:

> See, I have set before you today life and prosperity, death and adversity. If you obey the commandments of the Lord your God . . . then you shall live . . . and the Lord your God will bless you in the land that you are entering to possess. But if your heart turns away and you do not hear, but are led astray to bow down to other gods and serve them, I declare to you today that you shall perish . . . I call heaven and earth to witness against you today that I have set before you life and death, blessings and curses. Choose life so that you and your descendants may live.

The writer of Sirach clarifies, starting with verse 14, left out by the Elves:

> It was he [God] who created humankind from the beginning, and he left them in the power of their own free choice . . . he is mighty in power and sees everything; [nevertheless] He has not commanded anyone to be wicked, and he has not given anyone permission to sin.

In note 15.11-20 Burton Mack writes,

> The position argued against is that God ultimately must be responsible because he created the world in such a way as to make sin possible. Ben Sira argues that God is not responsible because humans have free choice. This is a theodicy similar to that argued by the friends of Job,

---

[35] *See* Raven, Appendix Two: *Holy Week: An Exploration of the Meaning of Kenosis.*

[36] Crossan and Reed, 288.

but quite different from that proposed by the author of Job.[37]

In the secular twenty-first century "God" is no longer an excuse or a reason for behavior, but the problem of evil remains. The debate now centers on human nature instead of "God." Crossan is adamant that "human nature" in itself does not result in collective systems that produce social, environmental, political injustice. The cause lies in the collective "normalcy" of civilizations that work to support and secure the collective well-being. This makes the call to act outside of unjust systems much more difficult than in earlier, simpler times. Paul could demand that his first century Corinthian friends not participate in Roman hierarchical social systems, which were clearly unjust and contrary to the egalitarian, radical abandonment of self interest modeled by the followers of the risen Christ. Twenty-first century would-be followers of Jesus's Way must balance individual integrity against the demands of corporate survival; and corporate survival no longer applies only to families, tribes, or nations but to all of humanity; not just to humanity, but to ecosystems planet-wide.

Crossan's kenotic choice invites us into what Paul called the mind of Christ: justice, life, and the presence of God. So long as injustice and death hold sway, the "spirit" remains hidden from the "flesh," and discernment of the mind of Christ is not possible.

---

[37]National Council of Churches, 1553.

Creating the Kingdom Part IV:
Subvert the Empire
Seventh Sunday in Epiphany

Matthew 5:38-48; 1 Corinthians 3:10-11, 16-23;
Leviticus 19:1-2, 9-18; Psalm 119:33-40

Once again, in the interest of Biblical literacy, the liturgist should reverse the order of scripture readings.

The selection from Psalm 119 continues last week's praises for God's law and prayers to keep God's law in the face of constant opportunities for selfish gain amid the vanities of conventional life. The NRSV describes Leviticus 19 as dealing with "ritual and moral holiness," laying out the requirements for priests responsible for the rule of law and basic justice for orderly communities. Most of the "Ten Commandments" that appear in Deuteronomy 5:12-15 (read in Year B) are covered: e.g., "you shall not steal; deal falsely; lie; swear falsely; or profane the name of God." But the rules in Leviticus add a level of distributive justice-compassion that may seem surprisingly applicable to twenty-first century civilization:

You shall leave some of the harvest for the poor and alien (9-10).

You shall not keep for yourself the wages of a laborer until morning (13b).

You shall not revile the deaf or put a stumbling block before the blind (14).

You shall not be partial to the poor or defer to the great: with justice you shall judge your neighbor (15).

You shall not profit by the blood of your neighbor – i.e., "don't stand by idle while your neighbor is in danger"[38](16b).

---

[38]National Council of Churches, n.19.16, 182.

You shall not take vengeance or bear a grudge against
any of your people and you shall love your neighbor as
yourself (17a, 18).

The creators of the RCL concentrate only on these verses.
Later, in Proper 25, these sections are revisited with the exception
of verses 9-14. It's far simpler to just eliminate the bulk of the
chapter than to pick and choose what might be relevant to post-
enlightenment society. The rest of Leviticus is ignored for the
entire three-year cycle. But underlying all the esoteric rules for a
premodern society in chapter 19 is a demand and expectation for
justice-compassion on the part of the religious leaders that
includes the alien and extends to the land itself. Verse 29 prohibits
making a daughter a prostitute because that would cause the land
to become depraved – perhaps a reference to the land as
Sovereignty, as Goddess, that the earth belongs to God as a
daughter belongs to a priest.

And the priest shall make atonement for him with the
ram of guilt offering before the Lord for his sin that he
committed; and the sin he committed shall be forgiven
him (22).
When you come into the land and plant all kinds of trees
for food, then you shall regard their fruit as forbidden
. . . . But in the fifth year you may eat of the fruit, that
their yield may be increased for you (23-25).
You shall rise before the aged and defer to the old (32).
When an alien resides with you in your land, you shall
not oppress the alien. The alien who resides with you
shall be to you as a citizen among you; you shall love the
alien as yourself, for you were aliens in the land of Egypt
(33-34).

There is enough here to convict twenty-first century national
and international policy and politics without looking at Paul's
paragraphs on the consequences of building on a different
foundation than one based on the wisdom of "Christ crucified," or
Matthew's recommendation to give up your coat, walk the extra
mile, and love your enemies. Paul was a Jew who knew the law
and the traditions. His letter to the Corinthians is not a "Christian"
letter; it is, however, an attempt on Paul's part to translate his

Jewish insight into the meaning of Jesus's teachings, death, and resurrection to a gentile Greek community controlled by Rome.

Unfortunately, the Elves leave out the central portion of Paul's illustration of exactly what he and Apollos had been attempting to do in this community, and what the consequences would be if the people decided to follow someone else. The analogy Paul uses is a master builder who lays a firm foundation on Jesus the Anointed. The danger is that someone else may build an inferior structure on top of that foundation. He acknowledges that some builders may indeed use valuable and long-lasting materials, but when the test comes – the trial by fire – an inferior structure will be destroyed.

Paul's point is not salvation from hell in the next life. His point is that if the body of the Anointed, the community he is building with the help of people like Apollos and Cephas, uses the conventional ways of the Roman world to construct its community, it will not stand. The creators of Mosaic law in Leviticus were saying much the same thing. When the people moved into the new land, they were not to abide by the social rules of the people in that land. Indeed, even if they planted their own fruit trees in the new land, they were not to eat any of the fruit from those trees for five years. Presumably by that time the new land would have been sufficiently purified (saved, claimed) by the righteousness of God's people for the harvest to be free of corruption – and probably well-acclimated to the new environment. Paul is saying that by following the teachings of the Anointed, the world, life, death, the present, the future – all belong to the community – the body – of the Anointed. "Everything is yours," he says, and you belong to the Anointed and the Anointed belongs to God.

The anti-Roman, anti-imperial subversion in Paul's assertion is obvious. The Anointed has been raised to God's realm, making a criminal executed by Rome more exalted than Caesar. Because of that exaltation, the people who follow Jesus the Anointed (Jew or Greek, slave or free) are also raised higher than Caesar, both in this life and the next. Roman rules governing patronage and social position no longer apply. The wisdom – the cleverness – the political games necessary for social advancement have now become empty foolishness. The craziness associated with people who follow Jesus's Way is actually the only sane way to live.

In a post-Christian, post-Biblical, secular world apocalyptic metaphors of exaltation or resurrection seem to have little relevance – which is why much of Paul's writings are difficult if not downright obtuse. The resurrection of Jesus has been literalized into meaninglessness, so that the idea of "rising up" into new life seems to have lost much of its power. But Westar scholar Bernard Brandon Scott argues that "we can reclaim the degraded view of resurrection that has dominated Christianity since the Neoplatonic revolution."[39] Resurrection – rising to new life – is collective, not personal, currently active, not future restricted.

In what is becoming a post-government world ruled by corporations, nonviolent resistance seems counter-productive. But salvation is liberation from injustice whether that injustice is codified in national law or in the rules and prevailing culture of corporations, large or small. Matthew's Jesus takes Paul's subversion into nonviolent passive resistance. Turn the other cheek; give up your inner garment as well as the outer one (if you have an outer one); carry the oppressor's armor a second mile. Loving your neighbor as yourself, as Leviticus says, is no longer enough. Even the oppressors do that. Love your enemies.

---

[39]Scott, 229.

Creating the Kingdom Part V: Trust
Eighth Sunday in Epiphany

Matthew 6:24-34;1 Corinthians 4:1-5; Isaiah 49:8-16a; Psalm 131

Perhaps in acknowledgment that some years will not have nine Sundays in Epiphany to prepare for Lent, the creators of the RCL embedded Matthew's admonitions about fasting and practicing piety in secret in the upcoming Ash Wednesday liturgy (Matthew 6:1-6, 16-21).[40] They also abandoned Matthew's version of The Lord's Prayer and Jesus's recommendation to lay up treasure in heaven (Matthew 6:7-15) in favor of Luke's treatment in Year C. Luke 11:1-13 covers petitionary prayer in a nutshell including Luke's shorter version of "The Lord's Prayer."[41] Scholars consider Luke's version to be closer to the original form of phrases in Q, but Luke changes the meaning from economic debt to personal sin (trespass). Postmodern scholarship makes a further shift in meaning from personal piety (sin) to economic justice. In Rabbinic literature (not Biblical literature) "sin" is considered to be a "debt" against God.[42] The unanswered question is why the creators of the RCL preferred Luke's context of petitionary prayer to Matthew's context of righteous humility. How "sins" and "debts" got translated into "trespasses" is yet another question. Can it be that the Church has been more interested in personal piety than economic justice? The curious aphorism about how the eye is the lamp of the body is ignored no matter which Gospel it appears in. Instead the readings fast-forward to the difficulty of serving two masters, and what has devolved into a postmodern heresy called "prosperity Gospel."

---

[40]*See* p. 81.

[41]Raven, 144.

[42]Levine, 1256, n11:1-4.

The Jesus Seminar scholars consider the series of pronouncements on anxiety in Matthew 6:25-30 to be possibly "the longest connected discourse that can be directly attributed to Jesus, with the exception of some of the longer parables."[43] Unfortunately some interpretations of Jesus's words in verses 31-34 can reverse the message. The pivotal verse is 33. The King James Version (the "authorized" version) says "But seek ye first the kingdom of God, and his righteousness; and all these things shall be added unto you" (KJV). One of the first "praise chorus" hymns that arose from the worship revival of the 1970s was Karen Lafferty's 1971 paraphrase of this verse:

Seek ye first the Kingdom of God
And His righteousness
And all these things shall be added unto you.
Allelu Alleluia.
Man shall not live by bread alone
But by every word
That proceeds from the mouth of God
Allelu Alleluia
Ask and it shall be given unto you
Seek and ye shall find
Knock and the door shall be opened unto you
Allelu Alleluia

Key words are "Kingdom of God" and "righteousness." The Kingdom of God traditionally has meant the universe of believers. To "seek first the kingdom of God" can mean (and has) working to establish Christianity as the world-wide religion. Seeking the kingdom of God is also understood in terms of personal piety: the acceptance of Jesus as personal savior, who has forgiven personal sin, and the continuing struggle to follow him in "righteous" living that will result in going to heaven at death. "Righteousness" is most often defined as being "right with God," complying with the Ten Commandments, and living a life free from such sins as unmarried sex, and drug and alcohol use. Missing in this interpretation of Jesus's words is the call to pay attention to God's justice-compassion. Jesus is saying look for God's rule, God's

---

[43]Funk, et al., 152.

domain, where distributive justice-compassion holds sway. The heresy is that Jesus's call for a radical abandonment of self-interest has instead become an expectation that wealth shall be *added* to you if you believe the story that Jesus died for your sins. Trust in the process of restoring God's original balance of distributive justice-compassion is not in the picture. Seeking God's realm – as these commentaries have defined it – means creating a life grounded in distributive justice-compassion here and now, requiring a radical abandonment of self-interest. Given the continuing difficult struggle in the face of the nearly overwhelming force that is the normalcy of civilization, anxiety about survival is to be expected. "Trust" is therefore the enabling power in this passage, not "reward."

Verse 24 provides the catalyst for Jesus's speech on anxiety. "No one can be slave to two masters," he says. "That slave will either hate one and love the other, or be devoted to one and disdain the other. You can't be enslaved to both God and Mammon. That's why I'm telling you, don't fret . . . ." Interestingly, "mammon" from antiquity acquired the meaning of "wealth" or "riches" or even "a bank account."[44] But the root meaning is "trust" or "reliance," as "that in which [other than God] one places one's trust."[45] The words snipped out of Paul's first letter to the Corinthians might be seen as relevant at this point, provided the emphasis is on "trust," not survival or acquiring wealth.

Paul continues to defend himself and Apollos as reliable – deserving of trust – and says that God will judge in the end who is to be commended or not. When the lord comes, Paul writes, "He will bring to light everything done in the dark and expose the motives of all human hearts; and then each of us will receive God's commendation." (The orphaned verses in Matthew 6:22-23 could serve here as an illustration of what Paul might have been talking about.) Paul goes on to remind the hearers of this letter (read by Chloe herself?) that they have already received "the world, life, death, the present, future" (1 Corinthians 3:22) because they belong to the Anointed Jesus. In 4:8 (never considered by the

---

[44]Funk, et al., 151.

[45]Levine and Brettler,14, n6:19-34.

Elves along with the rest of chapter 4 and all but two verses of 5), Paul says "Already you have it all! Already you have become rich! You have become kings without any help from us!" In fact, in contrast to the false leaders the Corinthians have embraced, he and Apollos get no respect. "I became your father in the community of the Anointed Jesus when I presented God's world-transforming message to you," Paul continues (4:15b-17). "For that reason I urge you to regard me as your model. It was for this purpose that I sent Timothy to you. He is my dear and faithful child in the service of the Lord. He will remind you of my views on our life as people who belong to the Anointed Jesus, just as I teach them everywhere in every community of the Anointed." Paul then promises to come to them soon to find out whether or not the words of the "pretentious people" who have been causing dissension in the community have any ". . . transforming power. For the empire of God is not just about talk; it's about the power that transforms the world."

Indeed, what greater power exists than distributive justice-compassion, which assures that the realm of God belongs to the poor; that those who grieve will be consoled; that the gentle [the nonviolent] will inherit the earth; that those who hunger and thirst for justice will have a feast? Psalm 131, echoed in Jesus's assurance, is a song of quiet, non-assuming, trust in God. Isaiah says "See, I have inscribed you on the palms of my hands." Matthew's Jesus cannot be more clear what it takes to fulfill the law – to do better than the scholars and Pharisees who are all talk and no action.

Transfiguration

Matthew 17:1-9; 2 Peter 1:16-2; Exodus 24:12-18;Psalm 2; Psalm 99

The creators of the RCL mercifully give progressive Christian preachers a legitimate way to avoid preaching on the Transfiguration by providing "Proper 4"[46] for "Churches whose calendar requires this Sunday, and do not observe the Last Sunday after the Epiphany as Transfiguration."[47] The story was first recorded by the writer of Mark, well before esoteric arguments regarding the divinity of Jesus began raging among the early creators of Christianity. Some scholars propose that the story may have originally been an appearance story that circulated among members of the Jesus movement. If it was, Mark was apparently not in agreement with members of communities who claimed a physical manifestation of Jesus's resurrection. Mark's Gospel has no appearance stories. The original ends with an empty tomb and terrified women who run away and tell no one. By the time the writers of Matthew and Luke came along, appearance stories were part of the landscape. Both Matthew and Luke lifted Mark's story wholesale, and the idea of a resurrected divine Christ within the human story of Jesus entered the stream of eye-rolling dogma.

Just in case sentiments such as those expressed in the above paragraph might have found a niche among second-century skeptics, the late second century writer of the purported Second Letter of Peter is adamant:

For we did not follow cleverly devised myths when we made known to you the power and coming of our Lord Jesus Christ, but we have been eyewitnesses of his majesty . . . . We ourselves heard this voice come from heaven, while we were with him on the holy mountain.

---

[46]*See* p.159.

[47]Consultation on Common Texts, 28.

Reinforcing Matthew's contention that Jesus was the new Moses by including in the readings Moses' meeting with God on the mountaintop does not lend credence to the transfiguration story. Suggesting with Psalm 2 that the Anointed (Christ) is established as ruler over the nations, or with Psalm 99 that the Lord (meaning Jesus) is king simply reinforces the imperial rule of the corporate church. Such proof-texting does nothing to further the restoration of a realm where distributive justice-compassion provides Covenant with a kenotic god.

Lent

It's That Time Again
Ash Wednesday

Joel 2:1-2, 12-17; Isaiah 58:1-12; Psalm 51:1-17; 2
Corinthians 5:20b-6:10; Matthew 6:1-6; 16-21

Ash Wednesday readings are the same for all three liturgical years – does that tell us anything?

The week leading up to Ash Wednesday culminates in "Fat Tuesday," when everything containing fat must be either eaten up or discarded in order to prepare for the great forty-day fast called "Lent," when not only is there food fasting, there is also fasting from entertainment, fun, and sex. It is time to "repent" of all the petty sins we may have done by omission or commission. But "repent" has come to mean "feel sorry about" rather than "turning around and away." Maybe that's why we have to continually repeat the process. Feeling sorry about something is no great motivation for changing – at least on a permanent basis. Some of the folks who ate and drank to excess during the carnival season are "repenting" of that behavior today, but come next carnival the party will undoubtedly be joined once more.

Ash Wednesday is all about imperial piety, which means marking believers' foreheads with a cross drawn with ashes, often made from burning left-over palms from the previous year's Palm Sunday. This makes a nice tidy connection: the palms symbolically waved to celebrate the triumphal entry into Jerusalem of Jesus the conquering hero are now used to mark us like Cain with the evidence of our sin. Doesn't all this fly in the face of Jesus's scorn for those who "make their faces unrecognizable so they may be publicly recognized"? Never mind that Jesus never said any such thing, and that Matthew added this to his collection of Jesus's sayings on his own. The point stands. Public piety does nothing but score points with the empire.

Ash Wednesday has its purpose, IF the paradigm is truly shifted, which a forty-day fast from the normalcy of civilization might possibly accomplish. Meanwhile, guilt is another word for cheap grace. Go ahead and eat your bread and soup meal this evening in honor of the illegal aliens who are denied basic humanitarian needs like food, shelter, and clothing – not to mention Iraqi children, refugees in Darfur, the list goes on and on. You can always go home and top it off with a bedtime snack (hmm... sounds like those awful Corinthians Paul was so mad at).

"God" is not going to listen anyway – as Isaiah makes clear. "Day after day they seek me and delight to know my ways, as if they were a nation that practiced righteousness and did not forsake the ordinance of their God." They have the nerve to ask God why God pays no attention to their fasts. "Like DUH!" Isaiah says, "You serve your own interests on your fast day, and oppress all your workers! HELLO!"

Repent for the Kingdom I: Choosing Justice
First Sunday in Lent

Genesis 2:15-17; Genesis 3:1-7; Psalm 32; Romans 5:12-19;
Matthew 4 :1-11

The five weeks of Lent in Year A explore the concepts of sin, salvation, and justification in Paul's letter to the Romans (and a diversion into pseudo-Paul's Ephesians), and the long theological discourses that John's Jesus engages in. Tradition defines "sin" in terms of conventional morality – especially sexual morality – and petty trespass. "Justification" usually means "rationalization" as in, "Anyone would be justified in demanding the death penalty in these circumstances"; or "abortion can never be justified under any circumstances." Even though the root of the word is "justice," and the true meaning is "to be made just," the usual understanding is less about reconciling transformation and more about coercion and retribution. Likewise "repentance," as pointed out in the Ash Wednesday meditation, has come to mean "feel sorry about" – i.e., cheap guilt to accompany petty trespass – rather than "turning around and away." Real crime, such as murder, earns its own conventional retribution, so doesn't enter the discussion. Murderers and other so-called "capital" criminals may indeed "repent" of their crimes, but "justification" for them is impossible on the earthly side of death – or so we have been taught for the past two thousand years.

For the first Sunday in Lent, according to the orthodox interpretation of the first reading from Genesis, the evil snake seduces the naive woman who in turn traps the all-too-willing man into disobeying God. In the last reading, the One who is to save humanity from the consequences of that original sin is made a similar offer and declines. In between is the Apostle Paul in one of his more inscrutable arguments. But if we let go of tradition and listen to scholarship, these readings take on a very different meaning that can provide leadership into a true and lasting repentance for this season of Lent and beyond. These stories are not about sex, nor are they about conventional morality and petty trespass. They are about human consciousness, and the choice each person has to make about whether or not to participate in God's ongoing program of distributive justice-compassion.

Non-human inhabitants of the natural world don't spend their time agonizing over "the problem of evil." So far as humans know, the rabbit does not have a last regret as her neck is broken by the fox's jaws. Justice in God's realm is profoundly distributive. To eat and be eaten is the Eucharistic law of the universe. But thanks to the Trickster in God's garden, humanity was given the ability to make value judgments about whether the rabbit "deserved" to die, and whether the fox's action is "violent." While what the snake told Eve is true on the surface ("if you eat of the fruit of tree of knowledge of good and evil you will not die"), in pure Trickster reversal, that knowledge brings the kind of death that separates us from God's realm, where the lion and the lamb lie down together in trust that the universe provides for equal life in balance – the radical fairness of distributive justice.

So into the fray of Paul's tortured language (Romans 5:15-16, NRSV):

> But the *free gift* is not like the trespass. For if the many died through the one man's trespass, much more surely have the grace of God and the *free gift* in the grace of the one man, Jesus Christ, abounded for the many. And the *free gift* is not like the effect of the one man's sin. For the judgment following one trespass brought condemnation, but the *free gift* following many trespasses brings justification" (emphasis added).

The *free gift (charis)* is the grace of God. One human (Adam/Eve) chose to live outside the distributive justice of God's realm (sin/trespass), thereby bringing injustice to humanity because of the human demand for retribution (payback) instead of the fair distribution of sustainable life. But God's distributive justice-compassion (righteousness) is freely available in God's realm – the natural world where there is no "good-evil" dichotomy because all inhabitants of the universe (God's realm, the natural world) live in a fair balance that sustains life for all. That is the *free gift* of grace – distributive justice-compassion – returned to humanity by Jesus, *if* humanity chooses to accept and use it.

Where modern and traditional theology loses its way is in the misunderstanding of death. Jesus did not come so that people would no longer die, or so that people might die now but be brought back to life later when Jesus comes back again to finish what he failed to do the first time. Death is a fact of life – even (or especially) in God's realm. Every being in the universe, from *eucharyotes* to saber toothed tigers to dwarf stars and planets has a life cycle that continues so long as there is a sustaining niche for it. As soon as the niche evolves away from sustainability, the life form dies – whether it is animal, vegetable, mineral, or gas. However, the good news from the scientific point of view (and surprisingly from the Apostle Paul's ecstatic mystical insight) is that matter cannot be created or destroyed, it can only be transformed. That continuing, eternal transformation is something that humanity participates in, whether individuals choose to believe it or not. That is God's *free gift* of eternal life.

But what Paul was talking about was not the natural order of the evolution of the universe. Paul was talking about how humanity can replicate the distributive justice-compassion found in God's realm. Back to Romans 5:17-19:

> If, because of the one man's trespass, death exercised dominion through that one, much more surely will those who receive the abundance of grace and the *free gift of righteousness* exercise dominion *in life* through the one man, Jesus Christ. Therefore, just as one man's trespass led to condemnation for all, so one man's act of righteousness leads to justification and life for all. For just as by the one man's disobedience the many were made sinners, so by the one man's obedience the many will be made righteous.

Here Paul shifts to *free gift* as *righteousness* – as being made just (justification). If humanity is to replicate God's distributive justice it *can only be* in this life here and now, as radical fairness – consciously choosing radical abandonment of self-interest (love) – as Jesus taught by the example of his own death at the hands of Roman imperialism.

Jesus taught that radical abandonment of self-interest as the way to live in the kingdom of God in this life. Whether Jesus or anyone lives in the kingdom of God in another life before or after this one is irrelevant. The non-human inhabitants of God's realm do not have the need or the ability to choose radical abandonment of self-interest. Only humans on Planet Earth (so far as we know) have that ability and – more of the Trickster's irony – the *need* if humanity is to continue for much longer as a conscious life form. The *free gift* of distributive justice is there, all we have to do is accept it and live it.

Matthew's story of the temptation of Jesus now begins to take on a metaphor that has meaning in a postmodern, post-Christian world. When the Devil (the same Trickster as appeared to Adam/Eve, the first humans) appears to the One whom Christians consider to be sent as the reconciler between God's realm and humanity, the Trickster offers all the ego-enhancing, self-serving powers and principalities of Empire, with its glittering theology: piety, war, victory, and – here comes the tricky part– uneasy, ephemeral, peace: i.e., retributive justice, which is injustice, that brought about Jesus's undeserved, unfair, unjust death. Matthew's Jesus says, "Get out of here, Satan! Remember, it is written, "You are to pay homage to the Lord our God, and you are to revere him alone." Jesus chooses God's realm, which is justice and life here and now. He is able to do it because of his extraordinary trust in God's free gift.

We have the free gift (*charis*) of grace that brings justice and eternal life because we are part of God's realm, whether we know it, believe it, or not. Jesus's choice provides us with the way to begin the process – the program – of conscious participation.

Repent for the Kingdom II: Choosing Trust
Second Sunday in Lent

Genesis 12:1-4a; Psalm 121; Romans 4:1-5, 13-17; John 3:1-17

Christian dogma is in full bloom in these readings: Abraham gained eternal life as the father of many nations because of his "faith" in God's promise, according to the story in Genesis, and the corroboration in Paul's letter to the Romans. The lawyer (teacher/leader) Nicodemus sneaks off to talk to Jesus in the middle of the night and finds out that the only way to "see the kingdom of God" is to be born again, by water and the spirit, and to "believe in the name of the only Son of God."

"Faith" is clearly "belief" as far as the writer of John's Gospel is concerned. "Trust" in God's promise – the Old Covenant – has been replaced with "belief" in a violent God that sacrificed his only son in order to save humanity from darkness and evil. But that action apparently was not enough even for John, because his Jesus says, "No one can enter God's domain without being born of water and the spirit," *i.e.*, baptism. In the synoptic Gospels (Mark, Matthew, and Luke) Jesus says that the way to God's realm of justice-compassion is open to anyone with eyes and ears; Paul insists that God's realm of distributive justice-compassion has arrived with Jesus's death and resurrection, and we are invited to participate in that realm here and now; in John's interpretation, the way is blocked by water as effectively as the return to Eden is blocked by guardian angel fire. Does "repentance" mean baptism, or a conscious, continuing struggle through the flames for distributive justice-compassion? The war between the worlds that defined Jesus's life and teachings has been joined.

The Elves should have continued the speech John has Jesus say to Nicodemus. That might have pointed to a possible dialogue with Paul's treatise on justification by faith (trust) in the free gift (grace) made possible by Jesus's death and resurrection, discussed in the readings for last week (Romans 5:12-19). After declaring all those who don't "believe" in him as condemned already, John's

Jesus continues: "And this is the judgment: the light has come into the world, and people loved darkness rather than light because their deeds [works?] were evil. For all who do evil hate the light and do not come to the light, so that their deeds may not be exposed. But those who do what is true [works?] come to the light, so that it may be clearly seen that their deeds have been done in [as part of] God." So there are good works and evil works. But John, where is the trust that God – through Jesus – has acted in the world to restore justice-compassion? Where is the invitation to join the risen Christ in the ongoing program?

John uses mystical language, which barely succeeds as metaphor in the twenty-first century because so much of it has already been interpreted to make Jesus's message exclusive. If John had Paul's letters to refer to, he either misunderstood them or rejected the argument. John clearly does not agree with Paul that "to one who without works trusts him who justifies the ungodly, such faith is reckoned as righteousness." What has become conventional interpretation (which began before John's Gospel was written) would insist that "the ungodly" are those who do not believe either in the Jewish God or the Christian Messiah. Paul is saying that whoever trusts the message – whether Pagan or believer – is made "righteous" [saved] through the free gift of God's grace. John insists that the "free gift" comes with a price. Repentance – turning away from "pagan" ways – is accomplished by water and the spirit in the ritual of baptism. Only then is grace bestowed and the realm of God found.

It is a short hop that requires no thought to arrive at the conclusion that the only way to be saved from sin is through baptism. Once "sin" became equated with "sex," and the dogma that all humanity is fallen beyond redemption because the only way that human life is transmitted is through sex (original sin), baptism became the only way that infants could be saved from eternal hellfire and damnation. The final act at the closing end of life became the words of absolution, and anointing with oil. What went on in between (faith as belief versus good work) was the subject of heated debate among theologians, and the source of constant, nagging doubt – if not despair – on the part of the people of ever being allowed into the realm of God. By the fourth century, this debate and doubt had become attached to political power, and the course was set for western civilization into piety, war, victory, and uneasy peace.

John equates darkness with evil, and light with good. But postmodern, post-Christian mystics know better than that. Only by embracing and living through the darkness can the turn be made once more to the light. Twelve-step programs ("tough love") hang all their effectiveness on the fact of human psychology that only after hitting bottom can people trapped in addiction – whether medical, chemical, or behavioral – begin to come back. Any artist will be happy to witness to the universal experience of creativity: the novel, the painting, the idea, the solution – comes from the darkness, from nothing. God's realm – the natural earthly world – teaches very clearly that only after a time of incubation in the dark earth does the seed sprout into life. Matthew Fox calls it the *via negativa*, in his countering theology of original blessing. That theology (Creation Spirituality) got him into permanent trouble with Pope Benedict (then Cardinal Ratzinger, in charge of church doctrine – the former Inquisition), and ultimately thrown out of the Dominican Order. John's Jesus did have it partially right. The church still prefers deliberate scientific ignorance that attempts to keep people in darkness about God's realm. But in Fox's words, "Christ is the light of the world, which we now know is made *only* of light. Flesh is light and light is flesh. We eat, drink, sleep, breathe, and love that light."[48]

Paul argues, "the promise that he would inherit the world did not come to Abraham or to his descendants through the law but through the righteousness of faith [trust]." Paul is not talking about Roman law in this instance. He is talking about religious law, which demands an outward sign of an inward covenant, such as baptism or circumcision, to separate "them" from "us." But separation, or hierarchy, are anathema to Paul, as they should be to Christians today. Once one joins the ongoing program, which is the great work of distributive justice-compassion, there is no longer any distinction to be made between male or female, slave or free, Jew or gentile, or any of the other means by which humans

---

[48]Fox, *Sins of the Spirit*, 271.

determine who is "in" and who is "out." So even though the community that John was writing for may have been in a struggle for survival that demanded a litmus test for membership, such a requirement flies in the face of Jesus's open and inclusive ministry.

Christian tradition that demands an outward sign to prove one's status as "saved" such as being "born again" through the "baptism of the holy spirit" or the public declaration that Jesus is your personal lord and savior, commits the same error as the Corinthian and Roman Christians that drove Paul crazy. "For if Abraham was justified by works, he has something to boast about, *but not before God. . .*" whose free gift is there for all without qualification.

Repent for the Kingdom III:
Accepting Grace
Third Sunday in Lent

Exodus 17:1-7; Psalm 95; Romans 5:1-11; John 4:5-42

Traditional Christian interpretation of how the "New Testament" replaces the "Old" is clear in the readings for this Sunday. The first reading is the familiar story from Exodus, where the Hebrew people complain that Moses has led them out of slavery in Egypt into the desert only to die of thirst. In order to satisfy their demand that Moses prove God's promise is reliable, Moses uses his staff to strike a rock and produce a rush of water. The Psalm confirms the moral: "Do not harden your hearts, as at Meribah, as on the day at Massah in the wilderness, when your ancestors tested me . . . For forty years, I loathed that generation . . . Therefore in my anger I swore, they shall not enter my rest." The portion selected from Paul's letter to the Romans confirms the tradition: "God proves his love for us in that while we were still sinners, Christ died for us." Like a good story teller, the Elves return us to the opening metaphor, as John's Jesus trumps Moses by supplying the enemy Samaritan woman not with physical water, but spiritual water – recalling last week's conversation with Nicodemus about the necessity of baptism for salvation.

Most traditional Christians don't even need to read the text. We already know these stories and their traditional meaning. But the "tradition" has been in danger of diverting into false paths from the beginning. One of those false paths, which is all too easily found in John's Gospel, opposes Christian "enlightenment" to the "darkness" of Jewish tradition. Another is the path that leads to collaboration with political Empire. Both result from answers to what I pose as the "four questions for the apocalypse," which have informed these commentaries since they began. The four horsemen of the apocalypse – War, Famine, Disease, and Death – galloping down the ages out of the Revelation of John of Patmos (*not* the author of the Gospel) – have brought humanity to the brink of extinction in the twenty-first century. We continue to terrorize ourselves with their seeming inevitability. Whether or not that metaphor is the one that prevails depends upon how humanity (not just Christians) decides to answer:

1)   What is the nature of God (or the universe)? Violent or nonviolent?

2)   What is the nature of Jesus'smessage (or any spiritual message)? Inclusive or exclusive?

3)   What is faith? Literal belief, or commitment to the great work of justice-compassion?

4)   What is deliverance? Salvation from hell, or liberation from injustice?

These are eschatological questions because the choices we make about each of these dichotomies determine not only the quality of our individual and corporate lives, but the sustainability of human life on the Planet. Indeed, to choose nonviolence, inclusiveness, justice-compassion, and liberation directly challenges violence, exclusiveness, literal belief, and salvation, which define the seemingly inevitable development of John Dominic Crossan's theology of Empire.[49]

The traditional interpretation of the stories chosen for consideration on the third Sunday in Lent in Year A assumes that the answers to these four questions must be 1) violent; 2) exclusive; 3) literal belief; and 4) salvation from hell. Therefore, these readings need to be carefully unpacked and reclaimed, if possible, in the light of postmodern scientific and political knowledge, and post-Christian scholarship.

Probably the most important question to start with in considering these particular readings is whether "faith" means "literal belief." Very few (if any) of the stories in the Bible are literally "history remembered." Certainly the magical qualities of these particular stories should be suspect: Moses uses his magic wand to hit the rock and produce water. Jesus supernaturally reads the Samaritan woman's entire sexual history when she lies, "I have no husband." Taking these stories as literal, physical truth robs

---

[49]Crossan and Reed, 72-73; 288 ff.

them of their meaning and power. Moses is reduced to a wizard controlled by a vengeful, violent God, who holds a grudge for forty years. Jesus is reduced to a New Age self-help guru, mobbed by clamoring fans.

The second most important dilemma to consider with these particular readings is whether God is violent or nonviolent. Taken literally – as it has been for most of Christian theology – Paul's language implies violence. "[W]hile we were still sinners Christ died for us. Much more surely [therefore], now that we have been justified by his blood, will we be saved through him from the wrath of God." What most Christians listening on Sunday morning have no access to is the footnote in the *Harper Collins Study Bible (NRSV),* which explains that "The wrath of God" is not God's anger – a human emotion – but "the rightful response to what humans have done"[50] – i.e., rejecting God's realm of distributive justice-compassion and embracing retributive justice – getting even – which is not justice at all. The Old Testament is chock full of cautionary tales about what happens when the people turn away from trust in God's realm of distributive justice (where the rain falls equally on the good and the bad) and begin to rely on human systems.

Third, is the message inclusive or exclusive? At first blush, John's story would seem to be inclusive. After all, Jesus – against all social taboo – speaks alone to a woman outside the town. Not only that, this woman is a Samaritan – the sworn enemy of the Jews. John's Jesus also says to her, " . . . salvation is from the Jews." But he goes on to make it very clear that "true worshipers will worship the Father in spirit and in truth," presumably as opposed to Jewish tradition and religious law. "[F]or the Father seeks such as these to worship him." John's Jesus seems to be saying that while "salvation" may have come from the Jews, it has not stayed with them, and furthermore, God himself no longer seeks them out as true worshipers. By contrast, the portion of Paul's letter to the Romans says that "Christ died for the ungodly," which means everyone. If the writer of John's Gospel had access

---

[50]National Council of Churches, 2117n1.18.

to Paul's arguments, he does not agree. This language is extremely dicey in today's world.

The last choice – salvation from hell or liberation from injustice – only becomes clear when the words – especially Paul's words – are translated correctly into contemporary language, and when the customary understandings of such first century concepts as "sacrifice" and "reconciliation" are explained in twenty-first century terms.

In the first century, "sacrifice" was a ritual act that served two functions, both having to do with the restoration of right relationship (reconciliation). One function was to restore the balance between human patrons and clients in the Roman world. Put in simple twenty-first century social terms, if somebody invites me to dinner, I am then obligated to pay them back by inviting them to dinner. If hosting dinners (or picking up the tab) begins to fall on me too often, then I begin to resent it, and if the "friend" or colleague doesn't get the hint that it's his turn, I'll stop inviting him. Newspaper advice columns are full of these kinds of conundrums. In the first century Roman world (which included the entire Mediterranean area), the social system of patronage prevailed on a vertical, class, basis. Dinners were given by patrons for clients below them, and were accepted by clients of patrons above them. The banquet restored the balance between patrons and clients. This spilled over into the spiritual realm when the meat for the banquet was first ritually prepared as a sacrifice in the local temple. The animal was sacrificed (made sacred) by being first ritually slaughtered, then burnt on the altar to restore the balance of relationship with God (or gods – or in some cases with Caesar himself, as the ultimate patron); then a portion of the sacred meal was brought back to be shared among the people, or political, social, and business clients. As John Dominic Crossan points out, no one ever imagined that the animal that was slaughtered for the sacrificial – reconciling – meal, deserved to die, or was killed as a substitute for the person holding the banquet.

Paul's language about "justified by the blood of Christ" does not mean that believers' lives are paid for with the murdered blood of Jesus. It means that everyone has been included in God's realm of distributive justice-compassion, and are *made just* – become just – are restored or reconciled in their relationship with God because of Jesus's death. In Paul's culture, Jesus was the *metaphor* for the sacrifice that restores right relationship. If Jesus's death is the metaphoric sacrifice, how is that sacrifice distributed to the people? Symbolically, through the ritual of the common meal; practically, through the acceptance by each person of the challenge and opportunity to participate in the ongoing, here-and-now, realm of distributive justice-compassion. That participation is the radical abandonment of self-interest, and Jesus's life is the model. The result is salvation as liberation from injustice.

Given all this, does the story of Jesus's encounter with the Samaritan woman at the well have anything to say to postmodern Christian exiles from traditional belief? Only in the sense that what Jesus offers is grace – free gift – automatic relationship with God in God's realm of distributive justice-compassion. Grace is not "pardon" for sinning with six husbands; grace is not letting anybody off the hook for petty trespass. Grace is the free gift of citizenship in God's realm extended to all, not just those who worship on the mountain or in Jerusalem. Grace is the free gift of eternal life, realized through trust in the nature of God's realm – where there is no death, only transformation. "I sent you to reap that for which you did not labor," John's Jesus says. "Others have labored, and you have entered into their labor."

Repent for the Kingdom IV:
Trusting the Promise
Fourth Sunday in Lent

1 Samuel 16:1-13; Psalm 23; Ephesians 5:8-14; John 9:1-41

The metaphor of baptism as acceptance into the community of Christ continues to flow through the stories from the Gospel of John, chosen for these readings in Year A. In the ancient world, anyone born with an infirmity was assumed to be paying the price for ancestral sin. Jesus sees a blind man along the road, and decides to use him to make a different point: "[H]e was born blind so that God's works might be revealed in him." Jesus then proceeds to use earth and water to cover the man's eyes, and tells him to go to the pool of Siloam in Jerusalem and wash away the mud. When the man does so, he comes back able to see. The song, *Amazing Grace*, comes to mind. But in the story of the man born blind, the question seems to be, who exactly is the sinner? The blind man's parents? The blind man himself? Jesus? Or the Temple authorities, who have promised to expel from membership anyone who "confesses Jesus to be the Messiah"? After two thousand years, the answer is obvious: it's those nasty "Jews," the Temple authorities, whose spiritual blindness is inexcusable. "If you were born blind," Jesus tells them, "you would not have sin" of your own. "But now that you say 'we see,' your sin remains." Cherry-picked pseudo-Paul agrees. "Take no part in the unfruitful works of darkness, but instead expose them. For it is shameful even to mention what such people do secretly."

To interpret John's story as literal dogma is disastrous on many levels. Certainly local and international, political and religious antisemitism is one. Another is the idea that someone was born with a disability "so that God's works might be revealed" through encounters with that person. This idea is pervasive, especially as a pious response meant to give comfort either to the disabled person, or to the family; but it transforms the

God of distributive justice and love into an interventionist monster that deliberately causes suffering in order to enhance "himself." The person with the disability is cast into an equally horrible role either as hapless victim, or pious example. The one is diminished and disempowered, personally, socially, and politically; the other risks becoming a kind of interpersonal, passive-aggressive blackmailer. A third evil that can and does arise from such interpretations is to deny the means to rectify the disability, either through prohibiting birth control and therapeutic abortion, or by preventing access to liberating medical care because the condition is "God's will."

The writer of John's Gospel might be appalled at such literal misinterpretations of his ecstatic mysticism, meant to encourage a second-century community of believers in a fight for institutional survival. What is more powerful than metaphors of earth and water, light and darkness, sin and salvation? Perhaps the power of those metaphors is what prompted the developers of the RCL to pair John's story of Jesus healing the man born blind by anointing his eyes with mud and the story of the prophet Samuel anointing the shepherd boy who became the great King David, the direct ancestor of Jesus. Certainly the reading that connects the two in terms of metaphor is the beloved 23rd Psalm: "Even though I walk through a dark and dreary land, there is nothing that can shake me. She has said she won't forsake me. I'm in Her hand."[51]

Taken out of context, the revelation to Samuel of God's new choice for king over the Israelites seems to foreshadow the gradual realization of John's man born blind that Jesus is the Christ, the anointed one. Jesse presents seven of his sons to Samuel, but none of them is accepted until Jesse admits that his youngest son is still out tending the sheep. "Now he was ruddy, and had beautiful eyes, and was handsome," gushes the Hebrew teller of the tale, "The Lord said, . . . this is the one." One wonders what the older brothers were like.

Contrary to Christian custom, the Old Testament story is where the real power lies in this series of readings, but the entire story has to be included: Saul and Samuel; Saul's beloved son

---

[51] McFerrin, Bobby, "The 23rd Psalm Dedicated to My Mother."

Jonathan (who became David's beloved companion); conquest, Covenant, blood sacrifice, imperial violence; and ego-driven failure to trust in God's word. Despite the fact that we are supposed to wait until Year B, please read 1 Samuel 8-17. You might want to pop some corn first or throw another log on the fire. It's a saga worthy of Shakespeare.

Briefly, the people of Israel want a king. All the other people in the neighborhood have kings. Why not us? And besides, Samuel is old, and his sons – who were supposed to act as judges and continue Samuel's work – have betrayed the work instead, have turned away from God, and generally screwed up. God does not want the people to have a king, because kings are notorious for imperially ignoring God's laws about distributive justice-compassion and for presiding over the inevitable march of the normalcy of civilization into oppressive Empire. The prophet Samuel agrees with God on this, but then God tells him to go ahead and listen to the people and give them their king. Only when they have one will they realize what a mistake it is. So Samuel finds and anoints Saul. Saul does a great job for about two years. Then one day when Samuel doesn't show up in time (maybe he couldn't get the donkey started, or a boulder had rolled into the path), Saul takes it upon himself to take matters into his own hands and performs a sacrifice to God. This was bad enough, but then when Saul proceeds to eliminate the Amalekites – as directed by God – he decides to save for himself the best of the flocks and the cattle "and all that was valuable," including – presumably – the king of the Amalekites, perhaps intending to exchange him for ransom later. God is so angry at Saul's disobedience that he tells Samuel, "I regret that I made Saul king, for he has turned back from following me and has not carried out my commands." This is terrible. Saul has caused God himself to change his mind. Such a breach of Covenant can only be rectified with the ritual sacrifice by Samuel of the king of the Amalekites – who was supposed to have been killed by Saul in the first place. "Then Samuel went to Ramah," his home – to which he had been trying to retire for eight chapters and several years of disaster on the part of Saul. "Samuel did not see Saul again until the day of his death, but Samuel grieved over Saul. And the Lord was sorry that he had made Saul king over Israel." (1 Samuel 15:34-35).

What a cautionary tale for an election year.

Time after time, Saul takes matters into his own hands instead of following God's command (and the laws of the land). And what is God's command – from Samuel to Isaiah to Jeremiah to the great commission at the end of Matthew's Gospel to Paul's letter to the Romans? Justice. Distributive, unconditional, free gift, grace-filled justice. But doesn't the violence in this story fly in the face of all that? God wants Saul to destroy all traces of the Amalekites – women, children, old people, men, cattle, sheep – maybe even scorch their earth with fire and sow it with salt. Instead of pardoning or rescuing the captured king Agag – which would have been a serious enough personal and political rebuke to Saul – Samuel cuts him up into pieces as a human sacrifice "before God"; and Agag knows he has met his own judgment: "Surely this is the bitterness of death," he says.

But it's not about political execution in the service of Empire. Samuel's act restores the Covenant the people of Israel had with God, which their king Saul had dishonored. Samuel's act is an echo of the earlier challenge that Saul had righteously and graphically delivered to the people who had agreed to surrender to a pagan enemy, and refused to join Saul's army against the Ammonites. In that case, the *people* had broken the Covenant with God. Saul chops up a yoke of oxen and carries the pieces around to all the camps, saying "Whoever does not come out [and support] Saul and Samuel, so shall it be done to his oxen!" So should it have been done to Saul.

Breaking Covenant with God brings war, famine, disease, death, economic, political, personal disaster. Instead of acting from radical abandonment of self-interest (love), which brings the restoration of God's rule, where the lion and the lamb lie down in distributive, balanced, justice and peace, civilizations are normally built through victory, whether military, economic, political, or personal, and only after such victory are justice and peace discussed. Justice in normal civilization is retribution: an eye for an eye. In Samuel's bloody, graphic demonstration, Saul's imperialism, which he chose for himself, is ransomed life-for-life.

God himself regrets ever choosing Saul as the people's king, and Samuel's personal grief is profound. The only recourse for God is to overturn convention and choose a lowly shepherd, the youngest of eight sons – David is not even the magical number seven.

Much later, as the writer of John's Gospel tells the story, God acts again to demonstrate to the blind people, who prefer the false brilliance of Empire, how to restore God's realm of distributive justice-compassion. This time the "king" is a powerless peasant who trusted the promise, even though it meant losing his life. But the community that John's Jesus was addressing did not go far enough. Then as now, joining the new Covenant means going beyond identity as "belief" to identity as purpose. Whether the first century or the twenty-first, acceptance of the new Covenant means choosing to participate in the program. That can only be accomplished by abandoning self-interest and trusting the promise. "If you were blind," John's Jesus says, "you would not have sin. But now that you say, 'we see, [and you do not participate]' your sin remains."

We have no excuse.

Repent for the Kingdom V:
Redeeming the Bones
Fifth Sunday in Lent

Ezekiel 37:1-14; Psalm 130; Romans 8:6-11; John 11:1-45

> "Dem bones dem bones dem-a dry bones . . .
> Now hear de word ob de Lord."

The sermon for this week is a cake-walk for literalists.

Ezekiel: "And you shall know that I am the Lord when I open your graves, and bring you up from your graves. . . . I will put my spirit within you, and you shall live, and I will place you on your own soil. . . ."

John: "Martha, the sister of the dead man, said to [Jesus], 'Lord already there is a stench because he has been dead four days.' Jesus said to her, 'Did I not tell you that if you believed, you would see the glory of God?' So they took away the stone . . . [and Jesus] cried in a loud voice, 'Lazarus, come out!' The dead man came out."

Psalm 130:   "Out of the depths I cry to you, O Lord . . . If you, O Lord should mark my iniquities, Lord, who could stand? . . . I wait for the Lord, my soul waits . . . more than those who watch for the morning. . . . For with the Lord there is steadfast love, and with him is great power to redeem. It is he who will redeem Israel from all its iniquities."

Paul: "If the Spirit of him who raised Jesus from the dead dwells in you, he who raised Christ from the dead will give life to your mortal bodies also through his Spirit that dwells in you."

All we have to do is repent from our postmodern skepticism and sin and *believe* that just as Ezekiel raised the army of dry bones in the desert using God's command, so Jesus, the son of God, in his most astounding miracle of all, raised Lazarus from the dead with his own divine power. God in turn raised Jesus from the dead, and so also will the spirit of the Christ who is now one with God raise bodily – physically – those who *believe*. Those who don't believe, as cherry-picked Paul says, "cannot please God. . . . To set the mind on the flesh is death, but to set the mind on the Spirit is life and peace." Is that really all we need, heading into the denouement of Holy Week and Easter Sunday?

Very little of Ezekiel is ever included in the Lectionary readings. Five selections are used in Year A, and three in Year B. The prophesy about the army of dry bones is used for two of the five celebrations in Year A: the fifth Sunday in Lent, and the Easter vigil. It is used again in Year B at Pentecost. None of these are combined with readings that deal with the subject that Ezekiel was most concerned about, which is exile. They are all used to bolster the Christian interpretation of salvation from hell through belief in the physical resurrection of Jesus, and the conveying of the holy spirit upon those who believe.

In the postmodern, post-Enlightenment, post-Christian twenty-first century, these readings are in real danger of being lost to ignorance of what they may have meant to the ancient Hebrew world and the early Christian way, and therefore lost to indifference about any prophetic relevance they may yet hold. But in a world bereft of meaningful metaphor that reflects current cosmology, Paul and Ezekiel may possibly be reclaimed. The story about the resurrection of Lazarus is more problematic. Second century people were no more likely than twenty-first century people to take such a story as literal truth, but nonetheless, to put it in contemporary terms, the story of the raising of Lazarus is perhaps about as useful as Elvis Presley sightings – except for one word that John's Jesus says to Martha: I *AM* the resurrection and the life. The verb is present tense, not past or future. The power of Jesus's message is the certainty of eternal life here and now, not there and then. That is a weak point to hang an argument on, even though Marcus J. Borg does so. "Martha spoke of the resurrection as future, as 'on the last day.' Jesus's response shifts to the present tense. . . . Martha thought of the resurrection as a future event at the end of time; but Jesus's response corrects her misunderstanding and speaks of resurrection as a present reality."[52] Nevertheless, Borg is the Biblical scholar who has done the research. If the writer of John's Gospel had Paul's extraordinary theology to refer to, all of Jesus's "I Am" sayings would have to be about present reality – realized eschatology – and would be an invitation to join him in raising the dead.

"Raising the dead" is not about bringing back Elvis. Raising the dead is about returning from exile. Millions of people on this Planet are in political, physical, and economic exile from homelands, and from the basic needs for human survival: food, clothing, shelter, education, and medical care. Millions more are in spiritual or religious exile, no longer able or willing to suspend disbelief in the premodern gods and cosmologies that continue to prevail. Still more are in personal exile from sustainable relationships, estranged from family, friends, and social networks. Nearly all of us think we are exiled from the interconnected web of our own biosphere.

For this reason, it is vastly unfair – if not unconscionable – to cherry-pick Paul's words from Romans 8 in order to perpetuate the very misunderstanding that John's Jesus gently pointed out to Martha. It is equally unfair to the shamanic experience of the ancient prophet Ezekiel, whose purpose was to encourage – that is bestow or invoke courage – on the demoralized Hebrew captives in Nebuchadnezzar's Babylon. We in twenty-first century United States are no less exiles than those of the sixth century B.C.E. from distributive justice, represented of old by the God of Abraham, Isaac, Jacob, and Jesus, and described by Jesus and interpreted by Paul as "the Kingdom of God." God will act to restore the people to their own land, promises Ezekiel. God will act to restore distributive justice-compassion, and the writer of John's Gospel and the Apostle Paul proclaim that God has acted through the life and death of Jesus, and continues to act to this day whenever anyone – believer or not – chooses to accept the invitation.

---

[52]Borg, 199.

If the Elves had allowed us to read to the end of Romans 8, the entire argument for this fifth Sunday in Lent would have been moot. "[I]n all these things we are more than conquerors," says Paul – more powerful than imperial rulers, because "neither death, nor life, nor angels, nor rulers, nor things present nor things to come, nor powers, nor height, nor depth, nor anything else in all creation, will be able to separate us from the love of God in Christ Jesus our Lord." The exile is over. The dead have been raised. The bones of the martyrs to injustice are redeemed and justified.

Further, the dry bones raised by Ezekiel become a metaphor for those who died in the service of God's justice; those who died working to restore God's distributive justice-compassion to God's earth, and who themselves never saw the transformed earth. The army of dry bones is an army exiled from justice. Fairness demands that if Jesus was resurrected into an Earth transformed into God's realm of justice-compassion, then all the other martyrs who died too soon should also be raised with him. "But in fact," Paul writes in 1 Corinthians 15:20, "Christ has been raised from the dead, the first fruits of those who have died." It is the Christ – the transformed and transfigured post-Easter Jesus – who has started that general resurrection, which restores justice-compassion to a transformed Earth. The transformation has begun with Jesus, and continues with you and me – IF we sign on to the program.

This is a far cry from feeling sorry about petty sin, (which is the dumbed down meaning that most people think "repentance" means); it is also a very far cry from the deep and unforgivable sorrow that somehow are personally responsible for Jesus's crucifixion (substitutionary atonement). Petty sin, feeling sorry, even deep sorrow over an impossible responsibility, do nothing to empower people to radically change the way we live. Further, when that sorrow is experienced as "unforgivable," the whole point of Jesus's message is overturned.

Finally, there is a fascinating anachronism in John 11:2, if John's Gospel is to be read as a chronological narrative: "Mary was the one who anointed the Lord with perfume and wiped his feet with her hair." This only makes sense if John was writing to a group of Christians who already knew the stories from Mark. Borrowing for a moment from the readings for Monday of Holy

Week (John 12:1-11), perhaps this time before Holy Week would be an appropriate time to create a ritual of commitment to follow Jesus into and through the coming days.

Invitation to Participate in the Kingdom Community

One: There is a story in the Gospel of Mark, chapter 14, about when Jesus was at Bethany in the house of Simon the leper. As he sat at table, a woman came with an alabaster jar of very costly ointment of nard, and she broke open the jar and poured the ointment on his head. . . . Jesus said, "Truly, I tell you, wherever the good news is proclaimed in the whole world, what she has done will be told in remembrance of her." And what was it that she did? Knowing she would probably not have the chance to do so if Jesus were executed by the Romans – which was highly likely – she anointed his body in advance for burial. So I invite us – in remembrance of her – to anoint one another as a symbol of our commitment to do what we can to live in a community of nonviolent justice-compassion, knowing that the struggle never ends.

[Start the oil among the people]

Invitation to the Meal

One: In Paul's first letter to the community in Corinth, he scolds them for falling out of the practice of justice-compassion, and getting sidetracked by the normalcy of injustice. He reminds the people that he received from the Lord what he also handed on to them. Jesus, on the night when he was betrayed by those who were trapped in the very same forces of injustice that affected the Corinthians, and all of us, "took a loaf of bread, and when he had given thanks, he broke it and said, 'this is my body that is for you. Do this in remembrance of me.'" If the Earth belongs to God, then participating in God's distributive justice means a radical denial of our own self-interest. As we share this bread, we share ourselves and make no distinction between them and us.

[Start the bread among the people]

One: Then Paul says, "In the same way he took the cup also, after supper, saying 'This cup is the new covenant written in my blood. Do this as often as you drink it, in remembrance of me.'" Again, in case we didn't get it when he broke the bread, Paul's Jesus says, the new Covenant – the new partnership with one another in God's Kingdom – is written in blood.

[Pour the wine and juice]

One: Whenever we eat this bread and share this cup, we proclaim our participation in God's ongoing, continuing work of justice-compassion until it is accomplished.

[Start the wine and juice among the people]

The Divine Warrior
Palm Sunday

Matthew 21:1-11; Psalm 118:1-2, 19-29; Isaiah 50:4-9a;
Psalm 31:9-16; Philippians 2:5-11; Matthew 26:14-27:66;
Matthew 27:11-54

Matthew's Gospel packs a great deal into the last week of Jesus's life after his "triumphal entrance into Jerusalem" – five chapters of teachings and stories, very little of which can be directly attributed to Jesus. The story is lifted wholesale from Mark, but Matthew conforms it with a prophesy from Zecharaiah and to images in Psalm 118. Even though Matthew's story is based on Zecharaiah 9:9, that passage is not read until much later in Year A. Zechariah 9 contains an oracle about a Divine Warrior, who arrives "humble and riding on a donkey" instead of imperial chariots and war horses – actually, the colt of a donkey, which is even less threatening. (The writer of Matthew's Gospel seems to have misunderstood the translation, and places Jesus atop *two* donkeys! So much for literalism.)

Because it is highly likely that none of this story ever actually happened, and because the only reading that changes each year is the one from the synoptic Gospels (Matthew in this Year A), it may seem pointless to revisit the scriptures that reinforce the tradition. As with all stories, however, the point is not whether or not they are factual, but what they mean. Perhaps we do not read Zechariah because the imagery does not match the traditional concept of Jesus as the "suffering servant" of Isaiah. Instead of being humiliated and vindicated, the Divine Warrior arrives with predictions of victory, pledges of security, and renewal of Covenant. Instead of passive acceptance of a preordained fate that supports the doctrine of substitutionary atonement, the Divine Warrior models resistance to empires that reject God's justice: "Then I will encamp at my house as a guard, so that no one shall march to and fro; no oppressor shall again overrun them, for now I have seen with my own eyes."

The Divine Warrior is a classic masculine archetype– not restricted to gender, of course. Warrior Energy is the energy of leadership, of protection, of moving outward, of exploration – as well as defense and conquest. Warrior energy inspires us – especially when we are young – to seek out adventure, to explore strange new worlds – to boldly go where no one has gone before ... Those strange new worlds might be galaxies, solar systems, planets, ecosystems, and they might be that spark of creativity that propels us outside the ordinary boxes of thought and into new paradigms, such as a commitment to the ongoing work of restoring God's realm of distributive justice-compassion. The Warrior is single-minded in his (or her) dedication to a cause that transcends Self, and is steadfast on the journey.

The Hero is another masculine archetype that according to Robert Moore and Douglas Gillette,[53] is more concerned with ego. The Hero's loyalty is to himself (or herself); the concern is with appearances, with impressing others with one's power. When paired with cherry-picked Paul, Jesus's triumphal entry into Jerusalem seems to mirror the imperial heroism and theology of piety, war, victory, leading to uneasy peace. But as Marcus Borg and John Dominic Crossan remind us,[54] Mark's original story is a caricature of the imperial *parousia*, the ticker-tape parade through the open gates of the city in honor of the returning conquering hero. Jesus's entrance is a deliberate parody – a political demonstration.

Like all archetypes, the Divine Warrior has two sides – a healthy, nurturing, positive side, and a negative, shadow, demonic side. Because the Divine Warrior is committed to a transpersonal purpose, and will give up his or her life in the service of that purpose, the Divine Warrior risks betrayal by the forces of conventional powers and principalities, and enslavement by its own demonic shadow. The Warrior denies himself for the good of the team. The Warrior believes what her leaders tell her. The dark side, the Shadow Warrior, may be seen in global warming, Native

---

[53]Moore and Gillette, *King Warrior Magician Lover,* 1990.

[54]Borg and Crossan, *The Last Week,* 2006.

American reservations, South African apartheid, religious intolerance, nationalism, and Empire.

Throughout Holy Week, beginning with Palm Sunday, runs the theme of the end of the way things have always been, the beginning of the transformation from oppression to liberation, from darkness to light, from sin to salvation – i.e., eschatology. The question is, what kind of eschatology? Apocalyptic – God suddenly intervenes; or participatory – human action in partnership with God changes the paradigm? Apocalyptic eschatology is by definition violent. God's direct intervention overthrows everything and forcefully establishes God's kingdom on earth, ready or not. The prime example is found in the Revelation to John. By contrast, participatory eschatology – which Jesus taught – establishes God's kingdom – God's realm – of justice-compassion through human action in partnership with God.

Whether participatory eschatology is violent or nonviolent may depend on the nature of the god that humanity is in partnership with. Covenant, nonviolence, justice-compassion, and peace is the theology of God's realm as taught by Jesus. The clue to the difference with imperial theology is found in Zechariah's Divine Warrior, who does not arrive as a conquering hero. Instead the Warrior has finished his work, and can now turn those energies to bringing God's peace to the people by restoring distributive justice-compassion with a sweeping demilitarization (Zecharaiah 9:10). Because of the covenant relationship that God has with the people of Israel, God will restore the people to the land, and will continue to raise up Divine Warriors as partners with God to assure future peace and security. The evidence points toward nonviolence throughout the Old Testament, and in everything Jesus taught, and in every action he took – even the trashing of the merchants in the Temple courtyard. As Marcus Borg points out, " . . . because some Christians have occasionally used Jesus's prophetic act . . . as a justification for violent action, it is important to underline that minor property damage in a symbolic act is very different from lethal violence against persons."[55]

---

[55]Borg, *Jesus: Uncovering the Life,* 247.

In late 2005, a Christian Peacemaker Team was captured in
Iraq and held for one hundred eighteen days. On March 9, 2006,
Tom Fox, one of the team members, was shot and killed execution
style, and his body dumped in a residential neighborhood in
western Baghdad. On March 23, the three remaining team
members, Jim Loney, Norman Kember, and Harmeet Singh
Sooden, were released by British forces. The captors had left
before the soldiers arrived. The surviving team members refused
to testify against their captors, and as a result, the people who
murdered Tom Fox were released. The reasons for not testifying
include that their captors would be subject to the death penalty,
and that they – like we – are involved in a struggle for survival.
James Loney writes in *Sojourners Magazine*, "We were given
birth to give birth, and every body is holy. The hardest birth of all
is dying. . . . Our job is to allow God to breathe us through,
together, in the mystery of incarnation . . . And peace – the
birthright . . . of every human being . . . I have come to cherish as
the dearest and most essential of all things, even more than life
itself. The gun, the bomb, the military-industrial office chair, the
words that carpet-bomb the garden God gave us to share: These
are anti-Christ indeed. . . . "[56]

In a time of bellicosity on the part of the last remaining
twenty-first century super power, as in the first century, perhaps it
is time for Zecharaiah's Divine Warrior to join forces with Isaiah's
suffering servant. Nonviolence does not preclude aggressive action
in restoring distributive justice-compassion. Aggressive action
does not necessarily mean physical action, such as pouring pig's
blood on missile nose cones. Aggressive action means
commitment to the restoration of distributive justice-compassion
by pledging resistance to the whole theology of imperial violence,
as suggested in the following portion of the *Litany of Resistance*,
created by Jim Loney:

All: With the help of God's grace
One: Let us resist and confront evil everywhere we find it
All: With the help of God's grace

---

[56]Loney, 12.

One:	With the waging of war
All:	We will not comply
One:	With the forces of fear
All:	We will not comply
One:	With laws that betray human life
All:	We will not comply
One:	With governments that are blind to the sanctity of life
All:	We will not comply
One:	With economic structures that impoverish and dehumanize
All:	We will not comply
One:	With the perpetuation of violence
All:	We will not comply
One:	With the help of God's grace
All:	We will struggle for justice, we will stand for what is true, we will love even our enemies, we will resist all evil
One:	Let us abide in God's love
All:	Thanks be to God

Easter

What Does It All Mean?
Easter Sunday

Acts 10:34-43; Jeremiah 31:1-6; Psalm 118:1-2, 14-24;
Colossians 3:1-4; John 20:1-18; Matthew 28:1-10

Peter's Sermon in Caesarea (Acts 10:34-43); Psalm 118; and the story of Mary Magdalene being first on the scene (John 20:1-18) are always offered as traditional readings for Easter Sunday morning. These are the pillars of Christian faith: Peter's sermon tells the story of Jesus in about 200 words, much as the story of the Hebrew people is told and retold at Passover and throughout the Jewish liturgical year. Psalm 118 becomes a song of vindication for Jesus as Lord instead of a song of praise at being able to once more enter the Temple in a condition of reconciliation with God. "[T]he stone that the builders rejected has become the chief cornerstone," appropriated from the original meaning, refers to the risen Christ as the foundation of the church. Finally, our favorite Mary, the forgiven sinner, walks in the garden alone and encounters the personal savior.

Easter Sunday is easy. The scent of forced-bloom lilies in the sanctuary is overwhelming; the local symphony orchestra's entire brass section has a paying gig – even the trombonists have been dispersed throughout the city. The choir turns its stoles to the gold side and screams Handel's Hallelujah Chorus. People show up who haven't been seen since Christmas Eve. The plate collection is the most lucrative of the year. The thunderstorms of Good Friday and Saturday are over and done, and the sun is shining. The Easter ham is slow-cooking in the oven, and the kids are stuffed with multi-colored Easter Peeps® and chocolate bunnies.

Who needs a sermon? Everyone who slides over the uncomfortable story about "resurrection" and talks about spring: New life from death – as though Jesus were planted like winter wheat and appeared along with the crocus and the daffodils to prove that nobody really dies, that "love is come again, like wheat that springeth green." These are perfectly usable and valid metaphors for the cycles of birth, life, death, rebirth – the archetype of the dying rising god, who brings renewal, fertility, hope. But if that is all Jesus's resurrection means, he is no different from the Celtic gods like Herne, or Lugh, or the Greek goddesses Persephone and Demeter.

Peter's sermon in Acts is no help. He reiterates the story, but already Jesus's Way has been watered down to forgiveness of petty personal sins. But then, Peter never did quite get what Jesus was all about, and very nearly joined Judas in opting for collaboration with the normalcy of Roman rule. The Colossians passage is just as bad: We are piously advised to "seek the things that are above, where Christ is." Authentic Paul's commitment to distributive justice-compassion has been eliminated by the usurper writer, along with Paul's passion about life transformed by participation with the risen Christ in God's kingdom, not the Emperor's. The creators of the RCL have eliminated the part where after the women have left to tell the men that Jesus will meet them in Galilee, Matthew suggests the distinct possibility of a hoax (Matthew 28:11-15). The tomb guards have run in a panic to the chief priests. Once the priests met with the elders, it was clear that a cover-up was necessary. The guards were paid "a large sum of money" to forget about angels and earthquakes, and to claim a "Passover Plot" perpetrated by Jesus's followers, "still told among the Jews to this day." To claim that Jesus's disciples stole his body and made up a story about a resuscitated corpse is no worse than dumbing down the message.

Throughout these meditations on the Revised Common Lectionary has run a thread called "Piety vs. Covenant," or the theology of Empire (piety, war, victory, peace) versus the theology of Covenant (nonviolence, distributive justice-compassion, peace). The only opportunity offered in the Year A Easter readings to claim something different from the imperial paradigm that still prevails in twenty-first century conventional Christianity is the Old Testament prophet of the Covenant, Jeremiah. So long as the people honor God's mandate for distributive justice-compassion, God will provide protection and prosperity. In the reading picked for this Easter Sunday, Jeremiah assures the "remnant" of the people left in Jerusalem that as a result of keeping the Covenant, they will be reunited with those returning from exile in Babylon.

What does it mean to keep the Covenant in a postmodern, post-Enlightenment, pluralistic, global, twenty-first century? Clearly the Way to keeping the Covenant is not to look "up" to God.

In Mark's original version of Easter morning, the women who found the tomb empty were so terrified they simply ran away without telling anyone. But the story could not have ended there, or this meditation would not have been written, and nearly two thousand years of Christian history would never have transpired. Somebody added a codicil in which the women did as the young man sitting in the tomb suggested, and they "briefly" told "those around Peter" what they had seen. In Matthew and Luke, angels explain what has happened. By the time John creates his version, there is only one witness – Mary Magdalene – who carries the story to the rest of the scattered followers. Regardless of how it is told, the story is the same: Jesus is not here. He is risen. That is a terrifying realization. If Jesus is not here, what happens to the message? What happens to distributive justice-compassion? What happens to those who had the courage to oppose the Empire? The visitors who find the tomb empty are confronted with a choice: If God's realm of justice-compassion is to be restored – as the Biblical record presents the argument – it will either be by the direct intervention of God alone (apocalyptic eschatology), or by the collaborative action of God in partnership with humanity (participatory eschatology).

For twenty-first century Christians, with Jesus seriously dead, and contemporary cosmology rendering theistic, personalized gods beyond belief, the only way to renew the Covenant is a participatory eschatology, through equal partnership with a kenotic God "whose gracious presence as free gift (Paul's *charis*) is the beating heart of the universe and does not need to threaten, to intervene, to punish, or to control. A God whose presence is justice and life and whose absence is injustice and death."[57]

---

[57]Crossan and Reed, 291.

Despite all the temptations that the Empire offers, the renewing of the Covenant is up to us. On Planet Earth, we can only look "out" (not "up") to find other planets and galaxies, and perhaps to discover something about the nature of the universe, the character of the spirit/creator we call "God," and the conditions in which humanity finds itself; but then we can only look "in" to ourselves to create the response that will result in the partnership.

> He had stood his ground honorably to the very end; he had kept his word. The moment he cried out "Eli Eli" and fainted, Temptation had captured him for a split second and led him astray. The joys, marriages and children were lies; the decrepit, degraded old men who shouted coward, deserter, traitor at him were lies. All – all were illusions sent by the Devil. His disciples were alive and thriving. They had gone over sea and land and were proclaiming the Good News. Everything had turned out as it should, glory be to God!
>
> He uttered a triumphant cry: "It is accomplished!"
>
> And it was as though he had said: "Everything has begun."[58]

---

[58]Kazantzakis, 496.

Reincarnation
Second Sunday in Eastertide

Acts 2:14a, 22-32; Psalm 16; 1 Peter 1:3-9; John 20:19-31

For the season of Easter in Year A, the Elves have us studying the First Letter of Peter, John, and Acts for six weeks. After the death of Jesus, the first question to be asked was, what happened to his followers? Once the idea of Jesus's resurrection began to be known, the question became how did the new story fit into Jewish community and religious life? Within a few years, what became known as the Way of Jesus proclaimed by Jesus's original followers began to develop its own communities, some still within the Jewish tradition, and others among gentiles and pagans.

Twenty-first century scholarship is beginning to come to a consensus that Acts was created in the early second century – perhaps as late as 150 C.E. Because whoever wrote Acts also wrote Luke, the impact of that timing on the interpretation of the content of Luke's Gospel is also being considered and debated by the Jesus Seminar scholars as they work to reconstruct the earliest Christian communities, from Galilee to Rome. Regardless of the timing, however, the point is that Acts is not history remembered. Like the Gospels and the various letters included in the New Testament, Acts was created in response to a need for standardizing an emerging Christianity that was moving farther and farther away from Jewish religion and from Jesus's original message.

Given that history and purpose, is there any point in pursuing the Bible study laid out for us between now and Pentecost other than to underscore traditional Christian belief and dogma? The time has come once again to revisit the four questions for the apocalypse, which are the underlying questions of these commentaries, and which provide a framework for reclaiming Jesus's message for a postmodern, post-Christian, twenty-first century:

1) What is the nature of God? Violent or nonviolent?

2) What is the nature of Jesus's message? Inclusive or exclusive?

3) What is faith? Literal belief, or commitment to the great work of justice-compassion?

4) What is deliverance? Salvation from hell, or liberation from injustice?

While keeping these questions in mind, the next six Sundays may be seen as an unfolding commitment to the work begun by Jesus for a developing Christianity, whether in the first or the twenty-first century. The journey begins with Doubt, and progresses to a dawning Recognition, formation of Community, committed Faith, continuing Revelation, and Salvation. The traditional theme for this week is, Even though you haven't physically seen the risen Christ, faith (belief) in his resurrection will save you.

Editorial writers for major U.S. newspapers are often tempted to weigh in on Easter Sunday (often a slow news day) with some theological or philosophical profundity. For example, "Easter – A Movable Feast"[59] captured the misperception of most of the non-Christian world that "The Easter story speaks to everyone about the universal fear of death" and that "[t]o believing Christians, the resurrection is literal. For others, it may be the hope that they will live on in their families, their friends and their society, and in the things they have done. . . . [Easter] has moved well along on the path to toleration and understanding, although, as always with such things, there are many miles to go." Indeed. Like the famous Doubting Thomas in the suggested reading from John's Gospel, the editorial writer couldn't see beyond the dichotomy set up between literalists demanding physical evidence and the depressing conclusion that eternal life is only available to famous people. The rest of us – who may have no children or grandchildren, or can't get a publisher to pay attention to our work – are doomed. Jesus's inclusive and anti-imperial message of distributive justice-compassion is then further eviscerated, and we are left with gutless liberal tolerance and vague attempts at "understanding" – ourselves? others? The writer did not say.

---

[59]*The Washington Post*, March 28, 2008.

Only one fact about Jesus's death and resurrection can be documented from the first century, and treated as factual, literal truth in the twenty-first century: Jesus died at the hands of the Roman Empire. The rest of the stories are attempts to reconcile that death with what Jesus taught about living in the kingdom of God's distributive justice-compassion. But the readings for this second Sunday in Eastertide tell us nothing about that. Instead, they are theological arguments that reinforce conventional piety.

The writer of 1 Peter points believers to heaven and the salvation of their souls. The people in this particular late first century Christian community are reminded that because of Jesus's resurrection, they have "new birth into a living hope" that they will inherit eternal life when they die because their souls have been saved. They were very likely under some pressure to conform to the society around them. The letter acknowledges that they may have to suffer "various trials," but their faith (belief) in the promise of heaven gives them the strength to resist. What do they resist? To take a sneak peek ahead – and into a section not included by the Elves in this six-week series – they are *not* resisting the injustice of Empire. Quite the opposite: "For the Lord's sake accept the authority of every human institution, whether of the emperor as supreme, or of governors, as sent by him to punish those who do wrong and to praise those who do right. . . . As servants of God, live as free people, yet do not use your freedom as a pretext for evil. Honor everyone. Love the family of believers. Fear God. Honor the emperor" (1 Peter 2:13-17).

Jesus never said to *dis*honor the emperor. But he did remind people that the emperor owns only the coin on which his likeness appears. The subversive meaning of Jesus's answer about whether to pay taxes to Caesar is lost to the letter writer, and to be fair, has remained a point of debate since the day it was uttered. *See* Mark 12:13-17; Matthew 22:15-22; Luke 20:19-26; Thomas 100:1-4: "Give the emperor what belongs to the emperor, give God what belongs to God. . . ." Anyone familiar with Jewish theology would know that the Earth, and all that is in it, belongs to God. But to "accept the authority of every human institution" means collaboration with the forces of injustice. Surely Jesus did not advise the poor to pay exorbitant taxes so that kings can go off to wage preemptive wars; surely he did not suggest that unskilled workers who clean corporate offices should be denied a living wage; surely he did not suggest that people should forfeit their homes to leveraged, multi-national, corporate debt. Nor would Jesus suggest, as the writer of 1 Peter would, that those suffering under oppressive systems should passively hope for a better deal in the next life. Jesus makes the point clear with his advice about how to respond when the oppressor insults you, or demands your coat or your services as porter. In case his listeners missed the point, he provides a personal physical illustration during the last week of his life with his parody of an emperor's triumphal entry into Jerusalem and his subsequent demonstration against Temple corruption. The crucifixion, of course, is the terrifying result his later interpreters are confronted with. Perhaps that is why they reduced the Way from radical, costly discipleship to conformity with powers and principalities.

The writer of Luke-Acts has the Apostle Peter (not the writer of 1 Peter) address the Jews in Jerusalem and Judea, accusing them along with God himself of being accessories to Jesus's execution: "[Whom], according to the definite plan and foreknowledge of God, you crucified and killed by the hands of those outside the law." Those "outside the law" (meaning outside Jewish law) are of course the Romans. With just this portion of Peter's Pentecost speech, even though God apparently planned the whole thing – which may excuse "the Jews"– the seeds of intolerant and exclusive antisemitism have been sown, along with the concept of a manipulative, interventionist God, who acts alone. Peter goes on to use Psalm 16 to argue that King David foresaw Jesus as the Messiah, and therefore, "God has made him both Lord and Messiah," and in case we didn't get it the first time, Peter reminds his Jewish audience that he is talking about "this Jesus whom you crucified."

Because these writings were created forty to one-hundred fifty years after Jesus's death, and no sooner than twenty years after the death of Paul, they cannot be read as definitive theology for twenty-first century Christians. Too much of what is known about Jesus's actual teachings has been recovered during the last century; too much careful Biblical scholarship has been accepted. The only phrase from the entire set of readings for this Sunday that has meaning for twenty-first century Christians is Acts 2:24b: "[I]t was impossible for [Jesus] to be held in [death's] power."

Why? What did Jesus say and do that death cannot destroy? Jesus's message went beyond resisting the normal injustices that come with human civilization, and certainly far beyond the easy admonition from 1 Peter (3:11) to "turn away from evil and do good." Jesus's message transformed Saul of Tarsus – whose job may have been to witness the stoning of Stephen on behalf of conventional Jewish piety – into Paul, who declares that nothing can separate anyone from the justice-compassion of God, seen in Jesus who became the Christ. Jesus rises from beyond death to remind us that God is not violent, and justice is not about revenge. God's distributive justice-compassion is not an eye for an eye and a tooth for a tooth, which is the normal course of justice in human civilization. God's distributive justice is radical fairness. When Jesus says, "love your enemies," he confronts us with an impossibility. In the words of Jesus Seminar founder Robert Funk, "those who love their enemies have no enemies." Loving our enemies flies in the face of every military action taken on the part of government anytime, anywhere. Loving our enemies means bringing nonviolent justice-compassion to every social and political situation that arises. Loving our enemies puts our lives and liberty at stake.

Whenever we take on that radical abandonment of self-interest – whenever we resist the forces of injustice in the workplace, in government, in our relationships with family, friends, neighbors, Jesus is reincarnated – rises again – in us. It is faith – trust – in that ongoing, ever-renewing resurrection that will save us, not from individual, physical death, but from the injustice that keeps us from recognizing our participation in the Kingdom.

Recognition
Third Sunday in Eastertide

Acts 2:14a, 36-41; 1 Peter 1:17-23; Luke 24:13-35;
Psalm 116:1-4, 12-19

These Year A Eastertide readings cover all the traditional Christian faith bases: deliverance from death, salvation from sin through baptism, deliverance from sin by blood ransom, and recognition of the risen Christ in the breaking of bread. For postmodern exiles, who want to commit to the work but reject the traditional fall-redemption theology as preached by the writers of Peter's First Letter and Luke-Acts, the time might be better spent looking at how the early followers of Jesus's Way recovered from a devastating setback, and what happened to Jesus's original ideas. Also appropriate may be to consider whether and how the foundational rituals of baptism and communion might be reclaimed so that they can continue to define a twenty-first century church that is faithful to the original – that is, to a Way for living life in the spirit that is not obscured by Greco-Roman philosophical overlays from the first and second centuries (and earlier); or the political accommodations of the fourth century and later; or the guilt-ridden, often blood-soaked, theories of substitutionary atonement and original sin.

The reading from the First Letter of Peter reinforces the disciple Peter's suggestion for gaining salvation from sin. Most Christians have no idea that the community described in Acts was founded in Jerusalem shortly after Jesus's death, but the community described in the First Letter of Peter likely was founded fifty or more years later. Most twenty-first century folks in the pews on Sunday morning are not going to make a distinction between the two Peters unless their ministers make it a point to do so. Once the point is made, the genie is out of the jug. Luke-Acts was not created until around the same time as the First Letter of Peter, if not even later, and perhaps well into the second century. Given that timeline, it is debatable whether the theology of salvation through baptism or the theology of blood ransom through Jesus's death were actually suggested by Jesus, or by Simon Peter. The argument is whether or not Jesus accepted John the Baptist's apocalyptic call for repentance. These commentaries have chosen the side that argues "no."

Unfortunately, the reading from Acts picks up where we left off last week, repeating the end of Peter's sermon, once more reminding "the Jews" to whom he was preaching that "this Jesus whom you crucified" was God's Messiah, sent by God to restore God's justice. This Peter then revisits John the Baptist's legacy, and insists that the only way for "the Jews" to save themselves from "this corrupt generation" was to repent and be baptized in the name of that same murdered Messiah. The writer of Luke-Acts reports that "about three thousand persons were added" to the community that day. Assuming (which historically, we cannot) that this happened fifty days after the death of Jesus (Pentecost), his original message of radically inclusive love and liberation from injustice apparently never made it out of the tomb.

All is not lost, however. Of all the appearance stories in the Gospel accounts, Luke's story about Cleopas and his companion who meet the risen Jesus on the road to Emmaus may be the favorite. The RCL recommends it be read every year, when the main Easter service includes a Eucharist on Easter day. In Year A, the story is also included in the readings for this third Sunday of Easter. In Luke's story (and it is only Luke's story), the Greek idea about fate being determined by God is put into Jesus's words: "Wasn't the Anointed one destined to undergo these things and enter into his glory?" Luke says, "Then, starting with Moses and all the prophets [Jesus] interpreted for them every passage of scripture that referred to himself" as a proof. But Cleopas and his traveling companion are still so "slow-witted" – as Luke puts it – that they do not recognize the risen Jesus until he shares bread with them.

If anything in these readings can be reclaimed for postmodern minds, it is this story. Theologies of fall-redemption, ransom, and substitutionary atonement no longer work, nor does proof-texting about Old Testament prophecies coming true hundreds of years later. What works is what Jesus did for the travelers on the road to

Emmaus: Hands-on, present moment action that reminded them what they were supposed to be doing. Review of tradition and history is very useful. Revisiting the prophetic voices of the Old Testament such as Amos, Jeremiah, and Isaiah can help postmodern twenty-first century Christians recall that the veil between the worlds of God's realm of distributive justice-compassion and the normalcy of human desire for retributive systems is breached whenever anyone acts in partnership with God to restore the balance.

The metaphor is the shared meal. Of course Luke's story is meant to be a miracle story about a mystical appearance by the risen Lord, who is only recognized when he breaks bread and passes it to the travelers. They remember that the last time he did that for them was the Passover meal, which – like others Jesus shared – was forever transformed. Jesus is reported in all the Gospels getting into trouble because he ate and drank with "sinners" – usually defined as tax collectors and other collaborators with the Roman occupiers – but his table was inclusive of all who were trapped in a system from which there was no escape. With Luke's institution of the "Last Supper," the old covenant secured by Moses was replaced by the new Covenant, sealed with the blood of the Messiah.

Twenty-first century exiles from any of the religions of the Book, but especially exiles from Christianity, no longer resonate with the metaphor of blood sacrifice that reconciles the relationship between God and humanity. The idea that Jesus's death is a sacrifice required by God as substitution for the death of sinners, or that Jesus's blood is somehow a ransom paid to liberate sinners from hell makes no sense in a post-enlightenment, non-theistic age. Instead, the communion meal offers postmodern, liberal Christianity a commemoration of both liberation from ancient political oppression and deliverance from injustice for all time. The shared meal is not a guilt-induced volunteer stint at the local soup kitchen (although whether inspired by guilt or not, the soup kitchens can use the help). The meal shared and recognized on the road to Emmaus starts with radical fairness: redistribution of access to power and wealth so that poverty and the conditions that cause poverty are eliminated; negotiation from the standpoint of a radical abandonment of self-interest to reverse hundreds of years of revenge and retribution among families, neighborhoods, governments, and nations.

Finally, in a postmodern, twenty-first century, where a non-theistic, kenotic God is present wherever life and justice are present, we can still join the psalmist who praises the God who delivers us from injustice and death. "For you have delivered my soul from death, my eyes from tears, my feet from stumbling. I walk before the Lord in the land of the living. I kept my faith. . . . ""

Community
Fourth Sunday in Eastertide

Acts 2:42-47; Psalm 23; 1 Peter 2:19-25; John 10:1-10

> *Oh the Mountain sheep are sweeter*
> *But the Valley sheep are fatter.*
> *Therefore we deemed it meeter*
> *To carry off the latter.*[60]

This week we have sheep and shepherds: Our favorite image of Jesus and his disciples in the first century, and the church and its bishops ever after, presiding over their "flocks" with their ceremonial shepherd's crooks. First we have the 23rd Psalm, read at times of personal or community crisis. Then we find in 1 Peter, reference to Isaiah 53 and the words used by G.F. Handel in one of the choruses from the Easter portion of the Messiah. (At least one choir director of my experience thought the musical emphasis produced on the English phrasing to be particularly amusing: "All WEE like sheep . . . have gone astray.") Finally, we have John 10:1-10, in which the sheep/shepherd metaphor is explored, ending with John's Jesus declaring that "I came that they may have life and have it abundantly." Emphasizing the comfort of the sheep/shepherd motif is certainly far less confrontational than considering the possibility that some first century Christian communities actually practiced communism and increased their numbers thereby. Nevertheless, this fourth Sunday of Easter mandates a look at the nature of community and leadership.

The shepherd metaphor is not particularly flattering, nor encouraging to twenty-first century hopes for global democracy. The people are sheep, who listen only to the known voices of their leaders. The people will not listen to anyone who comes in over the fence instead of through the gate. They will run away from that one, but will follow the true shepherd. Then John's Jesus tries to

---

[60]Thomas Love Peacock, *The War-Song of Dinas Vawr.*

explain what he means and says he is the gate. Presumably God is the gate-keeper who opens the gate so that Jesus the Shepherd can call the names of each one in his flock, and they will hear and follow.

Because of the infamous cherry-picking by the Elves, half of John's argument about the nature of the good shepherd is left out (John 10:11-18). In that section, the pivotal phrase, "lay down his/my life for the sheep" is repeated four times. Jesus claims the power to lay down his life and to take it up again as "received from the Father." By the end of the discourse, Jesus the good shepherd is seen to be in partnership with God the gatekeeper, even on behalf of "other sheep that do not belong to this fold." Here the metaphor breaks down. Unlike those other strangers, from whose voices the sheep will run, Jesus can jump the fence. "[T]hey will listen to my voice. So there will be one flock, one shepherd." The question arises, just who are the thieves and bandits here?

It is absolutely essential that these passages not be read as anti-Jewish. They are certainly anti-something. Whether the creator of John's Gospel was writing from within a Jewish context or from a non-Jewish pagan or Greek context is under current investigation by Biblical scholars. For the purpose of this discussion, which it was doesn't matter. John was probably railing against "thieves and bandits" in rival fledgling Christian communities who were siphoning off members using various interpretations of a developing Christianity. Perhaps John was referring to the likes of the leaders of 1 Peter's community. The sheep may run away from the thieves and bandits who jump the fence, but they cannot escape if the thieves grab them and carry them off.

The secret for a successful community that relies on commonality such as described in Acts lies in the certainty and trust that individual members have in the kind of realm described in Psalm 23. Even though the majority of twenty-first century, largely urban Christians have no clue what sheep are like, the 23rd Psalm attributed to the great King David resonates with other pastoral imagery of God's peaceable kingdom of distributive justice-compassion. Such trust allows the individual to walk through the valley of the shadow of death itself because evil is held in check by one's own integrity, partnership with the Creator, and trust that distributive justice can and does work.

With mutual trust, there is no need for authority. Or, as Paul puts it in 1 Corinthians 15:56, "the power of sin is the law." Extrapolating first century Paul to the twenty-first century is always a tricky exercise. Paul may have been talking about Jewish law that insists on physical signs to prove membership in a community; he may have been talking about Roman law, which solidifies retributive imperial power. But the relevance that remains in Paul's suggestion is that law expressed as power-over others prevents individuals from full participation in establishing just systems in a community, or participating with God in restoring distributive justice-compassion on earth, as in God's realm.

The interpretation of Isaiah's Servant Song (Isaiah 53) as ransom or substitutionary atonement theories, as 1 Peter does, has been accepted theology for nearly two thousand years. But being a servant-leader does not mean piously accepting abuse from the powers and principalities that impact the wider society, as 1 Peter implies. Without the second half of John's parable of the good shepherd who lays down his life for the sheep, Jesus's leadership falls far short of his dramatic demonstration of kenotic service found in chapter 13. Jesus's leadership model is the servant-leader who transforms societies because the servant-leader empowers others. The theology of 1 Peter amounts to heresy because leadership as the authority of human institutions acting with power-over others can never lead to distributive justice.

The Elves also conveniently skip 1 Peter 2:18, which advises slaves to "accept the authority of your masters with all deference," whether they are kind or "harsh." This is unacceptable on several levels whether in a first or a twenty-first century context. Slavery is outlawed world-wide in the twenty-first century, although of course it is practiced in all kinds of ways, ranging from sub-standard wages to human trafficking. Shall Christian communities indeed decline to work to eliminate this injustice? Following the slavery example, pious 1 Peter implies that if we allow injustice to not only exist, but to proliferate, "if you endure when you do right and suffer for it, *you have God's approval*." 1 Peter repudiates

Isaiah's suffering servant, negates the meaning of Jesus's own death, and cheapens the courage of selfless martyrs to justice in all times and circumstances.

Being an empowered partner in a community dedicated to the great work of distributive justice-compassion is not a passive role, subject to blindly following the leader. Kenotic servant leadership arises from and creates kenotic communities that bring about God's realm of distributive justice-compassion through radical abandonment of self-interest. But such radical abandonment is far from passive, and cannot happen without profound trust in the presence of justice and life. Participation then means active nonviolent resistance to the normalcy of unjust human institutional systems.

But beware of mixing the metaphor, as John risked doing with his parable, and the Elves have done with the choice of readings for this week. It is far more difficult to follow the true shepherd through the gate than it is to be kidnaped over the fence.

Faith (Not Belief)
Between a Rock and a Hard Place
Fifth Sunday of Eastertide

Acts 7:55-60; Psalm 31:1-5, 15-16; 1 Peter 2:2-10; John 14:1-14

With the exception of the Psalms, which the Elves use to reinforce orthodox dogma, all of the readings for the Sundays between Easter and Trinity Sunday (the first Sunday after Pentecost) are from the second century C.E. – sixty to one hundred fifty years after the death of Jesus. These are stories about how early Christians defined themselves against both the prevailing Roman culture, and the remnant of Jewish tradition after the fall of Jerusalem in 66-67 C.E.

The whole story Luke wrote about Stephen's arrest on charges of blasphemy and his inflammatory speech to the Jewish authorities is never read if the RCL is followed. As Stephen recounts the sacred story from Abraham to Moses, he focuses on Jewish disobedience to God. He conveniently leaves out the part about how God remains true to the covenant with the people, and continually redeems and forgives them. Stephen also implies that God cannot really be present in the Jerusalem Temple because it was made by Solomon, and "The Most High does not dwell in houses made by human hands." By the time he finishes his final insult, "You are the ones who received the law as ordained by angels and yet you have not kept it," the crowd is justifiably outraged. Luke's intention is to create a parallel between the death of Jesus and the death of Stephen. Twenty centuries later, the creators of the RCL are only too happy to continue the process.

Any attempt at finding some common thread or metaphor among the readings for the fifth Sunday in Eastertide is perilous. The First Letter of Peter might be mistakenly assumed to have been written by Simon Peter, the "rock" upon which Jesus supposedly said he would "build" his "church." The writer is building his case for claiming that converts to the Christian Way from outside the Jewish tradition have become the "chosen people" – replacing the original people of Israel.[61] He invites the people to "come to him [Jesus], a living stone . . . and like living stones, let your selves be built into a spiritual house, to be a holy priesthood, to offer spiritual sacrifices acceptable to God through Jesus Christ." He quotes Isaiah 28:16: "See I am laying in Zion a foundation stone, a tested stone; a precious cornerstone, a sure foundation"; and tops it off with Psalm 118:22: "the stone that the builders rejected has become the chief cornerstone." The psalmist (by tradition, assumed to be the great King David) proclaims that "The Lord" (understood by the early Christian community as the risen Christ) is his rock and fortress.

But the "rock" metaphor plunges over the edge with Luke's legend of the stoning of Stephen (the first Christian martyr), and the first appearance of Saul/Paul in Luke's two-volume narrative. With the declaration of John's Jesus that "whatever you ask in my name I will do," the conclusion that could be reached is that the "pagans" (Jews who did not believe Jesus was the Messiah) who stoned Stephen have become part of the "living stone" because Stephen forgave them in Jesus's name. According to Luke, after Saul's witness of the stoning of Stephen he continued to breathe "threats and murder against the disciples of the Lord" (Acts 9:1) until he made his life-transforming trip to Damascus. The connection between the stoning of Stephen and 1 Peter's "living stones" offering spiritual sacrifices acceptable to God has its own pious logic.

Neither Luke's story nor 1 Peter's disenfranchisement of the Jewish people from God's covenant are acceptable or useful to twenty-first century progressive Christians. What can be made of John 14? Certainly none of the Gospels can be read literally, and most assuredly, not the Gospel of John. As always, when attempting to reclaim ancient writings for contemporary minds, reading meaning back into it from our own point of view is not only a temptation, but is probably inevitable – even for scholars who know how to keep a wary eye on the work. The disastrous results that can come from such anachronism were spelled out

---

[61]*See* Levine and Brettler, 439n 2.4-10.

above.

The first order of business is to realize and accept the fact that the Gospel of John reflects the cosmology of the first and second centuries, C.E., not the cosmology of the twenty-first century. We have known since Copernicus that if there is a god out there somewhere, it shares the "heavens" with a lot of other stuff. Further, we know without a doubt that Jesus was and is seriously dead. All the Gospels make that point emphatically – the resurrection stories are not ghost stories. John's parable of the raising of Lazarus foreshadows Jesus's resurrection, but we are not talking about some kind of Zombie-like resuscitated corpse, still lurching along the highways and byways, terrorizing or shaming people into salvation.

Second, all of the Gospels reflect the times they were written in and for. Specifically, the Gospel of John was an extended, impassioned, possibly desperate argument whose purpose was likely twofold: first, to convince the community that the longed-for One, prophesied to be sent by God to restore God's kingdom of distributive justice-compassion was indeed Jesus, who had been executed by the Romans; and second, to somehow keep from exile the community who did believe it.

The way to possibly reclaim chapter 14 (in fact all three of the chapters at the heart of John's Gospel) is to revisit the Prologue.

In the beginning there was the divine word and wisdom. The divine word and wisdom was there with God, and it was what God was. . . . In it was life, and this life was the light of humanity. Light was shining in the darkness, and darkness did not master it. . . . Genuine light – the kind that enlightens everyone – was coming into the world . . . but its own people were not receptive to it. But to all who did embrace it, to those who believed in it, it gave the right to become children of God. . . . The Law was given through Moses; mercy and truth came through Jesus the Anointed One. No one has ever seen God; the only son, close to the Father's heart – he has disclosed (it).[62]

---

[62]Funk, et al., 401.

God is defined as "divine word and wisdom," revealed to everyone in the life and teachings of Jesus. John says, echoing the Apostle Paul, "the Law was given through Moses [but] mercy and truth [justice-compassion] came through the Anointed One." So the very nature of God is seen to be not the easy justice of retribution and pay-back, but the far more difficult distributive justice that includes mercy, compassion, and a transformation of thought: water into wine; food that nourishes the spirit because it is the work of establishing or restoring God's radical fairness. John 14 may be taken as an illustration of John Dominic Crossan's definition of a kenotic God – whose presence is justice and life, and whose absence is injustice and death.[63] Certainly that is the meaning that might be taken by twenty-first century non-theists, reluctant to condemn anyone for not "believing" literally the legend about Jesus's death and resurrection. Living in the absence of justice has been and continues to be a living death.

John's Jesus possessed within himself the confidence in the nature of God as distributive justice-compassion that eliminated any anxiety about death, whether physical or metaphorical. The judgment that is expressed regarding those who do not believe that to encounter Jesus was to encounter God, is simply the statement of a fact of life: those who do not love one another, who hate others, and do not live in distributive justice-compassion will suffer the consequences. They will not experience the peace that Jesus says he will leave behind. "What I give you is not a worldly gift," he says. The world with its systems of injustice and greed is not interested in creating systems of justice and sharing. To create such a world requires a radical abandonment of self-interest that few are willing to attempt.

---

[63]Crossan and Reed, 288.

Revelation
Sixth Sunday of Eastertide

Acts 17:22-31; Psalm 66:8-20; 1 Peter 3:13-22; John 14:15-21

Eastertide should mark the beginning of the year for Christianity instead of Advent/Christmastide. The fact that worldly time prevailed is evidence of the extent to which the Way followed by the early Christians eventually accommodated political realities. The series of readings for the Sundays marking the Easter Season in Year A (beginning with Easter Sunday) suggests a progression for Christian spiritual development: Doubt, Recognition, Community, Faith (Not Belief), Revelation, and Salvation. The theme for this sixth Sunday is the revelation of the true God.

All of the New Testament readings for this series reflect the vital organizational work of the early Christian movement. Especially after the destruction of the Temple, defining a new religion separate from Judaism became increasingly important as Jewish tradition shifted from Temple to synagogue, and began to include pagan (gentile) converts. All of the New Testament writings are part of that process. The synoptic Gospels are targeted to specific communities, and are focused on midrashic reconstructions of the life and teachings of the pre-Easter Jesus. The Gospel of John and the book of Acts were also written for specific communities, and are concerned with post-Easter themes. John especially presents a mystical, theological interpretation of who Jesus was. Some scholars argue that the Luke/Acts reports on the activities of the followers after Jesus's death – most specifically, the Apostles Peter and Paul – are fiction. Whether made up from whole cloth or not, nothing in the Book of Acts can be considered history remembered.

Claiming one "true God" among the pagan pantheon was a political necessity if the movement was going to survive on its own. The story about the altar to the unknown God has traditionally been understood as an indication of the universality of the Christian religion. Sunday school children are taught that the "pagans" Paul was preaching to believed in a pantheon of idols made of stone and wood, and in order to be sure they covered all the religious bases, they had this altar to any god they might have missed. Paul is credited with being especially astute in creatively seizing the opportunity to claim the "unknown god" as the Judeo-Christian God, whose son Jesus was crucified and raised from the dead to save sinners from hell. Paul then launches into standard lecture number one about how "God" does not live in a house made with hands and is not made of gold, silver, or stone, " . . . the art and imagination of mortals."[64] Finally, Paul gets around to talking about Jesus as the one who will judge the entire world on a day that God has already determined. The people are urged to "repent" from believing in false gods before it is too late.

The writer of Luke/Acts does not give us any numbers, but does say by the end of chapter 17 (not included in the readings) that while some scoffed at the idea of the resurrection, "some" joined with Paul – including a couple of named persons: Dionysius the Areopagite and a woman named Damaris (Acts 17:34). Unfortunately we don't hear anything more about them in the Bible, but legend has provided an interesting story: Dionysius the Areopagite was a prominent Athenian who converted to Christianity through the preaching of Paul on Mars Hill, the open-air supreme court of Athens (Areopagus in Greek). He later was appointed the first Christian Bishop of Athens, and then at the request of Paul, was sent to Gaul, where he suffered martyrdom by fire in Paris. His feast day is October 9th in the west and October 3rd in the east. Damaris apparently was an educated woman. Any woman who is named has to have been an important person.

---

[64]*See* p. 132, Fifth Sunday of Eastertide. The Elves skip Stephen's speech to his Jewish accusers in Acts 7:2-53, which includes a reference to God not living in a "house made with human hands." Stephen is stoned for implying with this phrase that the Temple was built as an idolatrous act. A.J. Levine points out that "Jewish tradition maintained that although God is universal, the Temple is no less a legitimate location where to worship." (*See* Levine and Brettler notes p. 213.) In contrast to the hapless Stephen, Paul uses the phrase as it was traditionally understood. What Luke may have been setting up and why will never be known; however, it seems that this is a place where the seeds of antisemitism could all too easily take root.

Inquiring minds might wonder what her relationship was to Dionysius, but given that the name is the Greek form of the name of the God of Wine (Bacchus) the entire point is easily muddled.

Meanwhile, John's Gospel continues with Jesus's final discourse to his disciples on the eve of his death. The portion chosen for this sixth Sunday in Eastertide is the promise of the Holy Spirit, who will come if the followers of Jesus remain faithful to him. The Advocate, the Spirit of Truth, will be in anyone who loves Jesus and keeps his commandments, and Jesus will reveal himself to them. These words – like many others attributed to Jesus by the writer of this Gospel – have been used for two thousand years to discredit, disinherit, and destroy political opponents, inconvenient alternative ideas, entire civilizations.

Yet these words have also been the foundation for speaking truth to power whenever that power has legitimized injustice in whatever form it appears. "I will not leave you orphaned," John's Jesus promises, " . . . because I live, you also will live. . . . I am in my Father, and you in me, and I in you." This is incarnational language, and it means that the spirit of distributive justice comes through Covenant with the realm/kingdom of God. This language empowers the work of justice-compassion, which has little if anything to do with the kind of docile piety dished out by the writer of 1 Peter – who is absolutely not to be confused with the original apostle. 1 Peter 3:13-22 could be construed as a call for nonviolent resistance to injustice, but only if taken out of the context of the rest of the letter, which is concerned more with obeying the authorities and rejecting "licentiousness, passions, drunkenness, revels, carousing, and lawless idolatry" (1 Peter 4:3). Nevertheless, the theme remains: Revelation of the true God and/or the Christ to all. But twenty-first century postmodern minds cannot accept Jesus's Way as the only legitimate one.

If there is any reclaiming that makes sense, it is the words that the writer of Luke/Acts puts in Paul's mouth: "The God who made the world and everything in it . . . does not live in shrines made by human hands . . . so that they would search for God and perhaps grope for him and find him – though indeed he is not far from each one of us" (Acts 17:24-27). We are tactile beings. We prefer the certainties of what we can see, hear, smell, taste, and touch. A non-theistic, non-corporeal, thought-form is hardly comforting in the middle of the night when the medics are on their way. But isn't that precisely what John's Jesus is pointing to? In the portion left out by the Elves, Jesus says, "Peace I leave with you; my peace I give to you. I do not give to you as the world gives" (John 14:27).

Those who live their lives as Jesus did ("they who have my commandments and keep them") are those who will experience revelation. But for postmodern Christians it is a continuing revelation, not one set in stone for all time. Twenty-first century Christians are confronted with choices about the nature of God – violent or nonviolent – and whether Jesus's message is inclusive or exclusive. Twenty-first century Christians must choose whether faith means literal belief, or commitment to the great work of justice-compassion; and whether deliverance means salvation from hell in the afterlife or liberation from injustice in this life.

Indeed, it is not only Christians who are confronted with these choices in these current times. The choices that people make, whether political leaders or common folk, regarding these questions are reflected in the results that are produced. Whether a Christian candidate for President of the United States, or a member of a religious sect that wishes to restore a lost legacy, for anyone who is unable or unwilling to separate ego from the role life has assigned, violent exclusiveness when paired with literal belief threaten the economic and political security of the entire Planet.

But those who live in Covenant with the kenotic God of distributive justice-compassion are already keeping those commandments John's Jesus is talking about. The Advocate, the Spirit of Truth, which John's Jesus promises, lives in anyone who chooses to participate in that great work. The Psalmist may yet have the last word: "For you, O God, have tested us; . . . we went through fire and through water; yet you have brought us out to a spacious place."

We shall see.

Salvation
Seventh Sunday of Eastertide
(Ascension Sunday)

Luke 24:44-53; John 17:1-11; Acts 1:1-14; Ephesians 1:15-12;
1 Peter 4:12-14, 5:6-11; Psalm 47; Psalm 68:1-10, 32-35;
Psalm 93

Ascension Sunday: The day for prayers for unity on the part of followers, and glorification by God for Jesus, as he takes off for Antares, promising to return in the same way he left on a day pre-determined by God, but not to be known by humanity. The roll is called among the remaining followers, who are reminded that everything written about Jesus in the Jewish scriptures and psalms must be fulfilled, and that repentance and forgiveness of sins is to be proclaimed in Jesus's name to all nations, beginning with Jerusalem. John's Jesus claims his own glorification, while Luke's Jesus confers "power from on high" upon the followers. Pseudo-Paul declares Christ the head of the church, which is his body, and the preacher using Peter's name reminds the rest of us that our job is to be glad for our own oppression, and to watch out for Satan, who "prowls around looking for someone to devour."

The creators of the RCL have defended the legitimacy – if not the message – of the writers of Luke/Acts, John, and even the First Letter of "Peter" for seven weeks; enough is enough. Even though these writings undoubtedly served the purpose of providing a new "Genesis" for the new diversion from Judaism, there is no more reason to take any of it as relevant to the twenty-first century than it is to believe the original sixth century B.C.E. creation story that kept the remnant of Judaism alive in Babylon. Repentance and salvation are the recurring themes of Luke/Acts, but "repentance" as turning away from wrong or unwise action seems to be in short supply in the twenty-first century.

The Planet continues its slide into the black hole of food and energy shortages, brought on by 1) a collective unwillingness to be concerned about anyone or anything beyond immediate and personal gratification; 2) unjustified wars perpetrated by right-wing zealots, some of are whom determined to bring about the "end-times" that will precipitate the aforementioned return from Antares by the "risen Lord" and the immediate conversion of all those "sinners" still holding out in Jerusalem; 3) environmental conditions that may or may not be part of the natural course of global weather patterns, but which certainly appear to be directly related to human misuse. The wealth of nations is flowing more and more into and through the deep pockets of the rich, who speculate on commodities futures, food futures, housing futures, as poverty rises steadily upwards through the economic strata, devastating the lower, middle, and upper-middle classes world-wide. Two percent of the population of the United States controls ninety-five percent of the wealth.

Even though the Elves divide 2 Samuel chapters 11 and 12 between Years B and C, the saga of the great King David and his affair with Bathsheba is the story for today.

This time of the year is Beltane, in the old Northern European/Celtic/Pagan tradition. It is the end of winter, and the beginning of summer, just as its opposite six months later (Samhain/Halloween) is the end of summer and the beginning of winter. Spring is the time when kings go forth to war. In the saga of the great king David, the springtime surge in military action allowed David the opportunity to also engage in the worst excesses of imperial power. He seduced the wife of his loyal commander, Uriah the Hittite, then arranged for Uriah to be killed in battle. Nathan the prophet then tells King David a story about a rich man with many flocks and herds who slaughtered the poor man's beloved lamb, which was all he owned. David is outraged at this gross injustice, and says that the man who would do such a thing deserves to die. Nathan says, "You are the man."

This parable of telling truth to power has been applied to many situations of injustice for thousands of years. It is an archetypal tale of the mindlessness of imperial power, and the traps that participants in imperial systems can easily find themselves in. But in today's climate in the United States, where injustice runs rampant among the poor and disenfranchised, where unjust wars continue, perpetrated and supported by lies that have long been uncovered and even refuted, prophetic voices that are raised in parable and protest are denounced and repudiated. When the story is told over and over again, instead of recognizing their complicity with unjust systems, the supporters of Empire scream "Bigotry! Racism!" From the Supreme Court to the bastions of journalistic righteousness, the guardians of democracy and liberation, freedom of speech, thought, and association, have sold out to the imperial theology:

Piety: "Faith" as "belief" in premodern cosmology; "faith" as "belief" in a resuscitated corpse; "faith" as the certainty that one religion (or political system) is the only true and legitimate one; "faith" as following the drumbeat of political expediency into

War.   Ostensibly wars are of liberation but in actuality all wars are of acquisition and affect the poor and disenfranchised, who have no other means of acquiring education, employment, and meaning for limited lives. Wars bring wealth to the suppliers of war materiel, but leave the veterans bereft of medical care, shelter, and the means of survival. *War* is not only military war. It is the war against those who would work for *distributive* justice-compassion: who would not just bail out the billion-dollar financial institutions, but would provide the greatest good to the greatest number with universal, single-payer health care, affordable housing, relevant education, job-training, in short, equal justice for all. In these wars, there can be no

Victory.   Instead there is only the prospect of continuing war, as "enemy" populations are devastated, and rise up again in desperate violence.

Peace   Like Victory, is promised but never comes. There can be no peace where free thought and speech are prohibited through intimidation and deliberate misinterpretation. There can be no peace when peace depends on the politically correct and expedient answers to lies that have been told in order to justify war – whether foreign or domestic.

This imperial theology is a corporate sin that seems to be so much a part of the body of postmodern civilization that it cannot be treated or removed except by radical redemption.

The final choice from the four questions for the apocalypse in this Easter series is the meaning of deliverance: salvation from hell? or liberation from injustice? And what are the radical acts that will ultimately redeem us – meaning buy us back – from the powers and principalities of Empire and restore us to God's realm of distributive justice-compassion? To choose liberation is to turn away from reactionary retribution. To choose liberation is to radically abandon self-interest and love enemies. Loving enemies means interacting, negotiating, listening, accommodating to the extent possible without losing integrity. To choose liberation is to speak truth to power no matter where it is. To choose liberation is to acknowledge our complicity with injustice, which is nearly impossible to avoid. The struggle is to learn to let go of the fear that keeps us trapped in the particular human hells of war, famine, disease and death; to trust in the kingdom that is available whenever we enter the silence outside of the theology of Empire: Piety, War, Victory, which brings only an uneasy, ephemeral peace.

Why is "the church" still standing around looking skyward?

Pentecost and Trinity

Still in Pharaoh's Fields
Pentecost

Acts 2:1-21; Numbers 11:24-30; 1 Corinthians 12:3b-13;
John 20:19-23; Psalm 104:24-34, 35b

Pentecost is perhaps the first festival appropriated from an ancient tradition to serve the purposes of the new Christian Way. In the midst of the celebration of "the Church's birthday," with glib assertions that "Christ is our Passover," thoughtful Christians may want to consider that the Jewish Festival of Weeks was really about life *after* liberation. (*See* Leviticus 23:15-21.) Fifty days after the commemoration of an archetypal deliverance from oppression and injustice, the Hebrew people were directed by the priests (God's representatives) to make holy offerings of grain, bread, lambs, and incense. In a very practical acknowledgment of the normalcy of human civilization after liberation is accomplished, the purposes of the ritual sacrifices were for sin (a goat), and for well-being (two male lambs). After that, it was party time, and work was forbidden. But just in case the people might forget why they were liberated in the first place, the priests made it clear that "when you reap the harvest of your land, you shall not reap to the very edges of your field, or gather the gleanings of your harvest; you shall leave them for the poor and for the alien: *I am the Lord your God.*" In the midst of a holiday, certain that sins had been forgiven and that future well-being was assured, the people remembered that God's kingdom, God's reign, God's imperial rule, means that God's people live in distributive justice-compassion.

What is missing from most Christian Pentecost celebrations is a sense of purpose, ownership, liberation, and commitment. Theologically, Jesus's death and resurrection supposedly replace any need for a "scapegoat" as a sacrifice for sin, and reconciles humanity with God's realm of distributive justice-compassion. But sin, and guilt about sin, continues to plague church-goers, as though Jesus's death and resurrection didn't really do the trick.

The reconciliation that Jesus's life and teachings illustrated was a profound oneness with a kenotic god, in a realm of distributive justice-compassion. Such an identification with God's kingdom conveys a sense of integrity, and thus the power to address systems of injustice. Sacrifice then becomes a symbolic action that bears witness to a transformed life. But postmodern Christians are separated from God's realm, unable to open our eyes and look and listen. Most of us have no personal stake in the conditions in which we live, or in which we observe others to be living. We have reduced "sacrifice" to an "offering" of money. We are unable to act with personal power.

The liberation struggle – for the ancient enslaved Hebrew population of Egypt and for any population held in thrall anywhere in any time – is first to realize that one is indeed oppressed. Those who collaborate with the oppressors (Bibically, "tax collectors and sinners") are especially prone to blindness about the extent of their involvement. The end begins to justify the means. Fruit growers and small farmers, priced out of the market, sell their land to developers and commodities speculators. Employed single mothers, with no skills, keep quiet about unsafe working conditions and below-minimum wages. High-priced law firms construct elaborate "Chinese walls" around the bankers on the third floor who fund the real estate developers on the fourth floor, preventing leaks of information to the litigators on the second floor, who are representing plaintiffs of unfair business practices. All are "enablers" of oppression, just as those whose friends or family members are addicted to drugs or gambling or alcohol, but cannot bring themselves to intervene. The struggle with denial and personal justification becomes a struggle against depression, apathy, and victimhood. After that, comes the struggle to realize that something can and indeed will be and is being done about the oppression. Only after reaching the depths of despair, the bottom of the addictive cycle, the nothingness and the void, is it possible to turn around – repent – and find the way out into the light once again.

The commemoration of liberation must include the acknowledgment and acceptance of the bitterness of existence under oppression. Only after that experience is it possible to celebrate forgiveness of sin, the grace of God's kingdom of distributive justice-compassion, and the certainty of future well-being.[65] The original Pentecost festival was held after the commemoration of liberation in the Feast of the Passover. For the primordial Hebrew people, God brought deliverance from injustice by direct action in the world. For the new Christian movement, God's direct action was manifested in the life, teachings, death, and resurrection of Jesus. So once the Passover commemoration is complete – including the acknowledgment of the bitterness of the oppression and the wandering in the wilderness of uncertainty about what to do about it – then it is time for true celebration. The spring mowing is done, and the hay is gathered. The fields are cleared and the seed is sown. The first spring vegetables and berries are ready for harvest. The time of hope has come. Party on! But don't forget the ones who still live in oppression – the widow, the orphan, the alien seeking hospitality.

If the New Testament is interpreted as the actualization of the Old, then Moses's wish in the passage cherry-picked from Numbers that all the people could be prophets comes true on the day described by the writer of Luke/Acts. The Holy Spirit, first given by John's Jesus, descends in tongues of flames on the Christian community gathered in Jerusalem. They are empowered to tell the story of Jesus – the new paschal lamb – in every language of the known world. Peter quotes the prophet Joel, that everyone who calls on the name of the Lord shall be saved. Paul proclaims, "For in the one Spirit we were all baptized into one body – Jews or Greeks, slaves or free – and we were all made to drink of one Spirit."

The imagery of fire represents the outpouring of the presence of sacred being and of creative power. Fire transforms, destroys, purifies, enlightens, inspires, and protects. But postmodern, "first

---

[65]Editor's Note: I have trouble with the idea that it is the acknowledgment of oppression that is essential. To my mind it is the conversion experience, the "turning around," the resolve to act against the oppression, and the subsequent action itself that can sustain a belief in forgiveness and a hope of future well-being. Christianity took the Jewish concept of the scapegoat carrying off the sins of the community (always the community!), but ignored the accompanying requirement for individual action to restore relationships. A fateful error. G.C.

world" people have no experience or appreciation for that kind of power. In order to live with and through the Pentecost fires – whether of ancient commitment and sacrifice, or of the certainty of a transformational message – would-be prophets must remember that fire does not care what feeds it. Fire can be fed by injustice as well as justice-compassion. Perhaps that is why the ancient priests were careful to remind the people to leave something for the poor and for the alien seeking hospitality in a hostile world. Prosperity can obscure the truth about one's condition.

Most Americans, Christian or not, have no concept of the struggle for true liberation that continues world-wide. Vast numbers of humanity are oppressed by imperial regimes, and by the unwitting and unwilling supporters of those imperial regimes. Prophetic voices have recently suggested that American society also suffers from imperial oppression. Wherever there are shortages of what is required for sustainable living, oppression exists: health care (not dependent upon commercial health insurance); affordable, safe housing; healthy food. The groundbreaking work done by the Union movement of the 1930s for protections for all workers has been all but overturned. Meaningful work that pays a living wage is non-existent in many areas of the country. Women especially are oppressed in this regard, as they earn seventy cents on the dollar compared to men in comparable positions. Workers in many low-paying industries and service-sector jobs must comply with unreasonable working hours and dangerous conditions. As for strictly "political" oppression, the U.S. Supreme Court has now opened the flood gates to state restrictions on voter registration; the Transportation Safety Administration – using soft lights and soothing music – lulls airline passengers into ignoring the fact that the new total body "security" scan is a violation of the Fourth Amendment to the Constitution; arbitration clauses attached to everything from automobile purchases to credit card agreements prohibit the right to jury trials; equal protection under the law is denied to anyone deemed an "illegal immigrant."

The ones still living in oppression are not the ones who do not yet know that Jesus is Lord. The ones still living in oppression are those trapped in various aspects of Empire: those who believe that loyalty to a political system is paramount; who believe that love of country can only be expressed with some outward sign such as a pin or scarf or loyalty oath; those who take government assurances of personal security at face value, and believe that if they have nothing to hide they have nothing to fear from imperial authority.

Twenty-first century American Christians are hardly ready to celebrate a true Pentecost. We've not yet left Pharaoh's fields.

Sound Bites
Trinity Sunday

Genesis 1:1-2:4a; Psalm 8; 2 Corinthians 13:11-13;
Matthew 28:16-20

The finale to the Easter Season, with the Church established at Pentecost, is Trinity Sunday. Liturgically, the year now looks to beginnings, as we are directed to read the first part of the Genesis story and its confirmation in Psalm 8. "God said, 'let us make humankind in our image, according to our likeness; and let them have dominion over the fish of the sea, and over the birds of the air, and over the cattle, and over all the wild animals of the earth, and over every creeping thing that creeps upon the earth.'" The Psalmist confirms this by asking, "what are human beings that you are mindful of them? . . . Yet you have made them a little lower than God . . . You have given them dominion over the works of your hands." But Matthew's Jesus claims, "All authority has been given to me in heaven and on earth." We, as disciples of the Christ who supersedes all other manifestations of divinity, are to make followers of all people, by baptizing them in the name of the Trinity. On this day we have the ultimate statement of faith in a three-part god: Father (creator), Son (Christ – Anointed One), and Holy Spirit (Holy Ghost), and the Apostle Paul closes his second letter to the Corinthians with a blessing in the name of the three-in-one.

This is cherry-picking *par excellence* on the part of those politically correct Elves. It is sound-bite theology, worthy of news organizations and partisans of all colors world-wide. In order to get your point across, whether it is marketing widgets or electing a president, concentrate on the shortest message with the greatest impact. Like the front-runner in a two-thousand-year long political contest, Jesus and his message have been defined by what has been said about him by the loudest and most well-connected of people in the shortest and most memorable ways. But before we join the vast army of Christian soldiers, carrying the cross of Jesus as though into war, we might wonder if that is who Jesus really was.

From the brief benediction at the end of 2 Corinthians, the eye strays back to the enlarged numerals marking chapter 13, and there in verses 1-2, the Apostle Paul is apoplectic: "This is the third time I am coming to you" Paul roars, " . . . I warned those who sinned previously and all the others . . . if I come again, I will not be lenient. . . . " Shades of Mom threatening dire consequences once Dad gets home from work. What's going on here? What happened to baptizing cute babies and blessing everyone in the name of the triune God?

Any seminarian with a decent New Testament professor, or lay-leader with access to a study Bible, has noticed that Paul likely wrote many more than two letters to the community in Corinth, and that the Corinthians were a recalcitrant bunch. What they were recalcitrant about is debated among some Biblical scholars, but John Dominic Crossan suggests that the problem was that the folks in Corinth were so deeply involved in their own first century version of bumper-sticker living that they could not imagine what Paul was trying to tell them about the Way of Jesus.

Roman life was a highly structured form of patronage in which all classes of society participated, from slaves to the Emperor. Political, social, and commercial life was carried out in a complex hierarchical system that could not be circumvented without causing disturbance. So when Paul came along and reminded Philemon that his slave Onesimus must be welcomed back into the community as an equal brother in Christ, the reverberations were felt for a considerable distance up and down the social strata of first century Corinth. When the good wealthy folk of Corinth came to participate in the Christian common shared meal and ran the risk of eating with people to whom they either owed social/political commerce (banquets and public sacrifices), or who owed to them, it made sense to eat at home first, and simply take a symbolic token of Jesus's common table.

When Paul baptized the family of Stephanas, and Crispus and Gaius (1 Corinthians 1:14-16), the community Paul had founded thought he was acting as a patron, representing Jesus as a supreme patron, and acting in competition with others who may also have baptized followers of Jesus's Way. What the Corinthians had so much trouble understanding is that Jesus's Way lies outside the normalcy of Roman (or any) civilization. Jesus's Way has nothing to do with normal, accepted social custom: "There is no longer Jew or Greek, there is no longer slave or free, there is no longer male and female, for all of you are one in Christ Jesus" (Galatians 3:28). Jesus's Way leads into the realm of God, where justice has nothing to do with payback, retribution, or what is or is not earned, owed, or deserved because of one's social, political, or legal circumstances.

Paul taught that participation with Jesus's program of restoring God's Kingdom of distributive justice-compassion means living kenotically. It means a radical abandonment of self-interest; a radical inclusiveness, in communities, business dealings, and political structures, that functions on a very different footing from the normalcy of civilization. So long as nobody asks any questions, civilization rolls nearly effortlessly into the normalcy of Empire. But, as John Dominic Crossan has put it, the ancient Hebrew people, who knew that God is just, and the world belongs to God, were in the habit of looking around and saying, "but the world sucks! What's wrong with this picture?" If God is just, and the world belongs to God, but the world is not just, then God – if God is indeed God – will have to act to do something about it. In Paul's brilliant realization, God's infinite grace is available to all who participate with Jesus in restoring that impartial, distributive justice to the world. The question then becomes, what does it mean to participate in that program?

Was Paul suggesting some kind of Trinity with his blessing at the end of 2 Corinthians? Or was the Trinity somehow "anticipated" in the beginning of 2 Corinthians (21-22)? No. The number three is a prime number, and has had mystical connotations for thousands of years before Christianity appeared on the Planet. The aspects of Goddess form a trinity (maiden, mother crone); the Moon has three phases: new, full, dark; ancient Celts turned around three times to raise protection of the elements around them; Brigid – a Celtic goddess who made the transition into acceptance as a Christian saint is a triple goddess governing poetry, healing, and the art of metal working. Paul certainly spoke in threes – any good preacher does the same. He says in 2

Corinthians 21-22, "But it is GOD who establishes us with you in CHRIST and . . . giving us his SPIRIT in our hearts as a first installment." It is God's action, through the life, death and resurrection of Jesus (another triad), that conveys the Spirit – that numinous, mysterious aspect of human consciousness that inspires and directs life outside the realm of ordinary human understanding. At the end of his letter Paul invokes the GRACE of the Lord Jesus Christ, the LOVE of God, and the COMMUNION of the Holy Spirit upon the community at Corinth. This is not a God divided into three equal parts. This is a three-part blessing with Grace, Love, and Communion. When all three are present, God's kingdom is found in the midst of that community, whether among the followers of Jesus's Way or not. In that elusive realm of distributive justice-compassion, where Grace, Love, and Communion are found there is no room for injustice.

The selection of the readings from Genesis and Psalm 8 is not so irrelevant as it may seem at first. While the soundbites are distracting (Dominion! Trinity!), a deeper reading suggests that one way to step into God's kingdom is to act with sustainable justice in our relationship to Planet Earth and the creatures that dwell here – including ourselves. Psalm 8 (NRSV) says, "Yet you have made [humans] a little lower than God." The Hebrew word is *elohim,* meaning divine beings or angels, which is the term used in the KJV. Angelic dominion is not about the physical space they control, but the human quality they have mastered and have become associated with. For example, The archangel Michael is a warrior; other angels are known as "Hope" or "Peace" or "Love," and may be called upon to act within their particular expertise. Guardian angels are frequently credited with intervening to save lives or property. So rather than taking God's granting to humans dominion over the earth as meaning domination, oppression, or subjection, the angelic meaning is closer to management, or "stewardship" – as the greener Christian denominations have long suggested. God's Earth has been placed in our hands as a trust. To accept the responsibility for its sustenance means acting for eco-justice in sustainable kenosis – the radical abandonment of self-interest. What impact would kenotic environmental attitudes have on oil, mountain-top removal, development of alternative energy resources, and the survival of endangered species – including those portions of humanity threatened with extinction by natural disaster?

The Priests for Equality of Brentwood, Maryland have the last word from *The Inclusive Psalms*: "From the lips of infants and children you bring forth words of power and praise, to answer your adversaries and to silence the hostile and vengeful. . . . You have made us responsible for the works of your hands, putting all things at our feet . . . Adonai, Our God, how majestic is your Name in all the earth!"

Ordinary Time

Proper 4
Faith, Works, Law, Who Cares?

Genesis 6:9-22; 7:24; 8:14-19;
Deuteronomy 11:18-21, 26-28; Psalm 46;
Romans 1:16-17; 3:22b-28, (29-31); Matthew 7:21-29

Now at last we launch the Year A Bible study of the Gospel of Matthew, along with three of the seven authentic letters of Paul. The Church's one foundation having been established, and the mission defined, the eternal *jihad* between faith and works, grace and law, justice and judgment is joined. So, into the fray:

We begin with Paul's argument about justification by faith, not by works. Since Martin Luther, this has meant that our actions are rationalized (we are right to do them) because of unquestioning belief in the literal, physical resurrection of Jesus from the dead. "Works" that the law requires do not count. Only actions that derive from belief will save us. The alternative reading from Deuteronomy could not be more blunt in its agreement: "See, I am setting before you today a blessing and a curse: the blessing, if you obey the commandments of the Lord your God . . . and the curse, if you do not obey. . . ." Matthew's Jesus presents the distinct possibility that acting in his name does not necessarily mean automatic acceptance into heaven. Indeed, Matthew's Jesus insists that to use Jesus's name without paying attention to Jesus's words subverts the law, just like a corrupt or foolish builder who builds his house on the sand. The cautionary tale of Noah and the flood leaves no room for misunderstanding. The "wicked" will be finally judged and destroyed.

Throw in a sentence or two about how "the Law" means "Jewish law," which has been replaced by the love of Jesus, reflected in the compassion God showed humanity after the flood, and this sermon should take about 6 minutes. Plenty of time to deal with First Sunday Communion, without going past the noon hour.

Problems: (1) Perhaps most important is the antisemitism that can creep in whenever the Gospel writers or the Apostle Paul engage in polemics about "the law." (2) Do Paul's obfuscations about whether faith (as belief) overthrows or upholds "the law" have any relevance to Christians today? (3) If God's justice is distributive, and the world belongs to God, what's with the collective punishment meted out to the entire creation who were not among the chosen few allowed into Noah's Ark? (4) Is this yet another instance where the Old Testament is supplanted by the New Testament?

The story of Noah and the Flood, Matthew's Gospel, and Paul's letters all have in common the purpose of defining for a people the nature of their God, and how to live in harmony with God's insistence on justice. For Matthew (and the historical Jesus), this meant keeping the movement within the boundaries of Mosaic law. For Matthew (not the historical Jesus) justice took the form of apocalyptic judgment. The story of Noah certainly lends itself to apocalyptic interpretation. But actually, it contains a thread of redemptive hope that runs throughout the Old Testament. In story after story a "righteous remnant" reconstructs, regenerates, and reestablishes the world of distributive justice-compassion after God has acted to root out (or drown out or burn out) the inevitable consequences of human civilization – i.e., injustice. Noah and his family are the remnant in Genesis. In Exodus, the righteous remnant of the original tribes of Israel who have remained faithful to God's distributive justice-compassion are delivered from Egyptian captivity and returned to the promised land. In the Babylonian exile stories, the prophet Jeremiah encourages the remnant left behind in Jerusalem to trust in the promise that the remnant carried off by the enemy will return to rebuild the temple within fifty years. The Servant Songs of Isaiah encourage those exiles.

Thirty years before the fall of Jerusalem and the great diaspora of the practice of the Jewish religion, the Apostle Paul defined a Christian movement within Judaism that was beginning to separate from the tradition. Included were non-Jewish people outside the synagogues as well as so-called "God Worshippers," who believed in the Jewish God but were not themselves Jewish. The Gospel writers' purpose was to encourage the remnants of those who followed Jesus's Way to remain faithful to his teachings, and to build faith communities, some within Judaism, and some without.

In the twenty-first century, Christians are debating the relevance of a belief system that depends on a premodern cosmology that clearly holds no scientific truth, and barely works as metaphor. Paul's first century arguments about who was a legitimate Jew (circumcised) and who was not, and whether one needed to be a circumcised Jew in order to join the Christians is meaningless except in the context of Judeo-Christian history. But who or what is a Christian today is the heart of the question, and Paul's argument about faith versus works (which is the whole point of his letter to the Romans) is worth looking at seriously.

If Paul's use of the word "faith" means "trust" in the basic truth of Jesus's life and teachings (which may be called simply "trust in Jesus") then perhaps what Paul was saying in the first century might be understood as follows: But now, in addition to God's law about living with distributive justice-compassion, and the prophets who preached about God's insistence on distributive justice-compassion, we recognize the distributive justice-compassion of God for all people, because of our trust in the basic truth of Jesus's life and teachings.

Paul is absolutely not saying that Jesus replaces God or the law or the prophets. Jesus instead fulfills, or actualizes, or brings into focus the law and the prophets, and if we follow his Way, we also participate in the fulfillment of the same law. And what is that law? It is the law of distributive justice-compassion, which applies to everyone, Jew or Gentile, whether one "believes" the resurrection story literally or not.

Proper 5
Promises Promises

Genesis 12:1-9; Hosea 5:15-6:6; Psalm 33:1-12; Psalm 50:7-15; Romans 4:13-25; Matthew 9:9-13, 18-26

The Call of Abram to establish his legacy in the land of Canaan is a powerful tale. The Lord God speaks, and Abram responds with an epic movement of family and possessions. He stops at a spot sacred to the Canaanites – an oak tree, or perhaps a standing stone – and claims the land for himself and his descendants. In an act that at once desecrates and resacralizes, he builds an altar to his own god. Then he moves on to the hill country, to the higher elevations at Beth-el ("house of God"), pitches his tents, and builds another altar. It is an archetypal saga of yore, on the order of Malory, Shakespeare, and Tolkien. The Apostle Paul updates and extends the promise made to Abram (Abraham) to "all his descendants, not only to the adherents of the law but also to those who share the faith of Abraham." Further, he tells his first century Roman community that the promise now rests on grace, extended to all those who trust that God is able to do what God promised.

This week's portion of Paul's letter to the Romans references the faith of Abraham – the trust that Abraham had in the promise received from God that Abraham and his descendants would inherit the earth. Just as actions that are required by law convey no credit for one's personal commitment to justice – such as wage/hour laws – Paul cautions that if the earth is inherited (appropriated?) by those who follow the law, God's promises are null and void. The law, Paul says, brings "wrath" – the rightful (just) response of God to what humans have done. Human civilization inevitably leads to retributive justice and ultimately to the kind of Empire that puts tariffs on food imports, or exports old-growth rainforests in defiance of God's distributive justice-compassion.

Behind all of Paul's circling language lies the conviction that the law – the normalcy of civilization – leads inevitably to injustice because the law requires retribution – payback. There is no grace (free gift) under the law. The law does not offer radical fairness. Under the law there must be winners and losers. But those are justified who trust in God's direct action in the world to establish God's realm of distributive justice-compassion, both through the life and sacrificial death of Jesus and participation with Jesus in that same program. Their trust is credited back to them as justice itself. Throughout his letter, Paul makes it clear that the promise of God to establish that kingdom preempts human law.

The Elves skip Paul's argument about how the purpose of circumcision was "to make [Abraham] the ancestor of all who believe without being circumcised and who thus have righteousness reckoned to them." Instead they cut to the chase: "For the promise that he would inherit the world did not come to Abraham or to his descendants through the law but through the righteousness of faith." Where there is no law [regarding circumcision], Paul says, there is no violation. By the same token, if there is no law regarding who owns what portion of the Planet, then the radically fair distribution of the resources of the land preempts any imperial claim.

What seems to be left out of today's portion of the argument is the choice that we have to join or not to join the ongoing program of establishing God's realm of distributive justice-compassion at all levels: individually, socially, politically, ecologically. Paul hints at the consequences of not joining the program when he speaks about how "the law brings wrath." Tradition interprets Paul's argument about the wrath of the law versus the righteousness of faith as meaning Old Testament retribution versus New Testament grace, earned by belief that Jesus died to pay for human sin. Certainly, cherry-picked Hosea warns of the consequences of abandoning the God of Abraham and following Ba'al. But Hosea is preaching about an eighth century B.C.E. political dispute between Judah and Israel about how to defeat the Assyrians. The Elves only included this reading because Matthew's Jesus quotes Hosea in a non sequitur – "Go and learn what this means," he says, and then quotes Hosea 6:6a:

"It is mercy I desire instead of sacrifice." The rest of the passage from Hosea 6:6 says, "[I desire] the knowledge of God rather than burnt offerings." This is a crucial redaction on Matthew's part. Hosea's point is that knowledge of the nature of God as distributive justice-compassion is more important to God than public ritual. Matthew's point is for pious Christians who were not comfortable with the kind of social company Jesus kept. Matthew's Jesus says "After all, I did not come to enlist religious folks but sinners!"[66]

The Elves dance through Matthew chapter 9, cobbling together a breath-taking combination of images. First, Jesus chooses "Matthew" as the first disciple. Then he challenges the Pharisees who questioned his judgment about "dining with toll collectors and sinners." Jesus says, "Since when do the able-bodied need a doctor? It is the sick who do," thereby setting up the story of healing Jairus's daughter, eight verses later, framing the story of the unfortunate woman who, if she lived in twenty-first century America would have had no health insurance, and would have been dead after twelve years of untreated vaginal bleeding. These stories seem to illustrate the "mercy" of God, as opposed to the retributive systems of the Pharisees. They are exaggerations, meant to convict members of Matthew's community, who perhaps had some doubts about whether the poor and disenfranchised deserved justice. These stories illustrate that sinners, collaborators, outcasts of any kind only need to trust in the power of Jesus to do what he says he will do. They seem to reinforce Paul's claim that God's promise extends to everyone.

Abraham did not "distrust" – Paul's word. Instead, he was fully convinced that God was able to do and would do what God promised. For sixth century B.C.E. people in Babylonian exile, this promise kept hope alive that they would be restored to their own land. Abraham's trust resulted in a reckoning – a distribution – of justice. Paul makes the intellectual leap that those who trust God's ability to raise Jesus from the dead will also have given to them the ability to participate in that same distribution of justice-compassion.

---

[66]Funk, et al., 163.

What happens in the twenty-first century to the promises of primordial gods and the updates to those promises by first century mystics? The metaphors in all these readings can quickly descend to twenty-first century irrelevance and dangerous Christian hegemony. The last time anyone did something similar to Abraham's action was in August 2007, when the Russians planted a flag under the polar icecap and claimed nearly half the Arctic seabed for themselves.[67] Needless to say, an American scientist is claiming that the technical procedures for the dive were his, and so the spoils are in dispute. Paul says that Jesus was "handed over to death for our trespasses and was raised for our justification." Watch out. Substitutionary atonement (invented nine hundred years after the death of Jesus) is out there, roaring around, looking to trap the unwary. "Justification" does not mean being "saved" or "paid for," "vindicated," or "acquitted," but means being made just – i.e., chosen, even ordained, as participants in God's justice-compassion. In addition, there is a subtle anti-Jewish note in the story of the healing of the woman with the twelve-year issue of blood if the woman is described as "unclean," and Jesus is credited with defying Jewish law by allowing her to touch the fringes of his robe.[68]

For twenty-first century Christians, these readings make three points.

First, in terms of twenty-first century political realities, there is no difference between the Russians planting their flag on the sea floor and Abram appropriating the sacred places of the Canaanites for his own god. Western world history is chock full of land grabs on the part of empires in the name of God and his Christ.

Second, taking Paul's point whole-heartedly into the present day, the laws that human societies create eventually evolve into the kind of empires that grab the natural resources for themselves and demand that everyone else pay, thereby rendering God's promise of distributive justice-compassion null and void. There are consequences to such violations of God's law by imperial

---

[67]http://www.nytimes.com/ 2008/ 02/19/ world/ europe/ 19 arctic. html?th&emc=th

[68]See Levine, *The Misunderstood Jew,* 24; 119-166.

injustice, which may not be apparent. The "wrath of God" – the consequences – may be long in coming, but as the psalmist warns at the end of Psalm 51 (left out by those discriminatory Elves), "What right have you to recite my statutes, or take my covenant on your lips? . . . you give your mouth free rein for evil . . . but now I rebuke you and lay the charge before you. Mark this, then, you who forget God, or I will tear you apart, and there will be no one to deliver. Those who bring thanksgiving as their sacrifice honor me; to those who go the right way I will show the salvation of God." Some of those consequences include global warming, sudden and catastrophic climate change, and mass extinctions of humanity and other (more essential?) life forms.

Third – and perhaps most startling – is Paul's insistence that faith trumps law every time. Everyone who lives in trust of God's realm instead of relying on law is guaranteed the promise of distributive justice-compassion. This is the grace of a kenotic god, whose presence is justice and life and whose absence is injustice and death. The struggle is to discern the difference.

Proper 6
A Priestly Kingdom

Genesis 18:1-15, 21:1-7; Exodus 19:2-8a; Psalm 116:1-2, 12-19;
Psalm 100; Romans 5:1-8; Matthew 9:35-10:23

Most ministers are skipping Romans and concentrating on the readings from Matthew's Gospel. The Gospel is much easier to expound upon, and little intellect is required to understand Church dogma. But if Christianity is to have any viable relevance to life in the third millennium, hard work is called for in comprehending, updating where possible, and reclaiming both the Apostle Paul's and the Gospel writers' interpretations of who Jesus was, and what his life and death means – to the first century as well as the twenty-first.

The Elves have paired the stories of Sarah's pregnancy with Isaac and the charge by God to the people in exodus from Egypt with Matthew's barely veiled hostility toward the Jewish tradition. Even though Sarah treated the promise of a son as a joke, the readings skip to assure us that Isaac was indeed born, and Abraham's covenant with God was confirmed by circumcision of the infant after eight days. In Exodus, God tells Moses to promise the people that, "if you obey my voice and keep my covenant, you shall be my treasured people. Indeed, the whole earth is mine, but you shall be for me a priestly kingdom and a holy nation." But it is Matthew's opinion (a millennium or two later) that the "lost sheep of the house of Israel" are in desperate need of a shepherd. Matthew's Jesus sends out the disciples, telling them to rely on the hospitality of the people for their sustenance rather than demanding payment for healing the sick, cleansing the lepers, even raising the dead. But there is a catch. Those who do not welcome the disciples or do not listen to them are to be abandoned to a final judgment. Worse, Matthew's Jesus expects that the [Jewish] councils and synagogues, governors, and kings will universally hate both the messengers and the message.

The anti-Jewish message is clear, and it must be countered

with scholarship. Matthew was a Jew, and he was likely the liturgical leader of a synagogue that had chosen to follow Jesus's Way. Matthew was writing – as all the Gospel writers were – well after the fall of Jerusalem and the destruction of the Temple by the Romans. That he constructed his Gospel as a liturgical replacement for Torah may be an indication of the bitterness of the disagreement between Jews facing the loss of their religion in diaspora, and fledgling Christians who wished nevertheless to be part of a synagogue. As the Jesus Seminar scholars remind us:

> The sayings in [these readings] reflect a knowledge of events that took place long after Jesus's death: Matthew is really depicting the situation as he knew it in his own time. . . . Persecution will cause the emissaries to flee from one city to another. But they will not have gone through all the cities of "Israel" before the end comes with the appearance of the son of Adam (. . . an apocalyptic figure). All this is far removed from [the historical] Jesus's perspective.[69]

My late father used to joke that the one thing Christians love more than Jesus himself is persecution. As soon as anyone objects to public prayer in schools or city/county council meetings, or whenever Christmas displays or representations of the Ten Commandments are barred from court house lawns and walls, the pious tie themselves to the stake, and beg for gasoline and matches. There is nothing more satisfying than to be hauled off to jail for disturbing the peace or disrupting a meeting, shouting the Lord's Prayer in defiance of godless liberalism. But Paul was not talking about easy piety when he wrote that "suffering produces endurance, and endurance produces character, and character produces hope, and hope does not disappoint us because God's love has been poured into our hearts through the Holy Spirit that has been given to us." The reading is the continuation of Paul's argument that Jesus died for the benefit of all people on the Planet, not just those who believe that Jesus rose bodily and magically from the grave. Jesus died in the attempt to reconcile humanity with God's realm of distributive justice-compassion. When we

---

[69]Funk, et al., 170.

live in Covenant with that realm, we participate with an incarnate Christ in making distributive justice possible in our personal, political, and social lives.

In that context, the charge from God to the Israelites at the foot of Mount Sinai becomes the source for transforming the theology of Empire (piety, war, victory, peace) to Covenant, nonviolence, and distributive justice-compassion. The instructions for how to do that can be reclaimed from Matthew's Jesus: "Go and announce: 'Heaven's imperial rule is closing in.' . . . Don't get gold or silver or copper coins for spending money, don't take a knapsack for the road, or two shirts, or sandals, or a staff. . . ." Trust in God's "imperial rule" sounds naive to sophisticated, third millennium, postmodern realists. But trust in the process of distributive justice-compassion to the radical extent demanded by the Covenant is just as dangerous in the twenty-first century as it was in the first. In the first century, outlaws, rough roads, Roman legions, wild animals, and extreme weather conditions would have added a high premium to the courage already required to tell the story of Jesus in a hostile world. Twenty-first century exiles face hostility ranging from professional media to political and religious fundamentalists, and ordinary folk, caught up in normal, conventional attitudes toward "justice," "peace," and integrity. Normal civil society seems intent upon deliberate misinterpretation of the motives of anyone insisting on eliminating the death penalty; providing universal, single-payer, government-subsidized health care; developing and promoting renewable sources of energy; controlling the availability of weapons of mass destruction; and negotiating with "terrorists" and other "enemies."

"Look," Matthew's Jesus says, "I'm sending you out like sheep to a pack of wolves."

Indeed, we respond.

"Therefore, you must be as sly as a snake and as simple as a dove."

Countering the normalcy of civilization means knowing the facts, framing the question, and presenting the argument so that the opposition is empowered to join the program. Tricky, but do-able.

"And you will be hauled up before governors and even

kings . . . so you can make your case to them and to the nations. And when they lock you up, don't worry about how you should speak or what you should say. It will occur to you at that moment what to say. . . ."

This is sailing a bit too close to the wind. Suppose I just vote, or buy organic, or – I'll march, but I really can't volunteer to get arrested in front of the White House. My [husband, wife, boss, children] won't let me.

" . . . You will be universally hated because of me. But those who hold out to the end will be saved."

Jesus never says it's going to be easy. He just gives us the choice: What is faith? Literal belief, or commitment to the great work of justice-compassion? What is deliverance? Salvation from hell, or liberation from injustice? When we choose liberation, we sign on to God's original Covenant as full partners in the struggle. We become a holy people, a priesthood, guides into the kingdom, and mediators of the sacred.

Proper 7
The King's Business

Genesis 21:8-21; Jeremiah 20:7-13; Psalm 86:1-10, 16-17;
Psalm 69:7-18; Romans 6:1b-11; Matthew 10:24-39

The readings for Proper 7 are all lifted wholesale out of context, and cobbled together like medieval motley. Even conventional dogmatic themes fail to form recognizable patterns in this "incongruous mixture" (as the Oxford Dictionary of American Language defines "motley"). Not to pursue this metaphor too far, but "playing the fool" by wearing motley implies astute criticism of the King's business. The Elves have not only missed the point of the King's business; they have failed to present any point at all. All bets are off this week. Pick a reading and preach on it.

Taken out of context, the reading from Genesis picks up at the end of the feud between Abraham's wife Sarah and Abraham's mistress, or second wife, or slave, or concubine – choose your epithet – Hagar. Ishmael was not really a bastard, but definitely not the fruit of the first womb. In order not to derail God's plan for Isaac, Hagar and Ishmael are thrown out into the desert. What a rich soup of themes for the twenty-first century: patriarchy; women's liberation; selfishness; stupidity; exploitation; breach of trust. But the story leaves us with too many questions: Did Ishmael really become the ancestor of Islam? Why did God intervene to save Hagar in the desert, but not in time to preserve family relationships in Abraham's camp? What is the connection with the Egyptians? Why are we reading this "text of terror"?

In the alternative Old Testament reading, Jeremiah is caught between what God demands that he say, and the social and personal consequences of saying it. He blames God for enticing him into the prophetic life, then abandoning him to the persecution of his enemies. Nevertheless, by the end of the reading, Jeremiah has to rely on God's promise of deliverance.

The portion of Paul's letter to the Romans is plucked out of the midst of Paul's argument about grace – the free gift from God that renders everyone just. The unwary may find themselves floundering in the waters that equate baptism with death and burial, and resurrection with a heavenly afterlife.

Finally, Matthew, the liturgist, strings together sayings of Jesus like a litany, designed to bolster the courage of believers under the constant barrage of criticism and persecution – much like Jeremiah. But Matthew ups the ante: "Whoever loves father or mother . . . son or daughter more than me is not worthy of me; and whoever does not take up the cross and follow me is not worthy of me." Judgment of unbelieving sinners is the name of Matthew's cherry-picking game.

"Context" here means consideration of two conditions. The first is the political, social, and spiritual milieu that gave rise to the original writings. If we look at the circumstances within which each of these readings was created, we find that they were all written under conditions of alienation and exile. The Abrahamic saga is part of the foundational myth of the Jewish nation and religion. Defining who is legitimately part of the authentic Hebrew people was vitally important to both the remnant exiled to sixth century B.C.E. Babylon, and those left behind in an alienated Jerusalem. The prophet Jeremiah was a living witness and interpreter of that time and place. Several hundred years later, the fledgling community of Christians in sacked Jerusalem faced the same kinds of issues: Who are we? Who was our spiritual leader and guide? What is our purpose? Who is part of our community, and who is not, and how do we decide? The Apostle Paul's letter to the Romans is a bit different. Written perhaps ten or fifteen years before the destruction of Jerusalem and the Temple, Paul thoroughly debates the definition of who is a Christian and what it means to follow Jesus. But even though Paul has chosen his mission to the Pagan/non-Jewish Roman world, he too is a political and religious exile. What can be more inflammatory to the Empire and to established religious tradition than to claim that "no human being will be acquitted in God's sight by deeds prescribed by the law, for through the law comes the knowledge of sin"? What greater threat to an economic and political system based on patronage than a community where everything is shared in common, and no one possesses more than anyone else?

The second aspect of "context" is the internal integrity of the story or argument. John Dominic Crossan makes it clear that the first order of business in scriptural interpretation is to "know the story and get it right."[70] It is vastly unfair – if not unconscionable – to cherry-pick Paul's words from Romans (or anywhere else) in order to perpetuate an institutional theological misinterpretation. It is equally unconscionable to misuse portions of foundational myths to the same end. When those myths are further bastardized to perpetuate present-day global political Empire, Paul's assertion that "the strength of sin is the law" takes on particular and tragic importance.

The Abrahamic story winds its way through the first five books of the Old Testament. To get the entire story straight and explore its meaning for twenty-first century political realities, is beyond the scope of this commentary. Perhaps this is the best argument for not following the Revised Common Lectionary, and instead concentrating on entire threads over a series of Sunday mornings. An alternative is certainly extended Bible study for all levels of church members, from pre-school to senior adults. The problem of course is curriculum. The straight story needs to be told from the cradle onwards, and without the dogmatic gloss that the New Testament supersedes the Old.

The prophets are no less prone to misinterpretation out of context, but their truncated stories are more easily dealt with in one sermon. Jeremiah wants the people to return to the old ways of the Covenant, and he is apparently willing to compromise with the Babylonians in order to avoid national destruction. This gets him in trouble with those who want to establish Judah as a kingdom in its own right. Jeremiah's dilemma is familiar to everyone confronted with the conundrums that accompany living in God's realm of distributive justice-compassion. He is compelled to speak truth to power, and we catch him at a weak moment – or would if the Elves allowed us to read on past the momentary relief Jeremiah finds in reminding himself that "[the Lord] has delivered the life of the needy from the hands of evildoers." But in the very

---

[70]Crossan, *God and Empire*, 128-131.

next verse, "Cursed be the day on which I was born!" Jeremiah sobs. "Cursed be the man who brought the news to my father, saying 'A child is born to you, a son,' . . . Why did I come forth from the womb to see toil and sorrow, and spend my days in shame?"

What Jeremiah prays for is deliverance. What the Apostle Paul promises in Romans 6:1-11 is transformation. For Proper 7, that transformation happens in the act of baptism: We are then dead and buried to the old life, which was defined by adherence to the law, and we are raised just as the Christ was raised to "walk in newness of life." The key words here are "death" and "life," not "crucifixion" and "resurrection." "Crucifixion" and "resurrection" are political terms, which Paul does not hesitate to use elsewhere. Jesus's death is not just a death. It happened in the context of Roman injustice. Jesus's resurrection is God's action in the world, continuing to counter imperial injustice. But using the words "death" and "life" confronts Christians with the day-to-day reality of participation with God in that same continuing action.

Returning to the opening metaphor, this day-to-day participation is indeed the King's business, which the Elves and the writer of Matthew miss. Once we know the political and spiritual context that Matthew was addressing, we cannot fault him for this; nevertheless, the aphorisms recorded by Matthew cannot be taken literally and applied uncritically to twenty-first century issues. Two of the aphorisms were agreed by the Jesus Seminar scholars as authentically going back to the historical Jesus. These are: "After all, there is nothing veiled that won't be unveiled, or hidden that won't be made known"; and "What do sparrows cost? A penny apiece? Yet not one of them will fall to the earth without the consent of your Father. As for you, even the hairs on your head have all been counted. So don't be so timid; you're worth more than a flock of sparrows." However, the original context for either of them has been long lost, and their position in Matthew's litany seems arbitrary – whatever Jesus meant when he said them, they have been reduced to non sequiturs, and their intent compromised.

Continuing the metaphor, and seriously playing the fool, the rest of the aphorisms listed by Matthew are clearly out of character with a Jesus who taught distributive justice-compassion. They are full of retributive judgment, and hints of violence against nonbelievers, and it is highly likely that Jesus never said any of them. They were essential to the survival of the early Christian community. But are they essential to a twenty-first century Christianity?

Crossan, in his book *In Search of Paul*, discusses Paul's theology, and specifically the letter to the Romans: "Christ's 'death' always meant for Paul the terrible death of an unjust execution, the horrible death of a shameful crucifixion. It did not mean death as the normal end of life. His theology was not actually built on Christ's death and resurrection as if Christ had died at home in Nazareth and rose there on the third day. That death meant injustice and violence. Here then, after two thousand years and especially as the twenty-first century's terrorism replaces the twentieth century's totalitarianism, we ask this question: Is it death or is it violence that is the last enemy of God? Or better, is it unjust and violent death that is the last enemy of God?"[71]

Here is the astute criticism the King's business demands.

---

[71]Crossan and Reed, 389.

Proper 8
Get with the Program

Genesis 22:1-14; Jeremiah 28:5-9; Psalm 13;
Psalm 89:1-4, 15-18; Romans 6:12-23; Matthew 10:40-42

"Paul, having mentioned sacrificial atonement by Christ, does not develop it further in any way, but speaks instead of *participation in Christ*, which . . . is the heart of his theology. And where *sacrificial atonement* got only one verse (3:5), *participation* gets a whole chapter (6:1-23)."[72] The Elves, of course, divided the chapter into two parts, thereby robbing Paul of the integrity of his argument. In the first half, Paul says that if we have indeed died to sin, by committing to living the same way of life as taught by Jesus, we shall then live not according to our own self interest nor according to the interests of Empire (foreign or domestic), but according to the kenotic (self-abandoning) rule of God. The "end" or result is "eternal life." The result of living according to the normal rules of civilization is death, says Paul. Not physical death, but spiritual death – the death of injustice, which also brings with it the death of God. But the free gift of eternal life (grace) here and now is extended to all who choose to participate with the risen Christ in God's realm of distributive justice-compassion.

The horrific story about Abraham's willingness to sacrifice his son to God has nothing to do with the "Christian God" sacrificing "his son" in order to "save us" from "eternal hellfire and damnation" (atonement – substitutionary or otherwise). It does, however, have to do with that same "free gift" in Paul's argument. The name "Isaac" means "God will provide." In the bare bones of the story, God provides the proper sacrifice and spares Abraham the barbarism of murdering his son. The story is so obscured with Christian gloss that it is nearly impossible to avoid the Christian metaphor. But in its own context, the story does two things: It illustrates an awakening spiritual awareness on

---

[72]Crossan and Reed, 384.

the part of humanity that human blood sacrifice is not necessary to become reconciled with one's gods; and the legend provides a graphic, pre-Christian demonstration of the level of commitment required to keep the Covenant. The old ways of literal blood-sacrifice of the first-born child were overthrown by the Covenant established for the people between God and Abraham. The Covenant continues, says the Apostle Paul, whenever anyone signs on to the program begun by Jesus.

Cherry-picking Jeremiah robs Jeremiah's witness to the will and wisdom of God of nearly all its power. All we hear from the Elves is that God's prophets always foretell gloom and doom, and the false prophets claim peace. Jeremiah tells Hananiah that when the prophesied peace comes, "then it will be known that the Lord has truly sent the prophet." The doctrinal assumption is that the Creation is "fallen" permanently into sin; therefore, any prophet has to be false who claims God's peace instead of God's "wrath" ("judgment"). A second assumption is that the reading simply reflects an ongoing rhetorical debate between false and true prophets, and we already know that Jeremiah is the good guy. Neither assumption honors the integrity of the story. Both lend themselves to pious self-righteousness.

In the encounter with Hananiah, Jeremiah has put an ox yoke on his own neck, demonstrating submission to the yoke of Babylon "until the time of his own land comes." Jeremiah tells the people, "if any nation will not serve this king, Nebuchadnezzar of Babylon, and put its neck under the yoke of the king of Babylon, then I will punish that nation with the sword, with famine, and with pestilence, says the Lord. . . . You therefore must not listen to your prophets . . . who are saying [the opposite] to you. . . . But any nation that will bring its neck under the yoke of the king of Babylon and serve him, I will leave on its own land . . . to till it and live there." (Jeremiah 27:8-11).

When we know the context we find that Jeremiah has had to resort to drama in order to get anyone to listen to him regarding the political fact that the Babylonians have won. But wait – doesn't that make Jeremiah a collaborator with the very Empire these commentaries have been railing against? Again, the answer lies in the context of the entire story of Jeremiah – who stayed with the remnant of Israelites in Jerusalem while the rest were exiled to Babylon.

> [T]he trick is to discover trust in that covenant regardless of the circumstances. As a demonstration of his trust in the covenant with God, the prophet Jeremiah buys a field at Anathoth on the eve of the Babylonian conquest, when the people of Israel are facing certain exile and slavery. This is a defiant – even a subversive – act in the face of Empire. He honors the Mosaic law spelled out in *Leviticus 25*:25-28, that allows – perhaps obliges – a family member to "redeem" land that is in danger of being lost to debt. With the Babylonians at the gates of Jerusalem, Jeremiah agrees to buy the field. It is an act of trust that the people will return by the Jubilee Year, 50 years after the sale is arranged, and the land will then be restored to them.[73]

God's plan is that the people make the best of a bad situation and live in safety in their own land. All they need to do is trust in God's promise to preserve that land for its own great destiny. But Hananiah has aligned himself with the politicians who want to overthrow the Babylonian empire and establish their own – despite the reality of overwhelming imperial military forces. Worse, Hananiah has the audacity to physically break the ox yoke that Jeremiah has attached to his own neck, thereby symbolically defying God's will. As Matthew's Jesus says, "The one who accepts you accepts me, and the one who accepts me accepts the one who sent me." The obverse – that the one who does not accept you does not accept me – means that if God's prophet is defied, God [himself] is also defied. In the part we are not supposed to read this week, Jeremiah goes back to Hananiah and warns him that because he broke the wooden yoke, an even stronger yoke of iron is now attached to the necks of all the nations conquered by the Babylonians, and furthermore, Hananiah will be dead within the year. Sure enough, "In that same year, in the seventh month, the [false] prophet Hananiah died" (Jeremiah 28:17).

An editorial in the *Christian Science Monitor* of June 18,

---

[73]Raven, 178.

2008, discussed the U.S. Supreme Court decision regarding Guantanamo detainees and habeas corpus. The Court divided 5 to 4 between the majority who held that "Liberty and security can be reconciled," and the dissenting view that "lower courts will almost certainly release dangerous detainees and cause more Americans to be killed." *The Monitor* concluded that "America's identity rests on its ideals, such as due process. They help preserve a quality of life that *may require a sacrifice of life*" (emphasis added). The editorial point concerns secular politics (and arguably imperial theology), not Covenant. Nevertheless, as Jeremiah demonstrated with his ox yoke (and perhaps underlying and informing the *Monitor's* view), the fact that Empire holds sway does not rule out distributive justice-compassion, which not only *may* require sacrifice. The readings for this Proper 8 assert that it does. Abraham was willing to give up any hope of realizing God's heady promise that he would be the father of a great nation in order to remain obedient to that same God of justice-compassion. Jesus gave up his life because of that same obedience to the rule of distributive justice in God's realm. The only time the prophet gets derailed is when she makes false promises of easy piety, war, victory, and peace. The trick is to distinguish between Covenant (nonviolent, distributive justice-compassion) and the easy piety of Empire. Anyone who thinks that participation with the risen Christ in God's realm of distributive justice-compassion is easy is listening to false prophets. The defining factor is justice – so long as justice is distributive and grounded in compassion, all is well. As soon as justice becomes retributive, and rooted in violence, the difference between the false and true prophets becomes clear.

Proper 9
The Burden Is Light

Genesis 24:34-38, 42-40, 58-67; Zechariah 9:9-12;
Psalm 45:10-17; Psalm 145:8-14; Song of Solomon 2:8-13;
Romans 7:15-25a; Matthew 11:16-19, 25-30

After all the heavy-duty theological argument of the past three weeks, we are rewarded with romance. Abraham's servant finds Rebecca as a bride for Isaac, and the two of them become one of the love stories of the ages. Psalm 45 is an Ode to a Royal Wedding; Psalm 145 is a Psalm of David, praising God; while the Song of Solomon celebrates spring, fertility, and the pagan rite of Sacred Marriage. The only sour note is old Paul, grousing on about how his "member" is at war with his mind, "making me captive to the law of sin that dwells in my members." What a curmudgeonly post-script to love, sex, and destiny! Those pious Elves probably think the Song of Solomon is an allegory of God's Love for Israel, or Christ's Love for the Church!

Meanwhile, Matthew's Jesus complains that "this generation" reminds him of "children sitting in the marketplaces who call out to others: 'We played the flute for you but you wouldn't dance; we sang a dirge, but you wouldn't mourn.'" He whines on: "Just remember, John appeared on the scene neither eating nor drinking, and they say, 'He is demented.' The son of Adam came both eating and drinking, and they say, 'There's a glutton and a drunk, a crony of toll collectors and sinners!'" Too bad we're studying Matthew's Gospel instead of John. If it were John's Jesus, he'd be attending the Wedding at Cana, and turning the water into wine instead of complaining about not making a difference.

Including a portion of Zechariah in Proper 9 seems another non sequitur. Here we are, three months after Easter, revisiting the aria from Handel's Easter portion of the Messiah: "Rejoice, daughter of Zion; behold your king comes triumphant and victorious, . . . humble and riding on a donkey." Looking at the cherry-picked portion of Matthew's Gospel, verses 25-30, Jesus is saying, "Come to me, all you that are weary and are carrying heavy burdens, and I will give you rest. Take my yoke upon you and learn from me . . . for my yoke is easy and my burden is light." Singers will find their minds going on in Handel's *Messiah* to the mezzo aria, and the accompanying chorus. Last week's reading in Jeremiah clearly references the yoke Jeremiah put on his own neck, and the false prophet Hananiah, who destroyed it. However, the traditional view tells us that Jesus redeems and actualizes the metaphor by declaring that unlike the yoke that Jeremiah took upon himself, the yoke that Jesus offers is easy. Is this a stretch or what? Especially given the fact that the Elves cherry-picked last week's Jeremiah to such an extent that the yoke is never mentioned in the prescribed reading. Nevertheless, look at Paul's lament in Romans 7:24b-25: "Who will rescue me from this body of death? Thanks be to God through Jesus Christ our Lord!"

Piety is easy, and the burden is indeed weightless.

Surely the point of the recommended readings is not that sex outside of marriage (defined strictly as between a man and a woman of course) is a sin. Wedding parties rule! Have a church picnic in the park instead of a service in the sanctuary! Read love poetry, including ee cummings and the entire Song of Songs!

For the purposes of liberal commentary, however, we owe it to Paul to reclaim Romans 7.

John Shelby Spong has theorized that the Apostle Paul was gay and his homosexuality drove him to seek salvation in Jewish law. Seeing that the new Christianity was beginning to overthrow that law, Paul became a zealous prosecutor, trying to stamp out a movement that threatened to overturn the very law (Torah) that "only by the most herculean efforts was holding Paul just above the abyss . . . ."[74] But then, like a bolt from the sky, he realized God's free gift of justice-compassion – grace – given to all those who participate with the risen Christ in establishing God's realm in this life and this time. This grace brought forgiveness of even the sin of murdering Jesus himself. Spong writes, "The being of Paul, a being he did not understand, a being he could not control, a being that all of the wisdom of his world and all of his sacred

---

[74]Spong, *Rescuing the Bible*, 116-120.

tradition condemned as worthy only of death, that being of Paul met the grace of God in the person of Jesus the Christ."[75] If Paul could experience this liberation, then everyone could.

Did Paul stop being who he was – whether a homosexual person or not? I would suggest that he became even more truly who he really was. If participation with the risen Christ means the radical abandonment of one's self-interest, the grace that is the free gift of God then is radical acceptance of one's own condition, and the conditions of others – or, as the Unitarian Universalists put it in their First Principle: "the inherent worth and dignity of every person." Reading from the beginning of Romans 7, instead of cherry-picking the most scandalous portion, Paul says, "But now we are discharged from the law, dead to that which held us captive, so that we are slaves not under the old written code, but in the new life of the Spirit" (Romans 7:6). Further, to take a sneak peak at next week's theme, "there is therefore now no condemnation for those who are in Christ Jesus" (Romans 8:1).

Whatever one might surmise about Paul's sexuality, and the liberating interpretation Spong presents, it is important to return to the guiding principles of context, and the integrity of the story. Paul is continuing his impassioned debate regarding works, faith, grace, and the law. He uses every trick of the trade, including hyperbole, and finally in chapter 7 resorts to the time-honored use of sex as a way to get his readers to listen to the radicality of his proposition. He starts with an anology of marriage, reminding people that according to the law, a woman is only married to her husband so long as he is alive. "If her husband dies, she is free from that law, and if she marries another man, she is not an adulteress." If that doesn't get their attention, nothing will. He is saying that participation in the kingdom as begun by the life and teachings of Jesus makes everyone who signs onto the program "dead to the law" that results in sin; or, in John Dominic Crossan's words, the law that inevitably leads to injustice – the normalcy of civilization. Is the law itself sin? No, rants Paul. But if not for the law, we would not know sin. This argument gets very close to the idea that we as humans cannot know good unless we have evil to

---

[75]Ibid., 122.

compare it with – a subject for a much wider debate. For now, suffice to say that these commentaries take the view that the nature of the known universe is good at best, neutral at worst. Humanity is the species that brought "evil" into the world because of our consciousness of consequences. Perhaps – for postmodern people – that is as close as we can come to Paul's point.

Paul then in desperation confesses his own personal weakness. The law is spiritual, he says, but I am trapped in a physical body. Even though the law mandates a particular behavior, and even though I may greatly desire to comply with that mandate, I cannot. This is the inner conflict – the personal *jihad* – the personal struggle to not only accept Jesus's invitation to participate in God's kingdom of justice-compassion, but to commit to that program, and stick to it.

We shall see if Paul does discover in the end that the yoke is easy, and the burden is light.

Proper 10
Insiders/Outsiders

Genesis 25:19-34; Isaiah 55:10-13; Psalm 119:105-112;
Psalm 65:1-13; Romans 8:1-11; Matthew 13:1-9, 18-23

The most obvious theme for these readings is the traditional Christian dichotomy: insiders who know the secrets and are "saved" versus outsiders who refuse to hear the truth and are condemned. Insiders/outsiders brings up the second question in the series of four that underlies these commentaries: What is the nature of Jesus's message? Inclusive or exclusive? The answer to this question determines believers' attitudes toward themselves, their families, communities, global relationships, and God's kingdom itself – the created universe.

The parables attributed to Jesus that are most likely authentically his creations always have an element of improbability or a joke that points to overturning social convention – whether in the first century or the twenty-first. The clue to the meaning of the parable of the sower is not found in Matthew's pious pontificating in 13:18-23. Nor is it found in the part the Elves skipped (13:10-17), where Matthew's Jesus complains about the political fact (still true today) that "to those who have, more will be given . . . and from those who don't have, even what they do have will be taken away." The clue lies in the outrageous yield the good earth provides: thirty percent, sixty percent, one hundred percent. The meaning of the clue comes into focus in commentary by Laurel A. Dykstra:[76] "Commenting on Mark's earlier version of this parable (Mark 4:3-8), theological animator Ched Myers says, 'The symbolic harvest represents a dramatic shattering of the vassal relationship between peasant and landlord.' Such a harvest would allow a peasant family to eat, pay rent, taxes, and debts, and even buy land, effectively turning the social order on its head."

---

[76]Dykstra, 49.

Matthew's Jesus provides an obvious and pious explanation that leaves us with the idea that only Christians can hear the message and understand it and profit from it. But, as the Jesus Seminar scholars insist, "This disposition is entirely alien to Jesus, but characteristic of some strands of the early Christian movement that were akin to gnosticism. The Gnostics claimed to be in possession of esoteric knowledge that was necessary for salvation."[77] For too long, Christians have bought into that idea and have made Jesus's message exclusive. The parable of the sower is not about "insiders and outsiders," as tradition and Matthew's Jesus tell us. It is about grace and justice.

Psalm 65 sings the joy of an abundant earth and a just God; Psalm 119 praises God's law, which sets up human society to live and prosper in abundance, justice, and peace. Isaiah 55 contains the original blessing, empowering us to go out with joy because our God is just and the world belongs to God. Jesus would not have said otherwise. As the sower scatters his seed, it falls wherever it falls. But when we live in God's realm, fairness and abundant life prevail.

Is the story of Esau and Jacob also about "insiders and outsiders" or is it about the liberation that comes from throwing over tradition? If we get outside the Christian gloss, we find that the story raises basic questions about good and evil, and choosing not only whether to participate in God's distributive justice-compassion, but how to do so.

Jacob and Esau are the prototypes for two types of souls, each with a distinct role to play in the fulfillment of the Divine purpose in creation. Maimonides calls these two spiritual types "the perfectly pious" and "the one who conquers his inclinations"; Rabbi Schneur Zalman refers to them as the "Tzaddik" and the "Beinoni." Humanity is divided into these two types, writes Rabbi Schneur Zalman in his Tanya, because "there are two kinds of gratification before G-d. The first is generated by the good achieved by the perfectly righteous. But G-d also delights in the conquest of evil which is still at its

---

[77] Funk, et al., 193.

strongest and most powerful in the heart, through the efforts of the ordinary, unperfected individual."[78]

Paul's argument tells us that the imperfect individual is the one who is awarded the free gift of grace, just because he or she joins the ongoing struggle for distributive justice-compassion, as Jesus taught during his life, and continued through his spirit after his death. Justice as retribution, payback, the normal course of civilization, lies well outside God's realm. The struggle is not only whether to redeem the world from its exile, but how. Christians should define themselves as those who model their lives after one who taught that the way to redemption was the radical abandonment of self-interest. "Belief" in life after death has nothing to do with it. Paul's point is that life in the spirit of the Christ is about radical inclusiveness. There are no "insiders and outsiders." There is only the free gift, available to all who choose to participate. But this begs the question, what about those who do not choose to participate?

Would anyone consciously choose not to participate in distributive justice-compassion? Suppose the answer to that is a resounding "no." Suppose that the reason for evildoers among humans is not that "When anyone listens to the message . . . and does not understand it, the evil one comes and steals away what was sown in the heart. . . ." (Matthew 13:19a). If our sense of justice was truly distributive, "evil" would be understood to be reversible. The Genghis Kahns, the Hitlers, the Stalins, the Saddam Husseins, would not be enemies to be destroyed, but fellow human lives to be redeemed into justice.

In the continuing foundation myth of Abraham his twin grandsons Jacob and Esau are archetypal. The privileged Esau, certain of his "birthright" as first-born of the two, demands food after an unsuccessful day of hunting. In the typical hyperbole of ego, he claims to be dying of hunger anyway, so who needs a "birth right"? Jacob is only too happy to oblige. Applied to twenty-first century global conditions, Jacob is the multi-national corporation that controls seed, land, markets, and commodities futures. Esau is the politically disempowered and the

---

[78]http://www.chabad.org/parshah/ article_cdo/ aid/15573/ jewish/ Jacob-and- Esau.htm

disenfranchised. Whether the Esaus of the Planet today are facing certain death anyway, or are caught in ideological systems that threaten well-being, they either are afraid to, or can't afford to consider the social, political, and environmental consequences of selling out. We can't push this portion of this foundational myth too far. Nevertheless, whether we see the incident as a clash of agrarian versus hunter-gatherer cultures or as an allegory of the history of the Hebrew people as they established themselves and became dominant in the ancient Middle East, or as a cautionary tale for children caught up in the battles of sibling rivalry, the story contains all the worst elements of human behavior: greed, treachery, arrogance, self-righteousness.

Romans 8:1-11 must be read in that light. Paul, after all, was a trained expert in Torah. He knew the stories and the traditions. When he writes, "To set the mind on the flesh is death, but to set the mind on the spirit is life and peace" he is not talking about premarital (or extramarital) sex. Paul has been arguing for eight chapters that participation with the risen Christ in God's realm of distributive justice-compassion brings life and peace. To refuse to participate is death and suffering. Why? Because God's law (not Roman law – or human law) is just. This is not about "believing" that a dead corpse came back to life, although Paul could only describe his extraordinary insight in those terms. "But if Christ is in you, though the body is dead because of sin, the Spirit is life because of righteousness." In other words, even though we are trapped in systems that perpetuate injustice and death – where there is no god – if we are participating with the ongoing program of restoring justice-compassion to the Planet, we live with the Spirit in that realm.

There is therefore no condemnation – not even for the killers of Jesus – for those who accept the challenge and participate in the great work of justice-compassion. This teaching means that not only is the death penalty in the United States inappropriate for those who rape children,[79] it is inappropriate for anyone no matter what the crime. The punitive, retributive system that controls how the United States deals with aberrant behavior is the opposite of

---

[79]Kennedy v. Louisiana, 554 U.S. 407 (2008).

"justice." Everyone deserves the chance to turn his or her life around and sign onto the program.

The gift of grace is free. This is an extraordinary claim. The free gift of grace is the same outrageous promise as the seed flung at random by the sower that produces thirty percent, sixty percent, even one hundred percent return.

Proper 11
Ladders, Circles, Covenant

Genesis 28:10-19a; Wisdom of Solomon 12:13, 16-19;
Isaiah 44:6-8; Psalm 139:1-12, 23-24; Psalm 86:11-17;
Romans 8:12-25; Matthew 13:24-30, 36-43

> *We are climbing Jacob's Ladder, soldiers of the cross.*
> *We are dancing Sarah's Circle, sisters, brothers, all.*
> *Every round goes higher, higher, soldiers of the cross*
> *Here we seek and find our story, sisters, brothers, all.*
> *Sinner do you love my Jesus? soldiers of the cross.*
> *We will all do our own naming, sisters, brothers, all.*
> *If you love him why not serve him? soldiers of the cross*
> *Every round a generation, sisters, brothers, all.*
> *We are climbing Jacob's ladder, soldiers of the cross*
> *On and on the circle's moving, sisters, brothers, all.*

The Abraham saga continues, with Jacob's dream. Christian dogma claims that Jacob's dream is about divinity interacting with humanity. The patriarchs of ancient Israel were all one hundred percent human, even though they may have dreamt of a great destiny. But Christianity trumps all that with the human/divine Jesus/God, who came to dwell among us. Cherry-picked Paul piously points orthodox theology into the apocalyptic future "while we wait for adoption, the redemption of our bodies." Matthew's Jesus rants that "The son of Adam will send his messengers and they will gather all the snares and the subverters of the Law out of his domain and throw them into the fiery furnace [where] people will weep and grind their teeth."

Jewish legend says that Jacob's pillar, which he set up to mark the spot of his prophetic dream, is the same spot where his father Isaac was prepared by Abraham for sacrifice; it is also the Temple Mount of present-day Jerusalem. There are global political and religious layers of meaning surrounding this story. It should be treated with respect, and not with glib literalism by anyone, including descendants of the People of the Book.

Recent Christian youth and feminist leadership has replaced the militant sexism of "climbing Jacob's ladder, soldiers of the cross" with "dancing Sarah's circle, sisters, brothers all." Somehow the original seems more honest. "Sinner do you love my Jesus? If you love him, why not serve him? Soldiers of the cross" can't be mistaken for peaceful coexistence with Jews, Muslims, or any other non-Christian spirituality. "Dancing Sarah's circle" sounds inclusive, but Christian hegemony lurks in the background like a watermark on fine stationery: "Here is where we find our story; we will all do our own naming; every round a generation, sisters, brothers all." The stories of Sarah, Keturah, Rebekka, Rachel, Leah, Dinah, Bilhah, Zilpah, and all the other women, named and unnamed, who contributed to the founding mythos of the Jewish people and the Jewish religion are not Christian stories except by "adoption" – and that is certainly not where Paul was trying to take his Roman community.

The power in these readings is the power of covenant relationship. In Jacob's dream, God's voice confirms the promise made to his grandfather Abraham and his father Isaac, that the land belongs to them and their descendants, and those descendants shall be as numerous as the grains of dust on the earth. God also promises that wherever Jacob and his descendants go, God is still their God. So God and God's realm are not confined to a particular geographical location, but reside in the hearts of those who accept the covenant. The Elves leave out Jacob's part of the deal. For the first time, the patriarchs make a promise to God. Jacob promises to establish the pillar as "God's house," and to return to God one-tenth of everything God gives to him (Genesis 28:19b-18). As the editor of the *Harper Collins Study Bible* wryly comments, "Jacob's faith is more markedly contractual than Abraham's" (p. 43).

The portion of Paul's letter plucked out of context for Proper 11 is also about Covenant. Whenever we join Jesus in the relationship with God that is so close as to be the same as a father, we are then children of God, and heirs of God. What do we inherit? Rather than one strip of real estate in the Middle East, the heirs of God, brothers and sisters of the Christ, inherit the realm/kingdom of God, where distributive justice rules. The caveat is that we "suffer" with Jesus. In other words, we participate with the spirit of Jesus in restoring/reclaiming God's realm of distributive justice-compassion. "Suffering" is not about persecution and torture for believing that a corpse came back to life. "Suffering" is what happens when we attempt to live in radical abandonment of self-interest and fail. "Suffering" is what happens when by extraordinary commitment we succeed in achieving that radical abandonment of self-interest, and the systems of retribution inherent in Empire intervene.

Paul rhapsodizes on: ". . . for the creation waits with eager longing for the revealing of the children of God; . . . that the creation itself will be set free from its bondage to decay and will obtain the freedom of the glory of the children of God. . . ." This is not about believers going to heaven in the next life. It is about partners actualizing the promise of God's rule in this life. The "children of God" are not some superior race. They are whoever joins the program – Christian or non-Christian, people "of the book" or not. Has this happened yet? No. "But if we hope for what we do not see, we wait for it with patience." The Elves cut him off here in mid-argument. The finale comes next week.

Meanwhile, Matthew's Jesus proceeds to further complicate and rob the parable of the sower of its covenantal, transforming power. He has apparently forgotten his own Sermon on the Mount and has sold out to fear. The parable of the sabotage of weeds introduces an enemy that comes in the night and sows weed seed in the field so that it is impossible to eradicate the weeds without also destroying the good crop. Sort of like that hapless Canadian farmer who was sued by Monsanto.[80] In a variation on the

---

[80]Monsanto Canada Inc. v. Schmeiser [2004] 1 S.C.R. 902, 2004 SCC 34 Supreme Court of Canada ruled that intentionally growing genetically modified plants constitutes "use" of the patented invention of genetically modified plant cells. The case is widely misunderstood to concern what happens when farmers' fields are accidentally contaminated with patented seed. However by the time the case went to trial, all claims had been dropped that related to patented seed in the field that was contaminated in 1997; the court only considered the GM canola in Schmeiser's 1998 fields, which Schmeiser had intentionally concentrated and planted from his 1997 harvest. Regarding his 1998 crop, Schmeiser did not put forward any defense of accidental contamination.

thirteenth century epithet, "slay them all, God will know his own," this apocalyptic Jesus says, "Let them grow up together until the harvest, and . . . I'll say to the harvesters, 'Gather the weeds first and bind them in bundles to burn. . . '" What happened to "love your enemies" (Matthew 5:44)?

Matthew's Christian community – which possibly had been thrown out of their synagogue, or had chosen to leave – was very likely under siege. Viewed with suspicion by their neighbors, confronted with the destruction of the Temple, under surveillance by the Roman authorities, who can blame them for finding it difficult to love their enemies? That first or second century community and others in similar circumstances were not much different from communities today. Certainly the governments and the people in the Middle East are still fighting the land battles described in all the foundational myths. Dictatorships and oligarchies from Asia to Africa to South America deny human rights to their citizens to the detriment of their nations' economic well-being. Further, since September 11, 2001, American society has been under political, social, and economic threat – mostly self-inflicted.

We do not need to follow Matthew's Jesus into paranoia and the fear-mongering that arises from it. As the Apostle Paul says, the present problems are nothing, compared with the transformation that is coming. The Elves should have had us read on in Romans 8 to verses 26-30. "The Spirit helps us in our weakness," Paul says. "We know that all things work together for good for those who love God, who are called according to his purpose." What is that call and purpose? To be partners with Jesus in bringing God's realm of distributive justice-compassion into human civilization. "For those whom [God] foreknew he also predestined to be conformed to the image of his Son, in order that he might be the firstborn within a large family." What God knows and does looks to us like prior action.[81] But Paul is not talking about the Calvinist doctrine of "predestination" that we are powerless to modify, which fore-ordains some to be "chosen" for "salvation" and others "chosen" for damnation. We are adopted

---

[81]National Council of Churches, 2127.

children of God, and because of that, we are conformed to the image of Jesus the Christ. The Scholars Version of these verses is much less confusing:

> Now we know that for those who love God – those who are called to live in accordance with God's purpose – God always collaborates for a good outcome. That is, God provided for those who are called, and God decided in advance that they would take on the form of God's "son," . . And those about whom God had decided in advance, God also called; and those God called, God also affirmed as getting it right; and those God affirmed as getting it right God also has transformed into something splendid.[82]

Wow. The crowd should be on its feet cheering. All we have to do is sign up. Those whom God/dess knew would be her own, s/hecalled. Those whom God/dess called and who responded were thereby made holy and just; and those who were made just, were celebrated as belonging to – even inheriting– the kingdom, without bargain or price.

The Circle is open but unbroken, and the traffic on Jacob's ladder is an interchange.

---

[82]Dewey, et al., 230.

Proper 12
Sex, Lies, and Standing Stones

Genesis 29:15-28; 1 Kings 3:5-12; Psalm 105:1-11, 45b;
Psalm 128; Psalm 119:129-136; Romans 8:26-39;
Matthew 13:31-33, 44-52

The Elves' focus on the patriarchs and the ancestral stories leading to Jesus misses the best parts of the Abraham saga. But to be fair, the reconstruction by the Biblical writers of these foundational myths only hits the highlights.[83] If we confine ourselves to the Elves' selection, Jacob is a hopelessly romantic naif. But if we read the whole story, Jacob begins to look more like the first practitioner of nonviolent resistance. After 20-plus years, two wives, two concubines, and eight or ten children, he finally has had enough. He declares his intention to return to his own country. Rachel grabs the family icons. Jacob tells off evil uncle Laban for all his cheating shenanigans. Laban capitulates (after being intimidated off his search of Jacob's tents by Rachel's claim that "the way of women is upon me"). Together Jacob and Laban create a cairn of stones and a menhir to mark their agreement never to trespass on one another's land again.

For those who want to cut to the chase without getting bogged down in all the sex, deception, and pagan magic between the portion of the story chosen for Proper 12 and the portion chosen for Proper 13, the Elves offer a snippet from 1 Kings. After the death of the great King David, Solomon asks for wisdom rather than wealth, and of course as we all know, he gets both. What a relief. No need for magic spells in order to assure that God's promise will be fulfilled. But Jacob, Leah, and Rachel have a more basic connection with the realm of God. They are people of the earth and practitioners of earth magic. When Leah's son Reuben brings mandrakes from the field, Rachel pleads with Leah to let

---

[83]For a midrash between the lines of Genesis chapters 29-35, see the now classic novel by Anita Diamant: *The Red Tent.*

her have them so she can use them herself and end the infertility she has suffered from. Leah trades them for a night with Jacob, which of course produces yet another son. But apparently the mandrakes work for Rachel, because at last she has a son, and that son is Joseph – the first savior of the Hebrew people.

Jacob does his own magic in order to assure the safety of his flocks of sheep and goats. He agrees to prolong his stay with Laban if Laban will pay him with black, and speckled and spotted sheep and goats. Laban promptly removes all of those from his herds and sends them off three days distance. Jacob then retaliates. He carefully takes branches from sacred trees: poplar, almond, and plane, and carves the bark to make poles that are striped and spotted with white. He plants them in the ground beside the watering hole whenever Laban's stronger flocks are there. When Laban's weaker sheep and goats are at the watering hole, Jacob takes the poles away. He separates his own flocks from Laban's. When Laban's stronger sheep and goats see the striped poles, they produce black and white offspring. The storyteller is gleeful: "Thus [Jacob] grew exceedingly rich, and had large flocks, and male and female slaves, and camels and donkeys."

Which is the greater wisdom? Solomon's wisdom, which is based on the written law, or the wisdom of Jacob and his people, which is based on their relationship with the natural world in which they live? Solomon – in all his glory – is defined by his piety and his strict adherence to the law. Jacob relies on his covenant relationship with God. Solomon is also a king – subject to all the temptations of Empire and the normalcy of civilization, despite his great wisdom. Neither Jacob nor Laban is interested in creating an imperial alliance. Jacob's honest cleverness has defeated Laban's selfish deception. The stone pillar marks their territorial boundary, and neither one will cross it.

Contrasting the imperial wisdom of Solomon's settled civilization with the tribal wisdom of a primordial people can only serve briefly as metaphor. The differences produced by the evolution of consciousness are too great. By the time Jesus walked the earth, the forces of Empire had become firmly established, and the struggle between the distributive justice-compassion of Covenant with God and the injustice inherent in human law had been documented and debated for thousands of years. Still, Jesus's parables called all who had ears to hear back into the covenant relationship with the wisdom and the realm of God.

The version of the mustard seed metaphor in Thomas 20:1-4 is thought to be closer to the original as told by Jesus because it has no interpretation attached to it: "[Heaven's imperial rule is] like a mustard seed. It's the smallest of seeds, but when it falls on prepared soil, it produces a large plant and becomes a shelter for birds of the sky." The tiny secret to the kingdom of God is hidden in plain sight. God's realm is not the big imperial power. As the Jesus Seminar scholars put it, "God's domain . . . was pervasive [like the mustard weed] but unrecognized, rather than noisy and arresting."

The parable of the leavening in the flour describing the nature of God's rule is thought to have come directly from Jesus because whether it occurs in Matthew, Luke or Thomas, there are no modifications or explanations. When was the last time one little packet of yeast – even if it was *Fleischmann's Rapid Rise* – was enough to leaven 50 pounds of flour? But first century people – rich or poor – did not get their leavening from little foil packets. Perhaps the "leaven" was a kind of sourdough starter. To use sourdough starter, you take a small amount and mix it in with the other ingredients and allow it to "leaven" the whole batch. The Jesus Seminar scholars point out that the leaven is "hidden," not "mixed." "Hiding" a bit of starter in 50 pounds of flour is an apt metaphor for the power of justice-compassion. Because it is not seen, acting with distributive justice-compassion – radically abandoning self-interest – as Jesus taught, at first seems ineffective and lost in the imperial injustice that holds sway among oppressed people. But eventually the movement grows until the whole population is involved, and liberation is won. As Victor Hugo said, "nothing is more powerful than an idea whose time has come."

As the man in charge of devious uncle Laban's fields, Jacob could have done something similar to the one who found treasure. A farmer in danger of losing his own land to the tax collector is forced to farm land adjacent to his own that belongs to the occupier. In the process of plowing the adjoining acreage, he discovers a buried treasure. He does not tell the land owner about the treasure. Instead, he covers it up, and sells his own land to buy that field. How is this kind of cheating representative of God's imperial rule? It is a perfect example of subversion of Empire in the name of the common man. The pearl of great price is actually worthless to the one who sells everything to get it. In order to live in the normalcy of civilization, he would need to sell it. But nothing is needed for living in God's realm.

Jacob's evil uncle Laban, like twenty-first century multi-national corporations, concedes defeat without admitting error, and invites a covenant with Jacob (Genesis 31:43-44). "May the Lord watch between you and me, when we are absent one from the other," he says. It is not a blessing. It is an invocation of God's judgment, should either one break the covenant represented by the cairn and the standing stone. But God's realm is not about judgment, despite the threat from Matthew's Jesus that "God's messengers will go out and separate the evil from the righteous and throw the evil into the fiery furnace. . . . " Matthew is stuck on fiery furnaces and payback, completely missing his own point. God's kingdom is not about Solomon's piety, war, victory. The way into the realm of God is Covenant with God. Rachel did not need to steal the household gods from Laban. God's part of the bargain with Jacob – marked with the cairn and the standing stone – is to be with him regardless of where he goes. The Apostle Paul is talking about the same secret. If God is for us, who can be against us? Who can separate us from the love of Christ? Indeed, Paul says, nothing can separate us from God's love. Nothing can keep us from God's kingdom, realized in the life of Jesus, and in the lives of anyone who signs on to the Covenant.

Proper 13
Put Your Own On First

Genesis 32:22-31; Isaiah 55:1-5; Psalm 17:1-7, 15;
Psalm 145:8-9, 14-21; Romans 9:1-5; Matthew 14:13-21

The Elves may have cherry-picked Romans 9 in order to avoid anti-Jewish preaching. The portions not included certainly could be read by the literal or unwary as a diatribe against Judaism. Paul's point of course is not anti-Jewish. He spells it out very clearly in those first five verses we are supposed to read: "They are Israelites," he writes, "and to them belong the adoption, the glory, the covenants, the giving of the law, the worship, and the promises; . . . from them . . .comes the Messiah." But he is disappointed that many Jews rejected the idea that Jesus is the Messiah. He argues that they relied on works mandated by law instead of faith in the ancient Covenant with God, which in Paul's mind was renewed and manifested in the life and teachings of Jesus. Therefore, God has extended to Gentiles the opportunity to sign on to the Covenant. Jews, of course, then and now, would disagree that they failed to measure up to the promise of distributive justice-compassion.

Whether Paul's polemics deserve attention or not, the whole series of readings for Proper 13 is about Covenant, starting with Isaiah 55. Just as God extended his covenant with David to include the entire nation of Israel, so God now extends to all the world the opportunity to participate in the ongoing restoration of God's kingdom of distributive justice-compassion. The Feeding of the 5,000 is an illustration of the God that Jesus preaches in the Sermon on the Mount (Matthew 6:25-30), and it is an illustration of the invitation to abundant life extended by the prophet Isaiah. "Listen carefully to me and eat what is good, and delight yourselves in rich food. Incline your ear, and come to me; listen so that you may live. I will make with you an everlasting covenant. . . ."

The story of Jacob wrestling with God (or the angel of God)

is also used in Proper 24, Year C – but there it is an alternative to Jeremiah, and is purported to be related to the Gospel and epistle readings.[84] In Year A, we skip the rest of the Jacob story, his reconciliation with Esau, and his establishment of settlement at Bethel (Jerusalem), so that we can go directly to the story of Joseph, and continue the lineage to the birth of Jesus. But the story of Jacob's fight with God is set in the middle of Jacob's dilemma about how to deal with the coming meeting between himself and his estranged brother Esau. After the fight Jacob is reborn/renamed as Israel (the one who strives with God) because he has striven with God (the angel) and humans (Laban) and prevailed. The next thing that happens is reconciliation with Esau – distributive justice.

The point is that Covenant – living in partnership with God in distributive justice-compassion – means life here now, not there then. In other words, reconcile with your brother and you will participate in the available abundance. When we fight with God about it, we always get hurt. In other words, if we resist dealing with the injustices in life – such as robbing our brother/sister of their birthright – we may well end up mentally and/or physically impaired. This is not "judgment." These are the consequences of not acting from radical abandonment of self-interest.

To return to Paul's argument, only the radical abandonment of self-interest counts. The law does not require such action. Only faith in God's realm produces salvation, which is life lived in partnership with God in justice-compassion. Works prescribed by law support the systems of injustice because we are not personally invested in them. We have a personal investment in reconciliation with friends, family, enemies.

Radical abandonment of self-interest (i.e., "love") is easiest to understand at the corporate level. Commercial, political, social "self-interests" are targets that attract money, media, and throngs of dedicated workers, whether for church mission fields, political action committees, marches, rallies, enthusiasm, or results. Political and social liberalism in the United States would be closer to death than it is without the willingness of people to abandon

---

[84]Raven, 188.

immediate gratification for the greater good.

But where the rubber meets the road, or perhaps where the Apostle Paul got it at the gut level (*see* Romans 7:21-25), is in the mundane realities of day-to-day intimate living with self, family, friends. Traditional teaching and understanding have it backwards. Sacrificial love is not about throwing yourself under the bus. Sacrificial love means letting go of guilt and ego involvement. It means taking a break, nourishing yourself, saying goodbye. The first instruction the flight attendant gives us when the oxygen mask comes down is to put your own mask on first, then help the one next to you.

In a crisis when Death is sitting on the chair beside your mother, we want God to intervene, to save, to prevent the inevitable course – whether it is dictated by the medical profession, the legal profession, or the Church itself. But look at what Paul says in the rest of his polemic in Romans 9:14-18: "[God] has mercy on whomever he chooses, and [God] hardens the heart of whomever he chooses." In other words, in God's realm, the rain falls on the just and the unjust.

Remember that the opposite to Covenant (nonviolence, distributive justice-compassion, peace) is the theology of Empire (piety, war [violence], victory, and conditional peace). The theology of Empire requires victims: victims of war, and of domestic or public violence. Victims are the result of a justice system that is based on judgmental retribution and payback, not neutral fairness. Under Covenant, there can be neither victims nor enemies, because those who live by distributive justice-compassion know that true power lies in trusting God's realm. Life under Covenant means the radical abandonment of self-interest. Those who love their enemies have no enemies.

When we are in alignment with that Covenant, intervention can be seen to be interference on the part of Empire, not the fulfillment of God's distributive justice-compassion. Paul says later in chapter 9:30-33: "Gentiles who did not strive for righteousness have attained it, that is righteousness through faith;

but Israel, who did strive for the righteousness that is based on the law, did not succeed in fulfilling that law. Why not? Because they did not strive for it on the basis of faith, but as if it were based on works."

When we let go and trust in the Covenant, everything falls into place. Does that mean that justice is served, or that suffering ends, or that miracles overturn the physical realities of the universe as we know it? Of course not. Death is part of life, and life is whatever happens to us. What "works" is the marvelous course that opens out before us as soon as we let go of any thought of making something happen that is not already in the offing.

A personal example: On the evening of July 3, a hospital dumped my mother into a "skilled nursing/rehab" facility, which I was unable at the eleventh hour to avoid. On Friday July 4, the biggest political patriotic holiday in the United States, I had to say goodbye to her and fly one thousand miles back to my home. All I could tell her was, I had done my best, and would have to trust the people in the system to do their job, and the creative forces of distributive justice to hold sway. Like a kayak in rapids, she and I had to just ride the river. Any attempt to intervene with a paddle or by shifting our weight would have wrecked us on the rocks. That is part of what it means to radically abandon self-interest.

Did I sue the hospital and take on the whole catastrophe of the U.S. medical system? Call Fox News and start an investigation into nursing home malpractice? Not directly. Those kinds of actions are usually self-gratifying, ego-justifying, Empire-supporting manifestations of works based on law, without faith, and outside the Covenant. Does that mean we just turn our faces to the wall and die? Absolutely not. We are not victims. Did my mother magically recover full strength and vibrant life? No. But, as Isaiah promises, according to God's Covenant, she shall go out with joy, and be led forth in peace. Those who live in Covenant with distributive justice-compassion are not victims, but victors. "The sting of death is sin, and the power of sin is the law," sings Paul in 1 Corinthians (15:56-58). "But thanks be to God who gives us the victory through our Lord Jesus Christ . . . because you know that in the Lord your labor is not in vain."

Proper 14
The Sound of Silence

Genesis 37:1-4, 12-28; 1 Kings 19:9-13;
Psalm 105:1-6, 16-22, 45b; Psalm 85:8-13; Romans 10:5-15;
Matthew 14:22-33

What new meaning can be wrung from the metaphor of Jesus walking on the water and pulling the unstable Peter to safety in the boat as the wind dies down? After two thousand years, we have certainly heard and said it all – including the defiant retort from the underpaid, overworked middle manager (or Greek slave – pick your era): "Sorry, I only pass water, not walk on it!" We could reach for a clue in the fascinating factoid revealed in the notes in the *Harper Collins Study Bible*[85] that ancient Jewish mariners used to carry in their boats a magical club engraved with "I Am" to shake at the storm threatening their safety – sort of like the land-locked witch who throws a silver dagger into the earth in the path of the cyclone, thereby splitting and defeating it. There may be a scientific possibility that such action on the part of the witch could rearrange the electrical forces generated by a tornado out on the prairie, and so it could be construed as trust in the covenant with the natural forces of the universe – but all we would be doing is joining the Biblical literalists, and the Elves who herd us willing or not along the supersessionist path.

Joseph's brothers seem to be understandably tired of Joseph and his special coat (with "sleeves" or "many colors"). Any little brother who rubs in the fact that he is Daddy's favorite by bragging about dreams of superiority is courting karmic consequences. But we blithely hit the highlights on the way to proving Jesus's ancestry, and don't worry about scaring our children with Sunday School tales of terror – not to mention justifying the worst examples of sibling rivalry.

Matthew's Jesus is Moses, constantly withdrawing to

---

[85]Council of Churches, 1885n14.27.

mountain tops to commune with God, then leading the people
through the Dead Sea waters. Jesus walking on the water evokes
God who "tramples on the sea" (Job 9:8), and "[whose] way was
through the sea, your path, through the mighty waters; yet your
footprints were unseen. . . ." (Psalm 77:19). The hidden realm of
God leads us to liberation through uncharted waters, leaving no
trace but righteousness (justice-compassion), which creates the
path for our steps.

Hello darkness, my old friend,
I've come to talk with you again,
Because a vision softly creeping,
Left its seeds while I was sleeping,
And the vision that was planted in my brain
Still remains
Within the sound of silence.[86]

Our favorite prophet Elijah is hiding out in his cave listening
to "the still small voice" of God, but we need to read the beloved
passage from 1 Kings carefully. According to the notes in the
Harper Collins Study Bible[87] the translation of the Hebrew is just
ambiguous enough to cast some doubt on whether Elijah (like Paul
Simon) heard anything other than his own despair in the silence
that followed the storm. God does speak to Elijah, *after* Elijah
repeats his tale of woe: ". . . I alone am left, and they are seeking
my life to take it away." God then tells Elijah to anoint a new king,
and to anoint a new prophet. "Thanks for your service, Elijah,"
God seems to be saying. "I accept your resignation as soon as you
have trained your replacement."

Fools said I, you do not know
Silence like a cancer grows.
Hear my words that I might teach you,
Take my arms that I might reach you.
But my words like silent raindrops fell,
And echoed
In the wells of silence.

The silence of the collective Church is deafening. Perhaps the

---

[86]Paul Simon, 1966 http://letsdown.net/download/1399.html.

[87]National Council of Churches, 551

silence rises and grows because the call from the liberal church for inclusive, distributive justice is drowned out by the fundamentalists' exclusive, retributive message, which the media have assumed defines "Christianity." Humans are normally able and all too eager to attach value to what attracts or repels. What is attractive is good; what is repellent is evil – except for those among us who have turned the logical experience on its head and insist that what is attractive is evil, and what is repellent is good. The torturers at Guantanamo Prison come to mind, along with the entrepreneurs who set up the market-based disaster called the United States "health care" system.

Some of the silence here is due to seminary training, which neglects the reality of a need for a course in "Crucifixion 101." Newly minted ministers may be grounded in postmodern theology, scholarship, and cosmology, but most are not equipped with the tools they need to lead parishioners out of the religious concepts of the nineteenth century. As a result, instead of reclaiming Christianity for a new age, ministers, in order to stay employed, preach what the people are used to and want to hear.

Some signs are appearing that the current crop of young adult evangelicals may be ready and willing for a kind of accommodation with the left in terms of social and economic justice, if not a transformation. But conflict between the radical inclusiveness that liberals are convinced was taught by Jesus, and the dogmas surrounding homosexuality and the sanctity of life that the conservative fundamentalists insist upon, still stands in the way. Liberals are accused and assumed to be unpatriotic with their opposition to war, their insistence on universal health care, radical response to climate change, prison and justice reform, etc. No wonder old Elijah emerged from the silence in such a negative state that God had to act to replace him.

And the people bowed and prayed
To the neon God they made.
And the sign flashed out its warning,
In the words that it was forming.
And the sign said, the words of the prophets
Are written on the subway walls

And tenement halls.
And whispered in the sounds of silence.

If one reads Romans 10:5-15 thinking that "righteousness" means politically correct piety, Paul's words are a call for crusade against everyone who does not sign up. "[I]f you confess with your lips that Jesus is Lord and believe in your heart that God raised him from the dead, you will be saved." What could be more clear? One's life is justified (rationalized) by belief in the life and death and literal physical resurrection of Jesus. "Everyone who calls on the name of the Lord shall be saved" from hell at the end of life. Hence the smug use of the aphorism, "there are no atheists in foxholes."

Christian "faith" has become believing in magic: walking on water, calming storms, curing terminal illness, finding parking places, or extracting cars from snowbanks. While there are no magic wands or crystal balls, the cross has nevertheless conveyed magic power. We make the sign of the cross over our own and other's bodies for protection or good luck. Crucifixes are always useful for waving in front of vampires or other forces of evil. Pieces of the true cross are still for sale by enterprising shopkeepers. But pious interpretations are not what is going on here.

Paul asks, "how are they to call on one in whom they have not believed . . . of whom they have never heard?" So the call goes out for witnesses, missionaries, to bring the "good news." These words just roll off the keyboard, as they have flowed from pens and from the extemporaneous artistry of countless preachers and theologians, most of whom have missed the point completely. The Apostle Paul's mystic insights are incomprehensible to most people, who only want to eat, sleep, make and raise children, be happy, be healthy, and live forever.

Christian "faith" is not about anybody coming back from the dead, nor is it about avoiding death altogether. Christian "faith" is trust in the distributive justice-compassion that holds sway in the universe, despite human social organization and understanding. Nothing distinguishes "Christian" from other faiths that have discovered the same truth except that Christian faith arises from the life and teachings of Jesus.

Chapter 10 of Paul's letter to the Romans continues his polemic against the Jewish communities who disagreed with his conclusions about who Jesus was. It is incomprehensible to Paul that anyone who heard the story would either not believe it, or not realize its radical meaning. Paul would make the same argument today. The cherry-picking Elves do a great disservice to Paul's theology by skipping around, perhaps hoping to avoid the anti-semitism that has plagued Christianity from the beginning. In the section skipped in Proper 14 (Romans 10:16-21), Paul quotes Isaiah: "I have been found by those who did not seek me; I have shown myself to those who did not ask for me. . . . All day long I have held out my hands to a disobedient and contrary people." Does this mean those who refuse to believe in the literal story about Jesus? Or does this mean that – as Jesus preached – the realm of God is all around us, ready for anyone to open their eyes and look and listen, and step into that realm?

People can only know if they are told, Paul says. "How beautiful are the feet of those who bring good news!" "Faith comes from what is heard, and what is heard comes through the word of Christ." The word has gone out through all the lands, through the best scholarship, through voices recovered from the past in Qumran and Nag Hamadi, through the work of "Biblical archeologists" excavating Jesus, and through the insights of cosmologists. The prophet Isaiah asks the same question Paul asks in his seminal letter to the fledgling Christian community in Rome (Isaiah 41:21): How can anyone not have heard? And once heard, how can anyone not get it?

Proper 15
What Would Jesus Do?

Genesis 45:1-15; Isaiah 56:1, 6-8; Psalm 133; Psalm 67;
Romans 11:1-2a, 29-32; Matthew 15: 10-28

Matthew's Jesus may have actually said that "it is not what goes into the mouth that defiles a person; rather it is what comes out of the mouth that defiles a person." The version in the Gospel of Thomas (Thomas 14:5) puts the saying in the context of Jesus's itinerant ministry: "When you go into any region and walk about in the countryside, when people take you in, eat what they serve you . . . ." Matthew's context has Jesus preaching to a crowd that includes those pesky Pharisees. Later, Peter (among the more dim-witted in the entourage, according to Matthew) insists that Jesus explain the "riddle." The explanation has for two millennia obscured the real point, which is not about sexual immorality, evil intentions, and blasphemies, as pious Matthew would have us believe. The real point is that living in God's realm of distributive justice-compassion obviates the need for any rules about what is or is not "kosher" or politically correct. The Apostle Paul is saying much the same thing behind all the polemics and despite the cutting and pasting by the Elves.

If we concentrate on Romans 11:29-32, with the story of Joseph's reconciliation with his dastardly brothers firmly in mind, then the message for today is a very pious one: Just as we all are "disobedient" to God's rules (regarding the Ten Commandments, abortion, same-sex marriage, "sexual sin," gun ownership), but have now received God's forgiveness (by believing that Jesus died in our place and was bodily resurrected), so "they" (by implication "the Jews") have also been disobedient and have also been forgiven (therefore, supporting the government of Israel regardless of the circumstances is "God's Will"). Then comes the kicker: "For God has imprisoned all in disobedience so that he may be merciful to all." Here is the monster God (graphically illustrated by Mel Gibson's 2004 film *The Passion of the Christ*), who deliberately causes people to fall into evil so that "he" can then save us and cause us to love "him." Such an interpretation is nothing more than a justification for abuse at every level of human experience – the exact opposite of distributive justice-compassion, and light-years from what the Apostle Paul was trying to say. The Elves strive mightily to avoid the antisemitism that can arise from an uninformed and literal reading of Paul's argument. But by not providing the context and allowing the full depth and breadth of Paul's polemic to be worked through, we are hard-pressed to arrive at any other conclusion.

Look at what Paul says in Romans 11:11-12: "So I ask, have they (the Jews) stumbled so as to fall? *By no means!* But through their stumbling, salvation has come to the Gentiles. . . . Now if their stumbling means riches for the world, and if their defeat means riches for Gentiles, *how much more will their full inclusion mean?*" And later in verse 15: "For if their rejection is the reconciliation of the world, what will *their acceptance* be but life from the dead!" (Emphasis added.) Apparently assuming we still won't get his point, Paul uses the metaphor of some branches that were broken from a healthy olive tree, and a wild shoot grafted into their place. Again, the argument takes some careful reading. Paul does say, "For if God did not spare the natural branches, perhaps he will not spare you. Note . . . [God's] severity toward those who have fallen, but God's kindness toward you, *provided you continue in his kindness;* otherwise you also will be cut off" (Romans 11: 21-22).

God's kindness is distributive justice-compassion, usually misunderstood as "mercy." "Mercy" as imperial theology uses the term most often means feeling sorry for a criminal, and converting the sentence from the death penalty to life in prison without parole. God's kindness under Covenant, on the other hand, means distributive justice-compassion: taking into consideration the entire context, then acting with radical abandonment of self-interest to ensure fairness. When Paul talks about "full inclusion" and "acceptance" of the Jews, he means what he said at the end of the eighth chapter of this letter to the Romans, that nothing can separate us from the love of God as evidenced and experienced in the life and teachings of Jesus, whom Christians call the Christ.

God has no litmus test for inclusion in the Kingdom except to do our best to live in distributive justice-compassion. No one is left out: neither slave nor free, male nor female, Jew nor gentile; and when we fail – because of a "thorn in the flesh" or any other shortcoming, we are saved by God's grace. Belief in a resuscitated corpse has nothing to do with it.

Nevertheless, don't get too smug about your salvation. God has always been very clear about the preference extended in God's realm to those who live in distributive justice-compassion. There are consequences for those who do not, generally having to do with becoming trapped in imperial forms of retributive justice, and theologies of piety, war, victory, peace – not to mention environmental holocaust. Consider what Joseph did when his brothers came looking for food-aid in a time of drought and famine in their own land. Joseph – now part of Pharaoh's imperial rule – could have enslaved them on the spot, or sent them away to starve and die. Instead, remembering that he was part of God's Covenant with his great-grandfather Abraham, his grandfather Isaac, and his father Jacob, he took them in. In the grand scheme of the Bible, of course, we Christians can make the next leap and claim that because of Joseph's justice-compassion, the Hebrew people did become enslaved, which allowed the great liberator Moses to appear on the scene, and ultimately, of course, Jesus, whom Christians call the Messiah. We can also "take in" the Jews by conversion – forceful or otherwise – as the dogma that underlies Christian Zionism assumes. But the point is the continuing development of human consciousness toward distributive justice-compassion, not supersessionary arrogance. The story is about the inevitable tendency of civilization to embrace the theology of Empire (piety, war, victory), and the ongoing struggle to remain true to the Covenant (nonviolence, distributive justice-compassion, peace).

For postmodern societies the aphorism Jesus might use to illustrate his reversal of imperial piety might be, "A victim is only a victim when personal power is unclaimed." Joseph certainly did not remain a victim of his brother's injustice. He took advantage whenever he could of the personal talents and power he had, and eventually won a place for himself that allowed him to rescue his entire family. Most extraordinary of all, he completely reconciled with his brothers – just like Esau did with Jacob. (That part was left out of the lectionary [Genesis 33].) There is a pattern here, if we are willing to see it. Jesus's Sermon on the Mount is about the empowerment of the poor and disenfranchised, victims of imperial power, which turns out not to be "power" at all. Once a victim is empowered, that person ceases to be a victim. Jesus himself did not die a helpless victim. Jesus died in active, nonviolent resistance to injustice.

How can a postmodern, market-driven society empower the powerless? Or, in the pious slogan of the late 1990s, What Would Jesus Do? First of all, what Jesus did, and what we must do, is drive a stake through the heart of our all-too-human desire for retribution. Second, we must reverse the insidious lie that takes literally the Pauline admonition that "I am content with weaknesses, insults, hardships, persecutions, and calamities for the sake of Christ." We must not be "content" with injustice. Nor must we be "content" with the easy hegemony that declares that anyone who does not believe that Jesus died for our sins is not a part of the kingdom of God. As Jesus said, it is not what goes into the mouth that defiles a person. What defiles us is the tacit agreement with imperial injustice and its accompanying theology.

Isaiah still has the last word: "Thus says the Lord: Maintain justice, and do what is right. . . . And the foreigners . . . all who . . . hold fast my covenant – these I will bring to my holy mountain, . . . for my house shall be called a house of prayer for all peoples."

Proper 16
Living Sacrifice

Exodus 1:8-2:10; Isaiah 51:1-6; Psalm 124; Psalm 138;
Romans 12:1-8; Matthew 16:13-20

How many sermons have been preached on the first two
verses of Romans 12? How many rituals of baptism, confirmation,
communion, invocation, confession, benediction? "Present your
bodies as a living sacrifice . . . Do not be conformed to this world,
but be transformed by the renewing of your minds. . . ." Plucked
out of the context of the rest of Paul's argument, these verses are
a reminder that Christians hold a special place in God's kingdom.
Christians do not live by the same rules as the rest of society.
Christians are able to "discern what is the will of God – what is
good and acceptable and perfect." This exclusivity is confirmed by
Matthew's Jesus, who rewards Peter's declaration that Jesus is
"the Anointed, the son of the living God" with the keys to the
kingdom. Whatever Peter binds on earth will be bound in heaven
(marriage contracts, peace treaties, tax breaks for corporations);
and of course the opposite is also true: whatever agreement Peter
releases on earth will also be released in heaven (voting rights,
environmental protections, social safety nets). That is an unfair
argument only from the point of view of church tradition that flies
in the face of Covenant and aligns itself with Empire.

Paul of course is not referring to accommodation with
political expediency. Paul's words are meant to encourage
subversion, the same kind of subversion that Moses's mother set
in motion with her little reed basket. Growing up in the midst of
imperial privilege was a tiny spark of God's justice-compassion,
a subtle and unsuspected link to Abraham's covenant. These
Biblical links in the great chain that is the story of the Jewish
people (and by adoption, followers of Jesus's Way as well) are all
individuals. The Apostle Paul is calling for a collective shift in
consciousness. "For as in one body we have many members, and
not all the members have the same function, so we, who are many,

are one body in Christ, and *individually we are members one of another*" (emphasis added).

But this is not an exclusive club. Anyone who wishes to participate in the program of restoring God's Covenant (nonviolence, distributive justice, peace) is part of the kingdom. The only requirement is the radical abandonment of self-interest: That is the "living sacrifice, holy and acceptable to God, which is your spiritual [or reasonable] worship." Sacrifice can only make sacred what is freely offered as a symbol of reconciliation with the realm of distributive justice-compassion that humans continually cut ourselves from. That life can only be acceptable as a sacrifice when self-interest is freely and radically abandoned in the service of the greater good.

In first century Rome, Paul's call to "present your bodies as a living sacrifice" meant declining to participate in the usual patronage system of public sacrifice and banquet, the purpose of which was to reconcile the participants with the gods and the emperor, and to restore the commercial balance between patrons and clients. Instead, by radically abandoning self-interest and sharing everything necessary for community without cost or price or condition, members of the Christian community restored God's realm of distributive justice-compassion here and now. This state of affairs is bad for business as usual, and is therefore unacceptable to Empire, as history has proven over and over again. Nor did members of the Christian community find this model easy – as evidenced in Paul's letters to the Corinthians. Following such a program gets awkward, if not extremely difficult. What about the slacker who joins the community just to get food, and never makes a contribution? How can your daughter get a decent marriage proposal without a dowry – which is only made possible because of deals you make in the course of business? If all property is owned in common, how can I get yours? In order to survive, the Church had to make some accommodation, and the accommodation began within a few short years after the death of Jesus.

In the twenty-first century, collective action to assure the well-being of human life on the Planet is essential. The time is long past for individual leadership on the order of the return of a Messiah, a prophet, or a liberator. Yet in the United States, national elections continue to focus on individuals who can win enough political support to bring their own ideas into power. Collective welfare, whether of education, medical services, employment benefits, or housing, is considered to be rewarding irresponsibility and encouraging criminal behavior at the expense of law-abiding tax-payers. The result is entrenched injustice.

Bob Dylan asked the question 40 years ago: "How many deaths will it take 'til we know that too many people have died?" He was singing about war, but any one of the above mentioned examples would do as an illustration of what the radical abandonment of self-interest might mean. For now, in what is becoming a continuing series, the question applies to the evils of market-driven medicine in the United States, which is also a war against human dignity, decency, common sense, and – oh yeah – love. Specifically, let's focus on one aspect of the medical system that impacts everyone, and that threatens to overwhelm the entire house of cards as the huge cohort of people born between 1945 and 1960 approaches our sunset years: end of life care.

When a nursing home prescribes medication that will stimulate appetite, but will not provide the assistance necessary for the person to eat, what is the point of providing food? A major problem in one particular state system is the failure of nursing home staff to turn patients every two hours, as specifically ordered by the physician, thereby worsening bedsores caused by archaic equipment, and creating more. What possible purpose is served in prolonging life for which there is no longer any discernible quality? Especially if one is trapped in the medical system that requires the sustaining if not prolonging of life, but denies the care required? At what point do we realize that the radical abandonment of self-interest might mean the active assistance of someone into death? This is not murder. Murder means to cause the involuntary death of another, whether at the hands of the state and its death penalty for criminals (Empire) or at the hands of a fellow human being who has become so involved with self-interest that s/he cannot discern right from wrong. Instead, such active assistance is the conscious choice on the part of the dying one and the assistant to ease into whatever adventure comes after this life.

If Christians "believe" that Jesus gave us "victory" over death, why should we be so afraid to welcome that release? As a society, we have been down this road with some tough cases: Terri Schiavo, and of course, Dr. Jack Kevorkian, who actively worked to assist terminally ill people with suicide, and was eventually convicted of second degree murder and delivering a controlled substance without a license. What is the nature of the god worshiped by the people who devised the rules and regulations that offer promises of "care," while denying access to that very care? And where is the Church (the Body of Christ) on these issues of death and dying? Somehow we consider the self-sacrifice of someone who saves another's life to be holy, but causing the humane termination of life is evil. Why am I allowed to kill myself to save another, but not to kill another in order to alleviate terminal and incurable suffering? In either case, death has happened, but one is noble, and the other is a crime.

Despite all the screaming about how the United States was founded as, and continues to be, a "Christian" nation, as soon as the radical abandonment of self-interest ["love"] includes active compassion – such as supporting the right to die, or increasing taxes to pay for a standard of living adequate for the health and well-being of self and family, retribution comes into play. Suddenly we revert to the prehistoric idea that anyone who is poor or dispossessed or ill or dying must either be a parasite on the community, or must have done something to deserve it.

We like to point to Abraham Lincoln's Gettysburg Address in which he declared that "government of the people by the people and for the people shall not perish from the earth." But the part that is overlooked is the responsibility the people have *for* the people. As the Apostle Paul says, "we . . . are one body in Christ, and individually, we are members one of another." Property rights, NIMBY, and "family values" belong to the theology of Empire: piety, war, victory. That theology is a theology of individual salvation rather than corporate distributive justice-compassion, and is aligned with the forces of evil, which work to convince us that the realm of God is closed to us, and the keys to the kingdom are lost.

"Present your bodies as a living sacrifice," Paul says. "Do not be conformed to this world," where the normalcy of civilization traps us into injustice, "but be transformed by the renewing of your minds so that you may discern" the will of God, which is distributive justice-compassion.

Proper 17
Call and Response

Exodus 3:1-15; Jeremiah 15:15-21; Psalm 105:1-6, 23-26, 45c;
Psalm 26:1-8; Romans 12:9-21; Matthew 16:21-28

If the people are calling for leadership and deliverance from unjust systems of war and greed (such as in an election year), the RCL readings for Proper 17 are spot-on. First comes the story of Moses and the burning bush. God calls Moses into leadership, ready or not. God also assures Moses that "I am who I am, and I will be what I will be." The Covenant with Moses's ancestors, Abraham, Isaac, and Jacob, is reaffirmed. The alternative reading from the prophet Jeremiah – writing from the remnant community left behind by the marauding Babylonians – has the same message: ". . . I am with you to save you and deliver you, says the Lord. I will deliver you out of the hand of the wicked, and redeem you from the grasp of the ruthless."

The Covenant is renewed in the Christian community founded by Paul in Rome. "Beloved, never avenge yourselves, but leave room for the wrath of God; for it is written, 'Vengeance is mine, I will repay, says the Lord.'" God's "wrath" is not human anger or revenge, but is God's response to human injustice. God's Covenant assumes nonviolent distributive justice, not violent retribution. God's justice is not revenge, but is the consequence of unjust behavior, and will be meted out, sooner or later. Meanwhile, Paul says, "if your enemies are hungry, feed them; if they are thirsty, give them something to drink . . . Do not be overcome by evil, but overcome evil with good." Finally, Matthew's group of Jewish Christians, under siege by the surrounding communities of Romans and members of local synagogues who did not accept the Christians' claim that Jesus was the Messiah, found inspiration in Jesus's words: "Those who want to come after me should deny themselves, pick up their cross, and follow me." While the passage from Matthew ends with a threat (". . . the son of Adam is going to come . . . and he will reward everyone according to their deeds"), these readings are not about judgment. They are about call and response.

Twenty-first century people are no more cynical than their first century counterparts. Anyone called to national leadership (then or now) runs the risk of corruption by corporate power, special interests, and the traps set by the normal human inability to distinguish between ego-driven power-hunger and the genuine compassion that propels some of us into action. What would the opposition party of today do with the fact that long ago, before he was called by God to lead the people to freedom, Moses killed an Egyptian who was beating a Hebrew? (Exodus 2:11-22.) What kind of "flip-flopping" politician was Moses? First he claims a heritage with the dominant Egyptians, then he aligns himself with the oppressed Hebrews. Who is this man anyway? He is a stranger in a strange land (Exodus 2:22b), a "resident alien" who has to prove his credentials as one of the people before the people will trust him enough to follow him out of bondage.

But what may be more important than individual national leaders is the ability of the people themselves to raise up leaders among their own local communities. Too often world history has illustrated that the normalcy of civilization always devolves from Covenant to Empire. The civilization may begin with a charismatic, visionary leader who embodies distributive justice-compassion, but so long as the people look to strong leaders and not to themselves, the danger is great that the civilization will develop the theology of Empire: piety, war, victory, and uneasy peace.

"Piety" means that those values (Biblical, family) that sustain civilization are primary. In ancient Rome, the emperor and his family were worshiped as gods; in the families of ordinary citizens, the man had absolute power of life and death over his wife, his children, his servants, slaves, and animals. Relationships among people and between levels of society were strictly controlled by the rules of religion, which leached into civil relationships, both commercial and private. In twenty-first century United States, worship of country has replaced the emperor and his family in a patriotism that presidential candidates ignore at their political peril; right-wing religious beliefs determine the rules governing marriage, childbirth, the criminal justice system, the medical system, economics – in short, all matters of life and death. Such piety has already resulted in various wars, both foreign and domestic: the war on drugs, terrorism, Iraq, Afghanistan. Wars must be won, according to conventional piety, making victory a prerequisite to peace. But that peace can never be true peace because piety – the worship of patriotism and conventionality – demands constant war against the adversaries: other countries, other ways of life, points of view in conflict with the prevailing civil religion. This constant war – pious, holy war – demands strong leadership.

In the great story of the Jewish people, God is the one who restores the Covenant after the people have fallen out of God's distributive justice-compassion. As we have seen in this Year A cycle, the Covenant was declared to Noah in the form of the rainbow after the flood; reiterated and codified to Abraham, and promised to his descendants. So long as the people live in justice-compassion, all is well. As soon as the people turn away from God's program, calamity strikes.

The secret to re-establishing and maintaining Covenant lies in the empowerment of each member of the community – which is what Paul's letter to the Romans is all about. Paul reminds his readers/listeners "not to think of yourself more highly than you ought to think" (Romans 12:3); and "do not claim to be wiser than you are" (12:16b). Instead, he says, follow the example of Jesus: "Rejoice in hope, be patient in suffering, persevere in prayer. Contribute to the needs of the saints; extend hospitality to strangers. Bless those who persecute you; . . . Rejoice with those who rejoice, weep with those who weep."

When we stand together, tyranny – whether of the majority or the minority – is overthrown. But individuals cannot allow themselves to be swayed by promises of first victory, then peace. Once again, the Elves have left out an important part of Paul's argument, which appears in the first seven verses of chapter 13. Perhaps they do so because those skipped verses seem to contradict Paul's entire polemic about how "the strength of sin is the law." What is going on here?[88] Consider what Paul is actually saying. "Therefore, one must be subject [to the representatives of the law – the authorities] not only because of wrath [the proper response to injustice] but also because of conscience." In other words, be subject to the law not only because of God's inevitable action in response to injustice, but because of individual conscience. He continues, "Pay to all what is due them – taxes to whom taxes are due, revenue to whom revenue is due, respect to whom respect is due, honor to whom honor is due." Behind these words is the call to resistance against unjust taxes, unearned and undeserved riches; resistance to those to whom no respect or honor is due because their actions do not command respect or honor.

So the marks of a true Christian, as spelled out in Romans 12:9-21 are about as far from conventional piety as one can get. Instead of unquestioning compliance with the law, Paul is saying, pick your fights with deliberation. Instead of lashing out in search of revenge, leave the consequences of evil action to take their own course, and practice that nonviolent resistance that "will heap burning coals on their heads." Despite the all-too-human certainty in Matthew 16:27 and 28 that judgment will arrive on the wings of God's avenging angels, Matthew's Jesus calls for all who would be followers to radically abandon self-interest. "What good will it do if you acquire the whole world but forfeit your life?" Jesus asks. "Or what will you give in exchange for your life?" Taking up your cross is not the struggle to stop smoking, give up chocolate, or tolerate your pushy sister–in-law. It is a call to participate in the ongoing program of restoring God's realm of distributive justice-compassion.

The imagery of taking up one's cross is identified with an exclusive Christianity that has changed the meaning from radical, nonviolent action for distributive justice to self-righteous martyrdom on behalf of religious ideology. But as the continuing story tells us, no one who answers the call and does the work is left out of the kingdom. "Vindicate me, O Lord, for I have walked in my integrity, and I have trusted in the Lord without wavering," says the Psalmist. What is your response?

---

[88]Crossan and Reed, 409-411.

Proper 18
Yes, But . . . :

Exodus 12:1-14; Ezekiel 33:7-11; Psalm 149; Psalm 119-33-40;
Romans 13:8-14; Matthew 18:15-20

The Elves must have tied on blindfolds then riffled the pages and planted a finger on the verses from Romans and from Matthew. How else to come up with opposing teachings from Peter's Jerusalem faction ("If [they] refuse to listen . . . treat [them] like you would a pagan or toll collector") and the Apostle Paul, sent off to bring the Jesus story to those very pagans, jailors, collaborators, and sinners throughout the Roman empire ("Love is the fulfilling of the law"). When confronted with blatant contradictions in the Gospels, go back to the four questions for the apocalypse:

1) What is the nature of God? Violent or nonviolent?
2) What is the nature of Jesus's message? Inclusive or exclusive?
3) What is faith? Literal belief, or commitment to the great work of justice-compassion?
4) What is deliverance? Salvation from hell, or liberation from injustice?

Matthew's Jesus is spelling out the ground rules for living in Matthew's Jerusalem community, bogged down in the minutiae of normal civilization where "justice" is based on what can be proved or witnessed to by at least two, but ideally three people. The Elves stop short of verses 21 and 22, where hair-splitting Peter demands to know how many times one person must forgive another.

This is easy piety. Paul is dishing out the rough stuff. "The one who loves another has fulfilled the law. . . . The [ten] commandments are summed up in this word: 'Love your neighbor as yourself.'" In that context, verses 11-14 of this amazing letter to the Romans cannot possibly be reduced to apocalyptic judgment upon petty sin. Paul did believe that the day of the Lord's restoration of the kingdom of distributive justice-compassion was imminent – and indeed it is. All that is required is to "lay aside the works of darkness and put on the armor of light. . . ." Just like Jesus said – the kingdom of God is here now, all we have to do is look and listen; all we have to do is step into that parallel universe.

Ah, yes, but . . .

Coal companies in West Virginia complain of lost profits because of increased government oversight of mine safety. Worse are the outrageous actions of Agriprocessors, a kosher meat-packing plant in Iowa.[89] After a raid by the Immigration Department in May 2008 arrested half its workers, the company continued to cut corners on wages, working conditions, health, and safety, and deliberately recruited workers from such disenfranchised populations as residents of a homeless shelter in Texas, Somali refugees from Minnesota, unemployable former prisoners from other states in the midwest, and unsuspecting people from the island of Palau who are not subject to U.S. immigration rules because they belong to a former United Nations trusteeship, now administered by the United States. One wonders where the U.S. government actually intervened in this case?

Meanwhile, back in the Old Testament, the Elves skip all the nasty plagues visited upon the hapless Egyptians and cut to the chase: The Passover ritual is a blood ritual that identifies clearly who belongs to God and who does not, and Ezekiel is the sentinel – the guardian of the faith, who warns the people when they are slipping into injustice and away from God's rule. In fairness to the creators of the RCL, the readings are not intended to coincide. The passage cherry-picked from Ezekiel is the "alternate," to be used in case it is more pertinent to the needs of the local congregation. Nevertheless, the exodus from Egypt after the commitment of the people to God and the later exile to Babylon might be seen as parallel metaphors. Both are mass movements of the Hebrew people from their settled existence. Both events were triggered by corporate injustice – the oppression of the Hebrew people by the Egyptian Pharaoh on the one hand, and on the other, the complicity with injustice by the Israelite nation in their own land.

---

[89]Jennifer Ludden, "At Iowa Meatpacking Plant, New Workers Complain," http://www.npr.org/ templates/story/story.php?storyId=94203311, September 02, 2008.

Moses is the leader of the exodus, Ezekiel is the prophet who went to Babylon.

God seems to revel in deliberately "hardening the heart" of Pharaoh, so that Moses can demonstrate God's awesome power through nine plagues. Only when the first-born children start dying does Pharaoh relent. Then he does not stop at merely letting the people go, he throws them out. God tells Ezekiel that if he warns the people about turning away from God, and the people pay no attention, then God will destroy the people, and their blood will be on their own heads. However, if Ezekiel does not warn the people, and they turn away from God, the people will be destroyed, and Ezekiel along with them.

The point seems to be that the leaders are accountable for the fidelity of the people to God's rule, which is distributive justice-compassion, and the leaders are equally accountable for the consequences of infidelity. What an interesting concept for twenty-first century civilizations, when the more closely a candidate for office is identified with conventional piety (sexual abstinence for the unmarried; social and political exclusion for GLBT people; unquestioning compliance with authority) the greater the probability that even the appearance of impropriety signals a lack of personal integrity. We may ask, who belongs to God today, and who are the sentinels?

Keeping the four questions and the partnership answers in mind, (nonviolent God, inclusive message, commitment to the great work, and liberation from injustice in this life, here and now), injustice must be recognized, named, acknowledged, and owned. The Ten Commandments (that great foundation for conventional piety) are irrelevant, says Paul. What matters is the radical abandonment of self-interest: ". . . make no provision for the flesh, to gratify its desires." This is not about petty sexual sin. It is about comfort at the expense of the environment; profit at the expense of well-being; personal advancement at the expense of relationship.

Participants in the program of restoring God's realm of distributive justice-compassion are the sentinels for our time, whether they are on the political left or the political right, whether they embrace Christianity or not. The proof lies in the results.

Proper 19
As We Forgive

Exodus 14:19-31; Exodus 15:1b-11, 20-21;Genesis 50:15-21;
Psalm 114; Psalm 103; Romans 14:1-12; Matthew 18:21-35

A conventional pass through the readings for this Sunday leads us to a vision of retributive judgment against the enemies of God: As Moses and the multitude of Israelites cross the Red Sea, God protects those who have signed on to the Covenant. The Elves tell us the alternative Old Testament reading (Genesis 50:15-21) is closely related to the Gospel reading. Joseph forgives his dastardly brothers, who sold him into slavery in Egypt. Sure enough in Matthew 18:21-22, Peter's question about how much forgiveness is enough is paired with the parable of the unforgiving slave, instead of with last week's admonitions about how to deal with recalcitrant members of the community. Matthew's Jesus threatens divine punishment of those followers who fail to forgive their friends and neighbors who might owe them a debt of money, gratitude, respect, or other payment for wrongdoing. Paul seems to agree, as he cautions the faithful not to judge one another, but to leave judgment to God. "We do not live to ourselves," Paul pontificates. "[W]hether we live or whether we die, we are the Lord's."

The Jesus Seminar commentators make a distinction between a *parable*, which has a single point, and an *allegory*, which "is coded theology."[90] By putting the story of the unforgiving slave in the context of how much forgiveness is required for salvation, Matthew turns the authentic Jesus's parable into allegory. In other words, instead of a parable with a confounding ending that causes the hearers to wonder what the trick is, Matthew's Jesus hits us over the head with piety: "That's what my heavenly Father will do to you, unless you find it in your heart to forgive each one of your brothers and sisters." Taking that point to its logical conclusion,

---

[90]Funk, et al., 218.

given the juxtaposition of this reading with Genesis, even Joseph, who suffered the ultimate betrayal and was sold into slavery, was able to forgive all his brothers. Surely Christians – who have overthrown all that Old Testament tribalism – can do as well, if not better than that.

Matthew's interpretation of Jesus's parable paints God as requiring retributive judgment. But Paul writes fifty years after the death of Jesus, "Why do you pass judgment on your brother or sister? . . . each of us will be accountable to God." Being accountable to one's "lord" is not the same as being judged less than moral by one's neighbors. Paul suggests that people may have been inviting others to join the Christian community in Rome as a set-up, or as Paul puts it, "for the purpose of quarreling over opinions." Dietary customs ("The weak eat only vegetables") are not usually fighting offenses in the postmodern world. Instead, the clash of opinions about gun ownership, reproductive choice, homosexuality, and theories about social and economic conditions has prompted deadly attacks on churches and communities from both the left and the right. In such a polarized environment, judgment wins the day, as complex thought is reduced to bumper sticker code that appeals to fear. Accountability is left for dead.

Paul's point is that judging others is a waste of time and energy because each of us is ultimately accountable to God. But to whom or what are we accountable in a post-Christian, non-theistic world? When the parable of the unforgiving slave is reduced to the bare bones of the story itself, when Matthew's opinion about God's avenging judgment is removed, we find that the slave for whom a vast debt is forgiven is held accountable not to his master, but to his own integrity.

Because Matthew is the only one who tells this particular parable, it is perhaps unfair to have it stand alone without Matthew's commentary. But the Jesus Seminar scholars thought that the story was the kind that Jesus liked to tell. So here we are around the camp fire. We come in a bit late, so don't hear what prompted Jesus to start the story the way he did. . . .

"Now I'll tell you why God's realm is like a land owner who decided to settle accounts with his slaves," Jesus says. He finishes off his last bite of fish, and licks his fingers. Mary Magdalene tucks a loaf of bread into the coals to warm, uncorks the wineskin, and starts it on its rounds. Andrew throws another log on the fire. Somebody hushes a child and points at Jesus.

"So the first account he looks at, the slave owes him $10 million."

"10 million!" "No way!" "No wonder the guy needed to close his accounts." "This crook ripped off his entire estate!"

Jesus goes on: "Obviously, he couldn't pay it back, so the land owner ordered him to be sold, along with his wife and children and everything he had." Jesus looks around at the company. "Sort of like you and Zach, Hannah." Hannah hugs the child, and Zach shivers and wraps his arms around his knees.

"Anyway, the slave begs forgiveness, reminds the land owner what an excellent steward he has been in other ways, and promises he will pay it all back." Jesus pauses for a moment. We are all expecting the worst for the slave for his impertinence: jail, torture, exile – but then Jesus says, "This land owner was compassionate. This master let that slave go and canceled the debt."

It's a joke. Several people start laughing. But Jesus isn't finished with the story.

"Wait," he says, "There's more. As soon as the slave got out of there, he jumped one of his fellow slaves who owed him $100 and demanded payment immediately. Well of course the guy begged for mercy, but the slave wasn't interested. Instead, he threw the guy in prison until he paid the debt. When the rest of the slaves realized what had happened, they complained to the land owner."

"Why? The slave was within his rights," says Judas.

"The land owner called the slave back and rescinded the agreement, and threw the slave into jail to be tortured until he could repay it all."

Silence. A twig snaps in the fire. Jesus pulls the warm loaf of bread out of the coals. He breaks the bread into two pieces, and lifts it up in his hands. Then he closes his eyes and says, "Abba, may your name be praised. You provide us with the bread we need for the day." Jesus passes the bread to the people on either side of him. "Forgive us our debts to the extent that we have forgiven those in debt to us."

In the stripped down parable, the subject matter is clearly economic debt – a life or death fact in the first century. The followers of Jesus presumably were the debtors, not the ones to whom debt was owed, hence the conundrum and the open meaning. What debt do we forgive, if no debt is owed to us? Debt is concerned with either the past or the future, never the present moment, which is all that matters in God's realm. In God's realm of distributive justice-compassion, where bread for the day is provided, where rain falls on the just and the unjust, debt has no power.

Proper 20
Harvest

Exodus 16:2-15; Jonah 3:10-4:11; Psalm 105:1-6, 37-45;
Psalm 145:1-8; Philippians 1:21-30; Matthew 20:1-16

Proper 20 finds the second harvest of the year underway in the Northern Hemisphere. Pumpkins and hay bales are beginning to predominate local farm markets. The last of the sweet corn, heirloom variety tomatoes, burgundy beans, zucchini, eggplant, and peaches are soon to be overtaken by the squashes, apples, sweet potatoes, and other root vegetables. Earth's bounty is there for the picking, canning, pickling, freezing. Matthew's parable of the workers in the vineyard is a harvest story.

As usual, Matthew's pious comment at the end has nothing to do with the point. The parable is not about the reversal of fortune for the greedy or the self-righteous ("the last will be first and the first last") but about frustrated expectations. Conventional fairness in the imperial marketplace certainly does get turned upside down, whether from the point of view of the rich proprietor, or the poor workers hired throughout the day. But Jesus is talking about more than frustrated expectations. Jesus is illustrating how in God's realm the reward is bestowed whenever the program is joined. That is the nature of God's Covenant.

"Covenant" is the defining word for all these readings, including the "alternative" portion of the story of Jonah, and the workers in the vineyard. In the Exodus story, the Covenant is clear, as God makes sure the people have the food they need for the day. Covenant is not so clear to Jonah, who is clueless from beginning to end. How can you throw a tantrum over a bush that is here today and gone tomorrow, God asks, when there are one hundred twenty thousand people whose ignorance keeps them in bondage? Never mind the non sequitur about the animals in sackcloth (Jonah 3:8) – perhaps they were in solidarity with the people who realized they needed to sign onto God's Covenant in order to save themselves. The part Jonah failed to realize is that

God's Covenant is extended to everyone who turns to God's way of distributive justice. No questions asked, no retribution for past sins required.

Read superficially, this feels suspiciously like "cheap grace." Certainly that is what Jonah thought. If God is going to settle for cheap grace, Jonah would prefer to be dead, thank you very much. The deadbeats hanging around the well all day pinching the women get the same wages as the pious ones who worked from dawn. The proprietor looks like a typical CEO, cheating his workers with bait-and-switch promises of a day's pay for a day's work without defining the length of the day or the rate. How fair or just is that? It's just like the old miscreant on his deathbed who confesses Jesus as Lord, and the angels waft him to heaven.

Dietrich Bonhoeffer, who wrote the book on grace, says: "The essence of grace, we suppose, is that the account has been paid in advance; and, because it has been paid, everything can be had for nothing. . . . Cheap grace means grace as a doctrine, a principle, a system. It means forgiveness of sins proclaimed as a general truth. . . . An intellectual assent to that idea is held to be of itself sufficient to secure remission of sins. . . ."[91] The key in Matthew's parable is the timing. God's reward is paid as soon as the worker agrees to the bargain. And what is the bargain? To be first? To be last? Far from a position in line, the bargain – the Covenant – is in Bonhoeffer's words, true (costly) grace: "the Incarnation of God." When Paul says in Philippians 1:21, "For to me, living is Christ and dying is gain," he is talking about incarnation – taking on the life and the purpose and the work that Jesus did. In Paul's experience, to die doing that work is deliverance. Bonhoeffer's "costly grace" is the radical abandonment of self-interest so that the great work of distributive justice-compassion can continue, and God's kingdom can come. The promised reward is deliverance from injustice – whether we live or die.

The Elves have conveniently abandoned the remainder of Paul's Letter to the Romans. Suddenly we switch to Philippians for the time leading up to Advent and Year B. Romans 15:4-13

---

[91]Bonhoeffer, 45.

was cherry-picked for Advent in Year A.[92] Romans 16:25-27 is used peripherally on the fourth Sunday in Advent, Year B (stay tuned). But despite the Elves' mysterious work, Paul's point still stands, whether it is by polemic in Romans, or by pastoral in Philippians. Like Matthew's parable and Jonah's tale, this is not easy piety, nor is it a children's story to be tossed off on a Sunday morning. Paul is writing from prison, where the conditions were primitive and horrific: so bad, that it is possible they made his friend Epaphroditus ill to the point of threatening his life. We don't know what Paul did that landed him in jail, but we can safely bet the rent that he wasn't preaching about salvation from hell in the next life, which poses no threat to Empire. Paul got into trouble for the same reason Jesus did. Preaching deliverance from injustice in this life calls into question everything that Empire does.

Radical abandonment of self-interest brings justice and life – the presence of God. The joke – which Jonah resented, Jesus knew, and Paul realized – is that the Covenant includes everybody and anybody who is willing to sign on. Jonah only went to Ninevah after his journey into death in the belly of the fish. But Jonah didn't die – he held onto his pious convention like a three-year-old. He would rather hold his breath until he turns blue than acknowledge that God cares more about saving one hundred twenty thousand sinners from injustice than one recalcitrant, self-righteous prophet.

Being willing to sign onto the Covenant and actually sticking to the agreement are not the same, however, as Moses found to his chagrin, and the Elves conveniently decline to include in the reading (Exodus 16:16-30). God might deliver us from the shadow of death, but as soon as times get dicey, we complain. God gives us manna from heaven – the perfect food – and the only requirement is that we trust it will be there. But we do not trust, we hoard – and find that what we have hoarded has rotted overnight. Not only that, God provides enough so that over the Sabbath – the holy day of rest – we do not need to go out and gather food. But we do not trust that what was provided will be enough, so we go

---

[92]See p. 19.

out on the Sabbath to get more and find none.

Twenty-first century life is largely divorced from the natural rhythms of the seasons and of the spirit of the land itself. Inhabitants of the civilized world have a long history of setting ourselves apart from and above that world. As a result, farmers – who should know better – over-fertilize, over-graze, over-plant, play the markets, and rely on chemical short-cuts for seeds, pest control, water supply. Commodities such as silver, gold, copper, coal, and oil are all exploited to the detriment of the Planet. "Mountaintop removal" – also known as "strip mining" – destroys in a day what took the Planet hundreds of millennia to create. "Surface mining" leaves slag piles in the middle of farmland and suburban areas. All of these activities are directly responsible for the decline in potable water and breathable air, and contribute to climate change world-wide that results in devastating storms, floods, droughts, fires, and mass extinctions of diverse life forms.

Ninevah's animals in sackcloth might be telling us that the "Incarnation of God" is not confined to humanity. In this time of harvest, Bonhoeffer's "costly grace" means the radical abandonment of self-interest toward all forms of life, including the non-human and (to us) non-sentient inhabitants of Earth: "Costly grace" means sustainable action; eco-justice.

Proper 21
It's the Economy, Stupid

Exodus 17:1-7; Ezekiel 18:1-4, 25-32; Psalm 78:1-4, 12-16; Psalm 25:1-9; Philippians 2:1-13; Matthew 21:23-32

The readings for this Sunday from Matthew and Paul's letter to the Philippians are usually construed as being about "belief" in Jesus's power to save us from hell. The overarching theme, however, when the prophet Ezekiel's word from God is also considered, is personal accountability in God's realm where distributive justice-compassion prevails.

The exiled Israelites in Babylon found God to be unfair, perhaps because God refused to allow them to blame either their parents or the people left behind in Jerusalem for their plight. To add insult to injury, the promise of salvation (life and justice) is extended to anyone, including the Babylonians, who "turn away from all their sins that they have committed and keep all [God's] statutes and do what is lawful and right." Matthew's Jesus presents a choice between a son who gives lip service but doesn't follow through, and a son who first refuses to comply with his father's request, but later does so. On its face, the story follows the lesson from Ezekiel. But Matthew's vignette is not a parable about justice; it is a cautionary tale about shame and honor in a first century Jewish culture. The one son first honors his father by saying he will do as asked, then shames his father by reneging on the promise. The second son first shames his father by refusing to follow orders, then honors his father by obeying. The end result is conventional piety, not radical love. Matthew then compounds his error by casting the lesson in terms of the failure of some in his Jewish community to believe the apocalyptic message brought by John the Baptist.

Not so long ago, Wall Street employees, from the janitors to the CEOs, believed the glory days would never end. Everyone was living the American Dream: Own your own home. No money down, no need to prove you are even employed. Borrow money to make money. Buy a house and flip it before the balloon payment comes due or the ARM readjusts upwards. The poor flipped foreclosed properties. The rich flipped whole subdivisions. Then the party ended, and the bull was hitched to the cart, hauling whoever was left into exiles called economic "austerity" and budget "sequester." Forty thousand people lost their jobs in New York City alone. The last investment banks standing (Goldman Sachs and Morgan Stanley) cashed in their chips and pledged to play by the rules. Surely Wall Street would never be the same.

"O House of Israel," Ezekiel reports God's voice: "Are my ways unfair? Is it not your ways that are unfair?" Whoever persists in unjust policies will die, according to God's imperial rule. "None of the righteous deeds that they have done shall be remembered; for the treachery of which they are guilty and the sin they have committed, they shall die." This is not retribution or payback. This is not God's version of the blood feud that involves generations. This is the consequence of failing to act with justice-compassion in one's own life. How quickly the conservative arch-capitalists dive for the socialist button. Who would ever have imagined that the Bush Administration would nationalize the U.S. financial system? But wait – who exactly was saved here? Who got the gold, silver, and green parachutes?

From prison, Paul writes his pastoral letter to the Philippians: "Let each of you look not to your own interests, but to the interests of others." Jesus's radical abandonment of his own self-interest meant he was "obedient to the point of death – even death on a cross." Paul is not talking about the kind of pious obedience demanded by the fictitious father in Matthew's sketch. Paul is talking about the kind of obedience that comes from total commitment to distributive justice-compassion. He is not talking about leveraging debt in order to amass fortunes that seduce others into debt they cannot afford. Paul is talking about creating the realm of God on earth by letting "the same mind be in you that was in Christ Jesus, who . . . emptied himself, taking the form of a slave." In such a realm, greed has no place, and debt has no power.

"Only the person who sins shall die" – no more serial retribution, says Ezekiel's God. But the heirs to this promise are not restricted to the people of Israel. Anyone who turns from sin lives. The Israelites in the sixth century B.C.E. said that's not fair. In the twenty-first century C.E., some called for the punishment of the speculators and managers who seemed to be responsible for the financial melt-down. Others held individual people accountable for making poor choices, or for not having the good sense to avoid the deal that seemed too good to be true. But this is pious revenge. If justice is distributive, there is no need for punishment beyond the consequences already befalling all of us who are caught in the system. If we truly turn from our destructive, unjust habits, the old patterns will not be repeated.

Meanwhile, the Hebrew people wandering in the Sinai desert – like the exiles in Babylon and the skeptics in Matthew's synagogue – also continue to not believe God's promises. They complained last week that God led them out of bondage in Egypt so that they could die of hunger. This week they moan that they will die of thirst in the desert. In neither case are they able to trust the Covenant. God brought them manna from heaven that magically appeared overnight. Moses produced water from a rock. What's next? Is there any miracle that will convince us to trust in the power of the Covenant today?

This metaphor risks getting stretched beyond recognition, but the point still stands: God's realm includes all of humanity. As soon as we abandon justice-compassion, or ignore the consequences of our actions that lead to unjust systems, we are caught in the powerful currents that propel civilizations into empires. This is not an indictment of human nature. Empire can happen when people begin to organize themselves into societies, but Empire is not necessarily inevitable. The primal myth of the Hebrew people tells us not to abandon hope. Sign onto the Covenant. Pick up your smart phone and start making sustainable deals that insure that no part of the interdependent web of life on this Planet is compromised. "I have no pleasure in the death of any [life form], says the Lord God. Turn, then, and live."

Proper 22
Murder in the Vineyard

Exodus 20:1-4, 7-9, 12-20; Isaiah 5:1-7; Psalm 19;
Psalm 80:7-15; Philippians 3:4b-14; Matthew 21:33-46

The Elves won't have it any other way for this Proper 22. The sermon practically writes itself: Choose from the Ten Commandments; the story of the leased vineyard, including "the stone the builders rejected has become the cornerstone"; or even the portion of Paul's letter to the Philippians, which lends itself to easy listening: "I regard everything as loss because of the surpassing value of knowing Christ Jesus my Lord." Any lay-leader worth his or her salt can write the liturgy for this Sunday blindfolded: The choir has to sing the chorus from Handel's *Creation* (Psalm 19): "The Heavens are telling the glory of God!" Use the litany responses from Psalm 80 in the Prayer of Confession: "Restore us O God of hosts; let your face shine, that we may be saved." Preface the sermon with "Let the words of my mouth and the meditation of my heart be acceptable to you, O Lord, my rock and my redeemer." Unfortunately, the sermon is going to take more work than might appear necessary at first glance.

To begin with, Paul's words are hardly easy listening if the dogma of two thousand years can somehow be put aside. Paul is not talking about *belief* in a story about someone who came back from the dead to scare us into piety. Paul is talking about the price paid daily for participating in Jesus's ongoing work of restoring God's realm of distributive justice-compassion on this Earth. Paul's sense of justice did not come from conventional rules and laws that keep empires in power. His sense of justice (righteousness) – his conviction of what is right – comes from his *trust* in the life example and teachings of Jesus, whom he dared to call "Lord" in the face of the Roman Emperor who claimed the same title. Paul hopes he can die for the same reason Jesus did, and somehow participate in the incarnation of God's realm – as

the Christ does. These are ecstatic, mystic words, which cannot –
must not – be taken literally. The parable of the leased vineyard
provides a clue into what Paul was trying to say.

Matthew's version of the leased vineyard story quotes the
imagery from Isaiah 5 as the introduction, and then closes with
Jesus's implication that he himself is "the stone that the builders
rejected." The vine and the vineyard have been used as a metaphor
for the chosen people of God since the beginning. Early Christians
would have had no problem using that metaphor to refer to Jesus,
Jesus's new Way, and ultimately to themselves as heirs of the
promise. The cornerstone or keystone metaphor is likely a
common early Christian reference to Jesus, who did become the
foundation for the new Way, after being rejected by both imperial
Rome and the traditional Jewish members of the synagogues,
whether in Jerusalem or the diaspora.

Some Biblical scholars disagree, but these commentaries take
the view that Jesus himself did not claim to be the Messiah. That
claim was made about him during his lifetime, but the seeming
prescience that he would suffer and die for sins was never part of
his message. Nor did Jesus's authentic message include
apocalyptic judgment, such as Matthew's Jesus continues to
threaten in this parable as well as others. Matthew's framework
transforms Jesus's parable into an allegory about himself for
Matthew's Christian community, thereby robbing the story of its
power.

The scholars of the Jesus Seminar consider the version of the
parable in Thomas 65 to be closer to the authentic historical Jesus
because it is not overlaid with Christian interpretation:

"A [. . .] person owned a vineyard and rented it to some
farmers, so they could work it and he could collect its
crop from them. He sent his slave so the farmers would
give him the vineyard's crop. They grabbed him, beat
him, and almost killed him, and the slave returned and
told his master. His master said, "Perhaps he didn't know
them." He sent another slave, and the farmers beat that
one as well. Then the master sent his son and said,
"Perhaps they'll show my son some respect." Because
the farmers knew that he was the heir to the vineyard,

they grabbed him and killed him."[93]

Stripped down to the story alone, the meaning is no longer so clear. When the story is seen in the context of first century Roman imperial oppression, the meaning is even less clear. Jesus's followers, far more familiar with the realities of tenant farming for absentee landlords, and the economic precariousness of everyday life, might well have asked, "What's wrong with killing the heir to the vineyard and keeping the crop for ourselves?" After all, as reported in Matthew's version, the people who heard it agreed: "[The owner] will [merely] lease the vineyard out to other farmers who will deliver their produce to him at the proper time." So why not take what we can? Why not lie in wait for the owner himself to show up and kill him too?

The Jesus Seminar scholars suggest that this parable as it stands on its own is comparable to the parable of the shrewd manager in Luke 16:1-7[94] because it deals with the economic realities of first century Palestine. Both parables could certainly be interpreted in terms of past as well as present economic realities in the United States. However, it is even more comparable to the parable of the unforgiving slave from Proper 19: "When the parable of the unforgiving slave is reduced to the bare bones of the story itself, when Matthew's opinion about God's avenging judgment is removed, we find that the slave for whom a vast debt was forgiven is held accountable not to his master, but to his own integrity."[95] Likewise, the scheming vineyard caretakers in today's parable might be justified in their desire for revenge against the unjust system that keeps them beholden to the land owner, with no recourse should the crop fail or should the owner demand the entire profit – either of which were distinct possibilities. The version of the parable in the Sayings Gospel of Thomas leaves us hanging. But Jesus would not have advocated a violent and unjust solution to an equally violent and unjust situation. Jesus always shows us the way to Covenant, never Empire.

Jesus probably was very familiar with the prophet Isaiah's

---

[93]Funk et al, 510.

[94]*See* Raven, 174.

[95]*See* p. 224.

Song of the Unfruitful Vineyard. What he would not have been able to do is transform the reference in verse 7 into his own death. Isaiah in Exile laments that the people have rejected the law – "The vineyard of the Lord of Hosts is the House of Israel . . . he expected justice, but saw bloodshed; righteousness [justice] but heard a cry [oppression]!" The Elves should not have stopped the reading there. The Song is not about foretelling the death of Jesus; it is about the failure of the people to honor God's Covenant: "[A]s the tongue of fire devours the stubble, and as dry grass sinks down in the flame, so their root will become rotten, and their blossom go up like dust: for they have rejected the instruction of the Lord of hosts, and have despised the word of the Holy One of Israel" (Isaiah 5:24).

In Jewish tradition the giving of the law is celebrated fifty days after the Passover. Christianity appropriated this festival, overthrowing the original meaning – the giving of the Jewish law (Shavuot) – and replacing it with the establishment of the church of Jesus Christ (Pentecost). The Elves constructed the Christian lectionary so that we arrive at one of the stories of the origin of "the Ten Commandments" three months later. What most Christians have never been taught is that the great law of Moses is far more than the first ten rules. The law codifies God's insistence on distributive justice-compassion, and the Old Testament is the story of the struggle to keep that law.

Jesus's followers would have known the whole law and the prophets. The metaphor of the lover's vineyard – God's realm, God's people – would also have been part of their daily mythos, as they suffered under Roman oppression and prayed for deliverance from injustice. Jesus's story about the leased vineyard may well have reminded them of Isaiah's Song, and the choice to be made. The recorder of Thomas' sayings Gospel ends many of Jesus's words with "Anyone here with two ears had better listen!" The Unforgiving Slave learned the hard way that in God's realm, debt has no power. Likewise, in God's realm, killing the heir will not restore the vineyard to the beloved.

Proper 23
Golden Bull, Golden Bear

*Exodus 32:1-14; Isaiah 25:1-9; Psalm 106:1-6, 19-23; Psalm 23;
Philippians 4:1-9; Matthew 22:1-14*

The Golden Calf! What a story for our times. The Elves have
set it all up for us, as usual. On the one hand, undisciplined people,
unable to wait for guidance from their leader who has gone up the
mountain to seek guidance from God Himself, have forgotten who
they are, and who saved them from the worst kind of oppression.
Psalm 106 tells how "Moses, [God's] chosen one, stood in the
breach before him, to turn away his wrath from destroying them."
But Matthew's Jesus has no time for compassion: "Many are
called, but few are chosen." On the other hand, Isaiah sings of the
great feast, the banquet on the mountain, prepared for the just at
the end of time. Paul exults in the nearness of the Lord, and the
beloved Psalm 23 leads us gently home.

The choice is clear, if stark: right-wing conservatism, or left-
wing liberalism; the proletariat versus the bourgeoisie; violent
apocalyptic judgment or nonviolent distributive justice-
compassion. The conflict is as old as time. Once more we are sent
back to the four questions for the apocalypse:

1) What is the nature of God? Violent or nonviolent?
2) What is the nature of Jesus's message? Inclusive or
   exclusive?
3) What is faith? Literal belief, or commitment to the great
   work of justice-compassion?
4) What is deliverance? Salvation from hell, or liberation
   from injustice?

The parable of the wedding celebration appears in three
versions: Matthew 22:1-14, Luke 14:16-24, and Thomas 64:1-12.
Matthew's version is the most elaborate, and the most
compromised with contemporary first century Christian concerns.
Jerusalem has been destroyed, along with Jewish temple-centered
religious practice; the Romanization of society has brought

systems of patronage and collaboration. Anyone who isn't properly dressed, who doesn't fulfill the proper qualifications, is subject to exclusionary judgment. Only the elect can be trusted to be part of the community.

The version in Thomas is much simpler. Here, a person is receiving guests, and has prepared a dinner party, not a wedding party. Thomas has no reference to invading armies that destroy the city. But the party-giver is frustrated when four invited guests turn him down. He has his slave go out and "bring back whomever you find to have dinner." Then the transcriber of the sayings collected in Thomas opines, "Buyers and merchants [will] not enter the places of my Father," which puts a very different spin on the story.

The third version in Luke is not included in any of the RCL readings for the three-year cycle. Apparently the creators of the RCL decided that Matthew's version is the definitive one for Christian theology and practice. However, the Jesus Seminar scholars point out that the version in Luke is likely the closest to what the historical Jesus would have told, although it too is permeated with early Christian piety. Imagine the scene, based on the stripped down version:[96]

> When Jesus is in Jericho, he encounters a head toll collector – a rich man named Zacchaeus. Later that evening, Jesus arrives for the banquet at Zach's house. After the meal, as the wine jug is passed among the reclining guests, Zach asks Jesus what is the Kingdom of God? What is it like? How do we find it?
>
> Jesus says, "There was a man who held an important position in Herod Antipas' administration. He wanted to give a dinner party for some local businessmen so that he could recruit them to act as liaison with the Roman proconsul. But they declined the invitation for perfectly good reasons – don't forget, it's the law that if the Romans draft you for some project, you can finish your own work first. So later, this guy sends his servant around again telling his cronies that the feast is ready, but they all refuse to come. In a rage, now, the host tells the

---

[96]Miller, *The Complete Gospels*, 296.

servant to bring in the poor, the crippled, the blind, and the lame . . . ." Jesus looks around at the group, but they don't seem to get it. He goes on: "When he sees that there is still room in his banquet hall, he sends his servant out into the countryside to round up people at sword-point."

This parable is a huge joke, which does not translate well in a twenty-first century world where the Roman patronage system no longer is in force. In first century Rome, everyone participated in the patronage system, from God to the Emperor, the noble classes, the merchants, the traders, the military, servants, slaves, and the totally disenfranchised. Everyone was either a patron or a client, and everyone had both patrons and clients, people to whom and from whom favors or commercial debt was owed. The way to repay the debt among the upper classes was to hold a banquet, usually a sacrificial banquet, in which an animal (or several) were slaughtered in the temple, the blood poured out for the gods, and the meat shared among the guests – all of whom were clients of the one giving the feast. For a guest to refuse to attend would be social, political, and commercial suicide, regardless of where one was in the social strata. For a host to then fill the banquet hall with people with whom one did not and would never do business would be ludicrous. There would be no possibility of ever receiving an invitation or favor in return.

But of such is the kingdom of God. This story is about grace, not apocalyptic judgment.

As for the Golden Bull, the temptation to extrapolate the metaphor to include pious diatribes against Wall Street greed is great, but irrelevant. Moses makes his own Wall Street deal with God when he reminds God that if God takes out his frustration and anger on the people, God will look bad in the eyes of all the surrounding tribes and nations, including – especially – Egypt. "And the Lord changed his mind about the disaster he planned to bring on his people." Then in the part we never read in any of the three-year cycle of the RCL (Exodus 32:15-35), Moses takes on the role of God and commands the sons of Levi (who answer the call to be on the Lord's side, and later become priests) to kill "your brother, your friend, and your neighbor." So a great blood bath ensues. Perhaps in order to reinforce the point, by the end of chapter 32, God has gone back on his promise to Moses not to punish the people, and sends a plague on them "because they made the calf – the one that Aaron made."

Taking Matthew's version of the parable of the wedding feast as definitive, and including the entire story about Aaron and the Golden Calf, puts postmodern, twenty-first century followers of Jesus in the same camp with an avenging, double-crossing Moses in the service of a capricious God. Is the nature of God then violent, and is Jesus's message then exclusive and relentlessly judgmental? Or are these stories illustrations of the constant human struggle with the normalcy of civilization, and the consequences of failing to act with distributive justice-compassion?

The relevance of the twenty-first century Christian message for sustainable life on Planet Earth depends on the answer we choose. As we have seen in the past several lessons, in the realm of God, the requirements of Empire for debt and death have no power.

Proper 24
Parousia – The Coming of the Lord –
Part I

Exodus 33:12-23; Isaiah 45:1-7; Psalm 99; Psalm 96:1-13;
1 Thessalonians 1:1-10; Matthew 22:15-22

The Elves in their wisdom have paired Matthew's version of Jesus's answer to the Pharisees' trap about whether to pay the Roman poll tax with the first installment of a five-week study of 1 Thessalonians. The themes seem to be unrelated. As the Christian liturgical year winds down toward the new season of Advent, Paul's only authentic letter to the Thessalonians conforms nicely with the dogma that Jesus is coming again. But if John Dominic Crossan's interpretation is correct, Jesus's advice to "pay the Emperor what belongs to the Emperor and God what belongs to God" sums up the key to the kingdom for both Jesus's followers during his lifetime, and Paul's Thessalonian converts to the Way twenty years later.

As with last week's parable of the wedding feast, the version of the story about the attempt to trick Jesus with a Roman coin appears in three of the four synoptic Gospels. Also as with last week's parable, Matthew's version is taken as definitive for Christian dogma. We never read the versions in Mark or Luke (and certainly not Thomas 100:1-4). The story really does not change much among the four interpretations. Jesus's reply to the loaded question is pure authentic Jesus, without any attempt at dumbing it down or re-interpreting the setting for pious purposes. The Jesus Seminar scholars even imagine that Jesus pocketed the coin while his challengers were trying to figure out what his answer meant![97] Traditional Christian interpretation of Jesus's open-ended reply has been to pay taxes, not to withhold them. The Apostle Paul spent some time struggling with the question

---

[97]Funk, et al., 526.

(Romans 13:1-7), and according to conventional interpretation, comes down on the side of paying, because political leaders are appointed by God. But as pointed out above in Proper 17, Paul is hardly abandoning his argument that the strength of sin lies in the law:

"Therefore, one must be subject [to the representatives of the law – the authorities] not only because of wrath [the proper response to injustice] but also because of conscience." In other words, be subject to the law not only because of God's inevitable action in response to injustice, but because of individual conscience. He continues, "Pay to all what is due them – taxes to whom taxes are due, revenue to whom revenue is due, respect to whom respect is due, honor to whom honor is due." Behind these words is the call to resistance against unjust taxes, unearned and undeserved riches; resistance to those to whom no respect or honor is due because their actions do not command respect or honor.[98]

Paul's response is just as subversive as Jesus's ambiguous answer. Any Jew would know that even though Caesar's image is everywhere – on coins, on monuments (the first century equivalent of billboards, advertising Caesar's divinity) – the earth belongs to God. "The earth is the Lord's, and all that is in it, the world, and those who live in it; for he has founded it on the seas, and established it on the rivers" (Psalm 24:1). "I am the Lord, and there is no other; besides me there is no god" (Isaiah 45:5). Caesar is entitled to his coins, but God owns the universe.

In Thessalonica, Paul was calling for allegiance to a God of distributive justice-compassion, and the radical abandonment of self-interest – the same message that Jesus preached during his lifetime, and for which he was crucified. In those opening words of the letter that seem so innocuous Paul was calling for people to serve "a living and true God," not the Emperor. As John Dominic Crossan puts it:

. . . Paul believes absolutely that "Jesus" or the "Messiah/Christ" or the "Lord" all refer to the same

---

[98]See p. 219.

person. . . . On the one hand, "lord" was a polite term usable by slave to master or disciple to teacher. On the other, "the Lord" meant the emperor himself. What we see here is what Gustav Adolf Deissman described . . . as "the early establishment of a polemical parallelism between the cult of Christ and the cult of Cesar in the application of the term *kyrios*, 'lord'" [citation omitted]. Or, if you prefer, polemical parallelism as high treason."[99]

Perhaps 1 Thessalonians is read at the end of Year A because Paul speaks in this letter about Jesus coming again. "Jesus, who rescues us from the wrath that is coming." For over two thousand years, these words have meant future apocalyptic judgment, not present-day participation in Jesus's ongoing program of restoring God's distributive justice compassion (the natural order of the universe). Jesus and Paul, and other martyrs to the anti-imperial Christian cause, have taught Covenant, nonviolence, distributive justice-compassion, and peace; not piety as social values violently enforced, war, and insistence on victory as a prerequisite to peace.

The words "wrath of God" are not generally understood to mean God's (or anyone's) proper response to injustice. Instead, those words conventionally mean judgment, leading to punishment for wrongdoing. But under a nonviolent Covenant the proper response from God or prophetic humanity is not judgment, but outrage that warns of consequences set in motion by injustice. Those consequences have nothing to do with retribution, payback, or punishment. The consequences set in motion by injustice include poor health, premature death, crime, drug abuse, economic collapse, war, and the extinction of life-forms (including human), among others.

After the outrage (righteous anger) comes the wrath of God as direct action. But direct action as Covenant is not violence. Instead, the "wrath of God" expresses itself in radical self-denial (kenosis).[100] *Kenotic wrath* in Covenant terms is the only proper response to injustice. The most obvious example for Christians is

---

[99]Crossan and Reed, 166.

[100]*See* Raven, Appendix Two.

Jesus – whom Paul and Christian theologians proclaimed was God's direct kenotic action on earth to restore God's distributive justice.[101] For postmodern, post-Christian, non-theists, a kenotic God is, as Crossan puts it, "the beating heart of the universe . . . [a god] whose presence is justice and life, but whose absence is injustice and death."[102] Kenotic action – whether on the part of God, Jesus, Paul, or anyone – requires a radical trust that is beyond simple piety.

In another seeming irrelevancy among the readings for Proper 24, Moses tries again to get God to pledge to stay with his people, for the sake of God's reputation if nothing else. God says he will stay with them, but he makes no promises about the outcome. "I will be gracious to whom I will be gracious, and will show mercy on whom I will show mercy." In other words, God will do whatever God will do, and meanwhile, you can see my backside. . . . Less polite language strongly suggests itself here. God is saying that nonviolent Covenant means distributive justice cannot be codified – despite Moses later carrying another copy of the Ten Commandments back down the mountain (Exodus 34:1-29). God is just, and the world belongs to God. Throughout the history of the Jewish people, God causes the rain to fall on the just and the unjust; God sometimes abandons his people, whether or not they have acted with injustice; and whether anyone believes in or accepts God as God, if justice is served, God favors that one. Isaiah 45:1-7 confirms God's alliance with the conqueror Cyrus.

One may well ask, why bother with this theological argument? Because if John Shelby Spong is correct, and Christianity must either change or die, one of the first changes must be to jettison the superstition that Jesus will return bodily from the sky to save the elect and condemn unbelievers. Such dogma might have made sense in the first century or two, but only if we assume that first century folk were unable to distinguish between metaphor and everyday physical realities. Beyond that, however, such dogma is highly useful to Empire, whether it be first century Rome or twenty-first century global entities. Magical,

---

[101]Philippians 2:1-13, (see p. 231).

[102]Crossan and Reed, 291.

otherworldly, life-after-death belief distracts people from the injustices they suffer, and robs them of the power to do anything about it. As soon as people start claiming the just consequences of kenotic wrath, the Empire is in jeopardy. Soon the prisons begin to fill, torture becomes legal, and heads begin to roll.

Proper 25
Parousia – The Coming of the Lord – Part II

Deuteronomy 34:1-12; Leviticus 19:1-2, 15-18;
Psalm 90:1-6, 13-17; Psalm 1; 1 Thessalonians 2:1-8;
Matthew 22:34-46

Paul's letter leads by stages into the heart of his pastoral message, which is meant to encourage and support the work of the community he founded. That community was likely a mostly Greek/pagan group of people, who may have been attached to a synagogue in Thessolonika. These folks would have accepted the Jewish God of the Covenant, and its insistence on justice, but likely would have balked at the more esoteric demands of Jewish law (*see* Leviticus 1-18, and 20-26, along with the verses skipped in Leviticus 19, which are never mentioned in the RCL). Once they accepted Paul's interpretation of the life and teachings of Jesus, they would have run into opposition from both the ruling Roman system and Jewish tradition.

In this week's section of Paul's letter to the Thessalonians,[103] he continues to remind them of their common experience together, and to assure them of their mutual love and support in carrying on the work: ". . . just as we have been approved by God to be entrusted with the message of the Gospel, even so we speak, not to please mortals, but to please God who tests our hearts." Then in verse 8 he says, "So deeply do we care for you that we are determined to share with you not only the Gospel of God but also our own selves. . . ."

The theme for the week is love, illustrated by Paul's pastoral promise, and emphasized by the story from Matthew, in which Jesus quotes his contemporary teacher, the Judean Rabbi Hillel: "You are to love the Lord your God with all you heart and all your

---

[103]2 Thessalonians was not written by Paul.

soul and all your mind . . . and . . . you are to love your neighbor as yourself." Matthew's Jesus reminds the Pharisees that "On these two commandments hangs everything in the Law and the Prophets." Indeed, the Elves not only cherry pick Leviticus to prove the point, they bring the story of the establishment of the Covenant to an end with the death of Moses. From this point on, we see the Hebrew people into the promised land, but the emphasis for the remainder of Year A and the season of Advent that opens Year B is on the prophets, who – according to Christian hegemony – foretell the coming of Jesus, the Messiah, the ultimate fulfillment of God's love for humanity (*see* John 3:16).

We could leave the sermon at that, which would cover all the bases usually covered by conventional Christian piety: Title: "Caring and Sharing"; content: Love God, love your neighbors, because Jesus/God loves you – as proved by the death of God's only Son in order to save us from sin. The closing hymn is St. Anne, based on Psalm 90. We can get out early in plenty of time to watch the game. The words in these readings are so familiar, and so buried in traditional theology, that it takes serious scholarly work to find out what the message really is.

Contrary to the conclusion hinted at by the Elves, the Covenant is far from fulfilled whether in the death of Moses, or the death of Jesus. Paul reminds the Thessalonians of how badly he and Silas were treated in Philippi, and how they apparently met the same kind of opposition in Thessalonika. We concentrate on the miracle in Philippi, recorded by Luke in Acts 16:16-40, where an angel releases them from prison, and they convert their fellow prisoners as well as the guard. What we don't consider is why they were arrested for disturbing the peace in the first place.[104] In addition, Luke/Acts suggests in Acts 17 that what happened in Thessalonika was a fight perpetrated by "jealous Jews." So long as Paul's message is construed as trying to convince people to believe in a resuscitated corpse, brought back to life to "save" sinners, and so long as we concentrate on the "miracle" of earthquakes causing prison doors to open so that the Lord's servants can escape their unfair imprisonment, Christianity will

---

[104]*See* Raven, 103.

continue to miss the point.

The point Paul was making was that Jesus died in the service of distributive justice-compassion, while pointing to the kingdom of God instead of the empire of Caesar. Local synagogue leaders in Thessalonika were likely miffed when Paul came along and poached their members away into his communities. But did those non-Jewish, pagan "God believers" join because of belief in a dead Messiah who promised to come again and violently overthrow the empire? Did they join because they could avoid the more difficult customs of Jewish law? Or did they join because they were deeply attracted to a radical way of life in which everything was shared in common, and from which no one was excluded? Were they excited by a community that offered an alternative to Roman imperial political systems that worked to keep injustice firmly in place? Did they prefer to give their spiritual allegiance to a *covenantal* God instead of the all too corruptible human emperor?

These questions lead to answers that are still dangerous in today's world. When Paul writes, "we speak, not to please mortals, but to please God who tests our hearts" he is not talking about trying to convince people to believe, but to trust God's justice (with all your heart, soul, and mind) and live in a radically inclusive, radically self-denying, way (love your neighbor as yourself). The heart test comes when the spiritual community you have been a part of all your life throws you out because your attitude violates the rules. The heart test comes when you lose your job for union organizing, or calling the boss on his sexual harassment. The heart test comes with the midnight knock on the door from the authorities, not from intervening divine judgment.

When Paul writes, "So deeply do we care for you that we are determined to share with you not only the Gospel of God but also our own selves," he means that he and his fellow travelers are willing to give whatever they have, including their lives, in order to further the work of restoring God's realm of distributive justice-compassion. Belief in a future apocalyptic return of an avenging Messiah has nothing to do with it. Paul was convinced that time was short for restoring God's realm of distributive justice-compassion. He was convinced that God would act again within his lifetime, as God had with Jesus, and that all those who signed onto the Great Work would see that kingdom come. For many twenty-first century thinkers, whether Christian or not, the time for turning humanity from its destructive imperial mind-set is also short. Some environmentalists now predict that the last of the great glaciers that provide living water for the driest portions of the Planet will be gone by 2035. That is well within the lifetime of the majority of folks today. The effect of such a loss on the planetary environment and on the quality of human life is unimaginable.

Some twenty-first century Christians are beginning to realize that the old idea that Jesus is coming again, so why worry about the condition of the world is not a wise position to take. "Stewardship" of the Planet for human use is not enough. Some are beginning to realize that life is a web, and all beings are part of it. Members of first century Christian communities were likely not thinking in terms of environmental justice. Twenty-first century Christians cannot afford to do likewise.

Proper 26
Parousia – The Coming of the Lord –
Part III

Joshua 3:7-17; Micah 3:5-12; Psalm 107:1-7, 33-37; Psalm 43;
1 Thessalonians 2:9-13; Matthew 23:1-12

John Dominic Crossan's interpretation[105] of the Apostle
Paul's theology as revealed in his authentic letters can be and is
debated among Christian scholars and theologians. That said,
Crossan's argument points the way for a transformation in
Christian thought that matches the postmodern, twenty-first
century intellect. Serious thinkers are not interested in a spirituality
that finds its meaning outside the boundaries of the known
universe – evidenced by the "brain drain," as disillusioned
Christians take their minds anywhere but church on Sunday
mornings.

The cherry-picked portion of Paul's letter to the Thessalonians
seems at first glance to hardly be relevant to how Christianity
might change, and thereby avoid the death foretold by John Shelby
Spong. Paul is reminding his readers how difficult the work was
in their community. "Night and day" – 24/7 – toiling to save
sinners: "pleading that you lead a life worthy of God. . . ." So often
leading a "life worthy of God" means following the Ten
Commandments, marriage between a man and a woman, no sex
outside of that marriage, and recently in the U.S., the right to keep
and carry guns of all varieties, and to do as we please with our
property – financial, commercial, agricultural, or personal.

But Crossan suggests that is about as far from what Paul and
the community in Thessalonika were doing as one can get. Paul's
message to the communities he founded around the Mediterranean
was that Jesus died because he preached a kingdom/realm of
justice-compassion ruled by a God – even a kenotic God – whose

---

[105]Crossan and Reed, 124-177.

distributive, radical fairness directly challenged Roman imperial theology. The 24/7 "labor and toil" that Paul and his companions engaged in was the highly dangerous project of preaching that same message and the absolute necessity of encouraging and supporting the members of the community to live the radical denial of self-interest that a serious acceptance of Jesus's message entailed. The "God who calls you into his own kingdom and glory" was not Caesar; therefore not only was preaching such a life and such a God – as Crossan says – high treason. Living such a life meant signing onto a continuing subversion. Martyrs were made.

In those circumstances, the only hope was a hope for vindication upon the return (*parousia*) of the Christ. Here's where after two thousand years of dogma, the Christian train is in danger of permanently leaving the track.

> Notice Paul's use of... technical terms for visitation and reception. He uses *parousia* for "our Lord Jesus at his *coming*" in 1 Thessalonians 2:19, "the *coming* of our Lord Jesus with all his saints" in 3:13, "the *coming* of the Lord" in 4:15, and "the *coming*" of our Lord Jesus Christ" in 5:23. . . . That metaphor controls the entire discussion (emphasis in text).[106]

Two of the above verses are left out of the readings cherry-picked for the next couple of weeks by our intrepid Elves. But it is important to read the entire letter, not just the portions selected to emphasize the meaning agreed upon by Christian Church organizers, who ended up collaborating with Empire, not disarming it. Writing about God calling people into his kingdom and the Christ coming again in glory were the second and third counts of high treason that could be charged against Paul. Only the emperor came as parousia – as procession, as visitation, as establishing and confirming his power over everything from coins to buildings to economies, to military control. The metaphor will be complete when Paul (and the Elves) gets to what happens along the parousial route into the city on the part of the Emperor, and into a transformed world on the part of the Christ. For now, Paul's

---

[106]Ibid., 168.

point is to bolster the courage of his people in the continuing struggle for distributive justice and peace.

The other suggested readings for this Sunday – often celebrated as Reformation Sunday and the Feast of All Saints – are not irrelevant to this discussion. Setting aside Paul's essay on the struggle to reestablish God's realm of distributive justice-compassion, illustrated by the profound difference between the coming of the emperor and the coming of the Christ, we still have the call to Covenant. Joshua's credentials as the successor of Moses are established as the story-teller's great leader motif continues. Not to press the metaphor too far, but the entrance of the Ark – the Presence of the Hebrew God – into the promised land resonates with the parousia of an earthly emperor. The very elements of the natural world stand back in reverence when the priests' feet touch the waters of the Jordan River.

But the march of the normalcy of civilization into retributive systems soon overtakes the best intentions of God himself. Some unknown hundreds of years after the arrival of the Hebrew people in Palestine, Micah – an eighth century B.C.E. prophet of the common people, not the intelligentsia – condemns Jerusalem and its rulers and prophets for their injustice. A millennium later, Matthew's Jesus begins a series of condemnations of corrupt "scholars and Pharisees," who only pretend to abide by Mosaic law. Matthew's diatribe is against the same kinds of prophets and rulers that Micah prophesied about. Matthew is defending his own fledgling community, under increasing threat from the equally endangered Jewish community, whose central home has been destroyed. The danger of losing any connection to Covenant, nonviolence, distributive justice-compassion, and peace is great on both sides. Matthew seems to be erring on the side of exclusive piety: Only Jesus can be called "Rabbi," he maintains. With Jesus, the prevailing order will be reversed: "Those who promote themselves will be demoted" and vice versa.

Matthew seems to have forgotten what he earlier reported Jesus had said about the way to counter the fear that he and his community were facing. Serendipitously, one of the readings for the Feast of All Saints in Year A is Matthew 5:1-12: "Congratulations to the poor in spirit! Heaven's domain belongs to them. Congratulations to those who grieve! They will be consoled. Congratulations to the gentle! They will inherit the earth. Congratulations to those who hunger and thirst for justice! They will have a feast. . . ." Do not be afraid of persecution, because you belong to the realm of God – the kingdom of distributive justice-compassion – heaven's domain. All you have to do is trust it – like the birds of the air and the lilies of the field.[107]

If anyone needs an example of how dangerous that message is for today's followers of the Christian way – or anyone who works to establish distributive justice-compassion as the grounding for human societies – we only need to consider the words of Sarah Palin, the 2008 Republican nominee for vice president. She defined the parts of the country that would vote for her and presidential nominee John McCain as "pro-America," leaving the obvious conclusion that anyone outside of those areas who might prefer the Democratic ticket is "anti-America."[108] Crowds in Palin's and McCain's rallies called for Barack Obama's death.[109] Indeed, one of the many threats against him in the last week before the election was serious enough to result in FBI arrests and media coverage.[110] Readers might argue that this is "politics." But – inflammatory reports notwithstanding – Barack Obama came from a Christian tradition that is steeped in distributive justice, civil rights, and liberation theology. Right-wing Christians are the ones supporting the Republican campaign, and encouraging piety, war, and victory as prerequisites to peace. Once again, "Christianity" – as it is defined broadly by the media – has aligned itself with Empire.

However, before liberal Christians claim Elijah's righteous mantle, strike the Potomac waters, and begin the triumphant parousia into world power, pay attention to Paul's words to the Thessalonians: " . . . [W]e dealt with each one of you like a father

---

[107]See p. 57.

[108]http://mobile.washingtonpost.com/ns.jsp?key= 295812&rc=trail_po

[109]http://www.huffingtonpost.com/ 2008/10/14/ palin-rally-kill-him-yell_n_134597.html

[110]http://abcnews.go.com/Blotter/story?id=6123157&page=1

with his children, urging and encouraging you and pleading that you lead a life worthy of God, who calls you into *his* own kingdom and glory." Micah spells out what the normalcy of civilization looks like: "Its rulers give judgment for a bribe, its priests teach for a price, its prophets give oracles for money; yet they lean upon the Lord and say, 'Surely the Lord is with us.'" As Matthew's Jesus said, as he sent his disciples out "like sheep to a pack of wolves . . . you must be as sly as a snake and as simple as a dove" (10:16). So vote, and stay awake. The fall out of Covenant and into Empire comes *like a thief in the night* (1 Thess. 5:2). By the time the warning sounds, it will already be too late.

Proper 27
Parousia – The Coming of the Lord –
Part IV

Joshua 24:1-3a, 14-25; Wisdom of Solomon 6:12-20;
Amos 5:18-24; Psalm 78:1-7; Psalm 70; 1 Thessalonians 4:13-18;
Matthew 25:1-13

The parable of the wise and foolish virgins cannot be attributed to the historical Jesus. The story makes a distinction between who is in, and who is out; who will be accepted, and who will not. It is Matthew's favorite theme, but it is not Jesus's message. It is Matthew's interpretation of that message, in the context of the destruction of the Jewish Temple, and the decentralization of the Jewish religion from Jerusalem Temple to local synagogue, or in John Dominic Crossan's words, " . . . the transmutation of Temple Judaism into Pharisaic and then rabbinic Judaism."[111] But traditional Christianity believes otherwise. According to Matthew's Jesus, he will come in the middle of the night, and those who are not ready will not be let into the kingdom of God. In this context, Matthew's parable goes right along with Paul's description of what fundamentalist Christians call "the Rapture": "For the Lord himself with a cry of command, with the archangel's call and with the sound of God's trumpet, will descend from heaven, and the dead in Christ will rise first. Then we who are alive, who are left [behind?] will be caught up on the clouds together with them to meet the Lord in the air. . . ." This is total nonsensical gobbledegook to postmodern, educated, scientifically sophisticated minds. Liberal Christians run screaming with laughter from that kind of preaching. If John Shelby Spong and the Jesus Seminar scholars are to be taken seriously, if Christianity is going to actually change and not die along with other discredited superstitions, the argument presented by Crossan and Reed has to

---

[111]Crossan and Reed, 173.

be worked through.

Crossan argues that Paul and the group in Thessalonika had come under heavy persecution by the Roman authorities. Some in the community may have been killed (martyred), while Paul himself managed to escape with the help of others. Paul's regret at the deaths that saved him may explain some of the defensiveness that arises in the letter (*see* 1 Thessalonians 1:7-8; 2:10). But what is more important is a question that was profound to first century Pharisaic Jews and others who believed in an eventual resurrection of all the dead when God at last establishes his kingdom of distributive justice-compassion. That question was, when God acts, what will happen to those who have already died in the struggle for justice?

Crossan talks about a Jewish apocalypse, written fifty years after the destruction of Jerusalem (which must have felt like the end for sure to those who lived through it). That apocalypse asks, "What will those do who were before me, or we ourselves, or those who come after us?" God answers that God's judgment is like a circle. There is no first, no last, no beginning, no end, but all are saved at once. The Gospel folk song, "Will the Circle Be Unbroken Bye and Bye?" asks and answers the question in the same way. But Paul's theology is different. His answer blows the tradition out of the tub. As pointed out in last week's discussion, Paul's use of the metaphor of parousia as it was experienced by first century participants in the Roman Empire controls the entire discussion.

The parousia of the Roman emperor was a visitation, a demonstration of total, complete power over the people. The Roman emperor was a god of the living and of the dead. In any first century town, the first encounter the emperor's procession would have had was with the city of the dead – mausoleums, graves, tombs – on the outskirts of the town. Then, the procession met the living citizens, who accompanied the conquering hero into the city, and presented him with the key – or feasting, or accolades, or tribute, or whatever. Paul – pressing mystical metaphor as far as it can go – says that when the Christ comes (parousia) the same thing will happen. But because God has already raised Jesus the Christ from the dead into God's realm, the people will have to meet him in the air – first the dead will be raised, then the living will join the procession. But the procession does not stay in the air, nor did the emperor's procession stay on the outskirts of town among the graves. The people met the procession, and accompanied it back into the city. In the same way, the living would accompany the Christ back to the world. But it would not be the same old world of retributive injustice. For Paul, "The parousia of the Lord was not about destruction of earth and relocation to heaven, but about a world in which violence and injustice are transformed into purity and holiness. And of course . . . a transformed *world* would demand not just spiritual souls, but renewed *bodies*."[112] The Gospel story about Jesus's triumphal entry into Jerusalem is a parody along the same lines.[113]

Without stealing a march on next week's reading, what is missing at this point is the timing. When will God's kingdom come? When will the Lord arrive? When will the transformation happen? Crossan sends us to 1 Corinthians 15 and 2 Corinthians 3:17-18: "And all of us . . . are being transformed into the same image from one degree of glory to another." The verb tense is crucial. It is not past, it is not future. It is present-perfect: we *are being* transformed. The work of restoring God's distributive justice-compassion was begun by Jesus, and continues with us.

With this interpretation, the alternative readings for Proper 27 from the Wisdom of Solomon are anachronisms. The Elves have cherry-picked a portion of the poem praising Wisdom (Sophia), which might seem to tie in with the cautionary tale told by Matthew's Jesus. But The Wisdom of Solomon has nothing to do with the context that Paul was writing about in 50 C.E. (whether Crossan's work is considered or not), nor with the judgmental opinions of the writer of Matthew 30 years later – even though the poetry includes the words, "the desire for wisdom leads to a kingdom." The metaphor could be stretched into something about the wisdom of the seamless realm of the natural world where Covenant happens without thought, but we have already redefined one metaphor (parousia) about as much as we can. Cramming the

---

[112]Crossan and Reed, 170.

[113]Mark 11:1-11; Borg and Crossan, 4.

Wisdom of Solomon into either Crossan's form, or the form put forth by those determined Elves is unnecessary, and unfair to the Alexandrian Jew who wrote it.

The story of Joshua, on the other hand, does remind us once more of the Covenant – the Covenant that is discussed and eventually agreed-upon by the people, not the "wisdom" of the natural universe. We skip most of Joshua's story, which is disappointing. For some reason, only children are allowed to learn about the Battle of Jericho – the template for future attempts by the U.S. Air Force to harass and capture Manuel Noriega, and for torturing prisoners at Guantanamo.[114] The story does its best to prove to us that Joshua was the proper candidate to replace Moses. He parts the waters of the Jordan River; he has a vision of God, who tells him to remove his sandals because he is standing on holy ground (5:13-15). He conquers most of the territory of Canaan, and divides it among the tribes. Finally in chapter 24, after several lost battles, he challenges the people to renew the Covenant with God. He warns them several times that if they enter into this Covenant, God will destroy them if they break it. The people pledge to forsake all foreign gods, and to keep God's laws. Then Joshua tells them they are therefore witnesses against themselves if they do not keep the agreement, and he sets up a stone as a witness.

Understanding Paul's theology about the "second coming" of the Christ is important because if Crossan is correct, and the theology is not about a future moment but a present, here-and-now, ongoing process of transformation, then we are talking about our own responsibility for bringing God's distributive justice-compassion into being. Just as Joshua told the Hebrews, once we choose God's Covenant and sign on to God's work, we have forsaken all other gods, including emperors living and dead, and the theology of empire. We no longer subscribe to piety, war, victory; instead we stand with nonviolence, distributive justice-compassion, and peace.

This is what the prophet Amos is calling for in his diatribe against the retributive injustice that holds sway in the world. All

---

[114]http://www.nowpublicom/ health/ david-gray-warns- torture- music-guantanamo

we have to do is "let justice roll down like the waters, and righteousness (just living) like an ever-flowing stream." Amos doesn't talk about some time in the future. He asks, who wants the day of the Lord (final judgment)? It is darkness, not light; it is ending, not salvation. Instead of praying for the "day of the Lord," Amos says, do justice now and live in the light of God's favor.

Proper 28
Parousia – The Coming of the Lord –
Part V

*Judges 4:1-7; Zephaniah 1:7, 12-18; Psalm 123; Psalm 90:1-12;
1 Thessalonians 5:1-11; Matthew 25:14-30*

The prevailing conventional theme for Proper 28 is judgment
– retribution – payback for sin. Because the Canaanites oppressed
the Israelites, God delivered their armies into the hands of Barak.
But in a nice twist, Barak doesn't get the credit. The seductress
Jael is the one who kills the Canaanite general Sisera, but we are
not supposed to read the whole story. The Elves apparently have
decided a) that God's stated intention is enough ("I will deliver
him into your hands"); and b) we should not look too closely at
exactly what Jael was doing under that rug with Sisera before she
pounded the tent peg into his skull. It's retribution, all right, but
maybe a bit too intense for Sunday morning (Joshua 4:8-5:31).

Likewise, Jesus's over-the-top joke about the normalcy of
civilization gets watered down by Matthew into a judgment
against people who don't have enough faith to wait for Jesus to
come again. The master leaves the first slave thirty thousand silver
coins. Assuming each coin is an ounce, that's three hundred
thousand dollars according to recent spot prices. It's also not a
great deal of money for the twenty-first century trading floor,
given the billions now required to rescue global financial markets.
But in the first century of the common era, the first two slaves
received a fortune, and the third received what amounts to about
twenty years of wages. By this time the disciples – who had been
with Jesus long enough to know what's coming – must have been
listening closely for the punch line. Unfortunately we don't really
know what the punch line may have been. The story certainly
reflects the unjust economics of Empire, but as it stands – whether
in Luke's version or Matthew's – the disciples must have just
shrugged. So what? The rich get richer and the poor get poorer.

Matthew resorts to stating the obvious, then adds insult to injury by having the master throw the slave – who was afraid to invest in the stock market on his behalf – into the utter darkness where, as the NRSV puts it, "there will be weeping and gnashing of teeth." Somehow "faith" or "belief" in Jesus acquires some means of being measured, and those who have more will get more, and those who have less will be thrown under the bus by a vengeful God.

Meanwhile, Paul says the Christ will come like a thief in the night, so we better be ready – sober, not drunk; awake, not asleep; morally pure, not caught in the night of darkness and sin like that hapless slave who buried his faith in the backyard. Ho Hum. Remove the Elves' insistence on "judgment," and what we have here is a series of completely unrelated snippets – cherry-picking, if not proof-texting, at its worst. Back to Crossan and Reed and the chapter on *The Golden Age, or As Golden As It Gets*.

This week's section of Paul's letter to the Thessalonians follows immediately last week's explanation of what the arrival – the visitation – the parousia – of the Christ will be like. The use of that word reminded Paul's community in Thessalonika that Jesus, who had become the Christ, was greater than all the emperors of Rome. The emperors come in war, and the people welcome the entourage into the city in victorious procession. But the Christ will be met in the realm of spirit, and will be accompanied by the living and the dead to a transformed earth where distributive justice is established at last, and the golden age can begin. The question is the timing. Crossan argues that Paul was convinced this parousia – and the transformation – would happen within his lifetime, or at least within the lifetime of the people he organized into communities. What is important to realize, however, is that the anticipation of the parousia is not passive. The work of restoring God's realm of distributive justice-compassion starts as soon as anyone accepts Jesus as Lord.

Those words, "accept Jesus as Lord," have become a litmus test for belief in a resuscitated corpse instead of a radical repudiation of the authority of the emperor – or the president, the prime minister, the bishop, the pope, the stock holders, the boss – whomever or whatever stands in the way of distributive justice.

Christianity long ago jumped the tracks, and likely within a few days of Jesus's death. By the time Paul began organizing communities, the inevitable tension with imperial authority had split the followers of Jesus into several sometimes feuding factions. Some of this is reflected in Paul's letters to the Corinthians, as well as 1 Thessalonians, and in the contradictions found in Luke/Acts and the letters attributed to Paul, but not accepted as genuinely Paul's.

To accept Jesus as Lord means signing onto the program. Once everyone is participating in the program – the restoration of God's distributive justice – we have a transformed world into which to welcome the returning Christ. But Christianity soon found itself not only sidetracked, but propelled into a virtual train wreck of exclusivity, intolerance, and deliberate ignorance of the world we live in. Worse, is the embrace of the theology of Empire (piety war victory), and the repudiation of Covenant (nonviolent, distributive justice-compassion, and peace).

The Elves have also misused the prophet Zephaniah's warning about the great "day of the Lord." The selective words go along with the sentence that Matthew's Jesus suggests should be meted out to the slave who buried his talent and his master's reputation. But Zephaniah's "judgment" is about the need for religious renewal in this world. The prophet is calling for commitment to God's vision of a world without violence, injustice, and oppression. Last week's quotation from Amos was more direct: He asks, who wants the day of the Lord (final judgment)? It is darkness, not light; it is ending, not salvation. Instead of praying for the "day of the Lord," Amos says, do justice now and live in the light of God's favor.

> Paul, like Jesus before him, did not simply proclaim the imminent end of evil, injustice, and violence here below upon this earth. They proclaimed it had already begun (first surprise!) and that believers were called to participate cooperatively with God (second surprise!!) in what was now a process in human time and not just a flash of divine light (third surprise!!!).[115]

---

[115]Crossan and Reed, 176.

Even though the timing has been shown to be wrong (so far), Crossan continues, " . . . the first and fundamental challenge they offer to Christian faith is this: Do you believe the process of making the world a just place has begun and what are you doing about joining the program?" The real story Jesus told as he and his band camped beside the Sea of Galliee, not far from Tiberias, probably went like this:

"There was a rich man who was planning an extended marketing trip to the Roman colonies in Syria. Before he left, he turned over his business operations to three slaves."

One of the women is cleaning fish poached from the lake and throwing them into a cauldron steaming in the fire. She pauses a moment and says, "I heard something about this from Mary's uncle Mordecai not two hours ago."

Jesus looks around at the company. They have seen that look before. "To the first he gave thirty thousand silver coins . . ."

Several snickers are heard as several more fish find their way into the soup. The woman starts shaking her head. A child runs into the group, screaming about some outrage his brother has perpetrated. Another woman catches him, and quiets him down to listen.

"He gave twelve thousand silver coins to the second, and to the third, six thousand silver coins. The first slave immediately used his master's name to buy the most lucrative farm within miles, and sure enough, when the crops were harvested he had increased his investment ten-fold."

"Sounds like that thief Jered," grumbles one of the men. "Put my whole family off the land and here we are."

"The second tripled his money by seizing all the land bordering the lake and charging the fishermen for access, and requiring that they buy back the fish they caught before selling them in the market."

Nothing is heard now but the bubbling stew. This is too close for joking. They wouldn't be throwing contraband fish into a pot liberated from someone too rich to miss it if not for the recent edict handed down by Herod Antipas.

"The third slave took his six thousand pieces of silver and buried them in the master's kitchen garden."

Jesus smiles a private smile, reaches for a loaf of bread, breaks off a hunk, chews, and waits.

Proper 29
Liberation – Christ the King

Ezekiel 34:11-16, 20-24; Psalm 100; Psalm 95:1-7a;
Ephesians 1:15-23; Mathew 25: 31-46

Matthew's Jesus once again has contradicted himself. With his parable of the vineyard laborers (Matthew 20:1-16), Matthew's Jesus illustrated the nature of the Covenant offered by God.[116] The parable was not about the reversal of fortune for the greedy or the self-righteous ("the last will be first and the first last"). Jesus was illustrating how in God's realm the reward is bestowed whenever the program is joined. That is the nature of God's Covenant. But by the time the writer of Matthew got around to chapter 25, he was more interested in maintaining law and order in his early Christian community. Anyone who does not provide food, drink, hospitality, and healing for the poor (or, as the Jesus Seminar scholars put it, "the most inconspicuous" in the community) will be separated forever from God's realm. The writer has forgotten how in God's realm the rain falls on the just and the unjust. He has forgotten Jesus's prime directive: Love Your Enemies. He does not understand (authentic) Paul's breakthrough concept of grace.[117]

Nevertheless, among the most beloved phrases in Christianity (in addition to John 3:16), is the last judgment by Matthew's Jesus: "I was hungry and you gave me something to eat; I was thirsty and you gave me something to drink; I was a foreigner and you showed me hospitality; I was naked and you clothed me; I was ill and you visited me; I was in prison and you came to see me." The astounded followers were told that whenever they did any of these things for the "least of these" (NRSV) they had done them for Jesus; they had participated with Jesus in God's great work of distributive justice-compassion. These words are words of empowerment as well as challenge, inspiration as well as

---

[116]*See* p. 225.

[117]Raven, 115.

admonition. These words are the catalyst for countless church programs from soup kitchens to homeless shelters, and for institutions such as World Vision, Church World Service, and Habitat for Humanity, without which the Planet would be in worse shape than it is.

Unfortunately, these words have become easy piety, evoking guilt among the faithful of a Sunday morning. Who has time to volunteer at the soup kitchen, or start a thrift shop, or join a hospital or prison ministry? So we dig into our wallets and give a little extra to support the church's "outreach" programs, especially in hard economic times. But deep down, we know it's not enough. "Cheap grace" is exactly that. We know we are really part of the goat troop that will be sent over the cliff into "eternal punishment."

The portion selected from Ephesians is not much help in this regard. By the time this letter was written, in the last third of the first century, the Apostle Paul was long gone, and a cosmic view of the Church of Jesus Christ was well underway. "Paul's Prayer," as the reading is named in the NRSV, has little to do with either final judgment as preached by the writer of Matthew, or justice, as called for by the prophet Ezekiel. Instead, the pious "saints of the Church" are called to realize some future hope in a glorious inheritance yet to come to those who believe. For people oppressed by various forms of Empire, there is no way out. There is only the uncertain hope for a better life after death. The Church itself is caught in the seemingly inevitable march into the normalcy of retributive systems.

In 1987, I went to Esteli, Nicaragua, with a group called "Escuela Nica." The purpose was to bring North Americans to the heart of the Sandinista movement, to see the other side of the Contra War being waged by the United States in an effort to restore the Samoza regime to power. For five weeks we were to study Spanish, get to know the Nicaraguan culture, history, and people, and along with that, study liberation theology as expressed in Ernesto Cardenal's *The Gospel in Solentiname*. What an opportunity for direct action, for making a difference in people's lives, for learning how the poor and disenfranchised live, and doing something about changing it!

I very nearly was not accepted to the program because of my answer to one question, discussed in a preliminary interview. The question was, What do you hope to gain from this experience? What is in it for you? The question confused me. It's not about me, I explained. It's what my particular expertise can bring to the people there. I listed my qualifications: leadership, education, music, organizational skills. But that is not what was wanted. Terms like "poor and disenfranchised" "victims," "the least of these," or as the Jesus Seminar scholars put it, the "inconspicuous," denigrate and disempower the people they describe. What the interviewer wanted me to realize was that the people I was going to visit had a tremendous gift for me. My job was to discover that gift and bring it back.

Here it is: Forget grandiose ideas about saving the poor, transforming their lives, making a difference, winning the Nobel Prize for Peace. The way to empower people is to work in partnership with them to improve their lot – whatever it is. The concept is as old as time: Give a man a fish and you feed him for a day. Teach a man to fish and you feed him for a lifetime. Behind the saying is the realization of a profound equality that overturns oppressive thought forms about "power-over" others. The mission is to recognize the inherent power of oppressed people. When people are empowered, they can pull themselves out of the worst kind of oppression.

In El Salvador, in 1991 (this time on a trip sponsored by CISPES[118]), we visited a village of returnees from exile who had created a neighborhood in the heart of San Salvador on top of a waste dump site. They had tapped into the city water supply (illegally), and built houses literally in the midst of mud and garbage, which ran down the middle of the mud-packed streets. Inside the tin-roofed cinderblock houses, the packed earth floors were spotless. Behind the houses, flying in the sunlit breezes, was bright-colored laundry: jeans, dresses, jackets, shirts. In front of the houses, within mere feet of the open sewer, were flower and herb gardens. Little girls with dirty bare feet chased each other around the yards in immaculate dresses.

---

[118]Communities in Solidarity with the People of El Salvador.

The Great Work of restoring Covenant, nonviolence, distributive justice, and peace to the Planet begins, as Dorothy said, right in our own backyard. My backyard in West Virginia looks out over some of the worst poverty in the country. West Virginia is near the bottom of the scale on income, affordable housing, education, and health when compared to other states. The following story may be apocryphal – but a friend who is the wife of a dentist swears it is true: One day a twenty-one-year-old man came to the office and said it was time to get his false teeth. Even though his teeth were in fairly good shape, it was a right of passage to have them all pulled and replaced because they would all rot anyway. Mistrust of "the government," "liberals," and outsiders is so great that the people believe that government guidelines for a healthy diet are a socialist plot whose purpose is to control their lives. Daddy ate hotdogs, Granddaddy ate hot dogs, and no government is going to tell us what to eat – let alone force us into anti-smoking programs, drug addiction counseling, AA, and other "liberal, socialist schemes" (such as mandatory seatbelts) that threaten individual freedom and property rights.

The struggle for liberation is a struggle because it is so much easier to disregard people with less education, less money, less opportunity. It is so much easier to stay away from neighborhood meetings that bog down in petty arguments between people who seem incapable of seeing the bigger, sustainable, picture that could transform their lives if only they would open their minds. Liberation is a struggle because the would-be liberators' minds are just as closed by attitudes that are determined by the labels we use, which keep oppression firmly in place.

Nothing opens minds more than respect for who one is, and the realization that we hold the keys to our own empowerment. But that kind of leadership ends all too often in death: Mohandas Ghandi was murdered by one of his own. Martin Luther King was shot down by a previously nameless drifter. Jesus himself, according to profound Christian myth, was betrayed into the hands of the Roman Empire by a follower who could not imagine a realm of distributive justice-compassion.

Look now at the reading from Ezekiel. Strip away the implied references to Jesus, the savior of the world. Imagine Ezekiel in his own milieu – exiled from Jerusalem, cut off from religious and cultural grounding. Yes, the situation is much like Matthew's Jerusalem community. Matthew may have been thinking of Ezekiel's prophetic call for judgment when he penned his own story about Christ the King, the Good Shepherd. After all, Ezekiel points out that God "will set up . . . one shepherd, my servant David, . . . and I will make with [the people] a covenant of peace. . . ." (Ezekiel 34:23-25). But what is Ezekiel really saying? The "day of the Lord" (*dies irae*) has already happened. The people have been forcibly removed from Judah to Babylon. To those survivors, Ezekiel says, the reason you are exiled is because your leaders, your shepherds, paid no attention to God's justice: "Ah, you shepherds of Israel who have been feeding yourselves! . . . You eat the fat, you clothe yourselves with the wool, you slaughter the fatlings; but you do not feed the sheep. You have not strengthened the weak, you have not healed the sick, you have not bound up the injured, you have not brought back the strayed, you have not sought the lost, but with force and harshness you have ruled them" (Ezekiel 34: 2b-5). This portion is (of course) not part of the readings for Proper 29.

Ezekiel's point is that if the leaders abandon their responsibilities, then God himself will lead the people, and will feed them with justice. The people are held accountable, and are therefore empowered. Likewise, Psalm 95 tells us that it is not only the leaders that God holds accountable, but the people as well. "O that today you would listen to [God]'s voice! Do not harden your hearts, as at Meribah, as on the day at Massah in the wilderness, when your ancestors tested me and put me to the proof, *though they had seen my work*"[119] "For forty years [God] loathed that generation and said 'They are a people whose hearts go astray, and they do not regard my ways. Therefore in my anger I swore, they shall not enter my rest.'"

Are we and the Psalmist blaming the victims here? Of course not. But the consequences of injustice apply to everyone. God's judgment (wrath) must be understood to be the proper response to injustice. We don't have to wait for some kind of "afterlife" to see

---

[119]*See* p.91.

what that wrath brings. It includes failing schools, overwhelmed medical systems, bankrupt industries, collapsed markets, political apathy, fear, violence, dysfunctional families, and a degraded biosphere.

> *Felipe: I see that when Christ spoke of the Last Judgment he didn't speak of religion, prayers, ritual; he spoke only of social needs.*
>
> *Alejandro: Let's make no mistake about that; there are religious people who think they are good people because they give aid, alms, old shoes. That's not what Christ demands in this Gospel; it's a total change in the social system.*[120]

That is the liberation struggle.

---

[120]Cardenal, Vol. 4, 52.

Bibliography

Bibliography

Bonhoeffer, Dietrich. *The Cost of Discipleship*. New York: Macmillian Publishing Company, Inc., 1976.

Borg, Marcus J. *Jesus: Uncovering the Life, Teachings, and Relevance of a Religious Revolutionary*. New York: HarperCollins, 2006.

_____ and John Dominic Crossan. *The Last Week*. San Francisco: Harper SanFrancisco, 2006.

Cardenal, Ernesto. *The Gospel in Solentiname*. Maryknoll, NY: Orbis Books, 1982.

Consultation on Common Texts. *Revised Common Lectionary*. Nashville: Abingdon Press, 1992.

Crossan, John Dominic. *God and Empire*. San Francisco: HarperSanFrancisco, 2007.

_____ and Jonathan L. Reed. *In Search of Paul: How Jesus's Apostle Opposed Rome's Empire with God's Kingdom*. San Francisco: HarperSanFrancisco, 2004.

Dewey, Arthur J., Roy W. Hoover, Lane C. McGaughy, and Daryl D. Schmidt. *The Authentic Letters of Paul: A New Reading of Paul's Rhetoric and Meaning*. Salem, OR: Polebridge Press, 2010.

Diamant, Anita. *The Red Tent*. New York: St. Martin's Press, 1997.

Dykstra, Laural A. "Living the Word," *Sojourners Magazine* (July 2008).

Fox, Matthew. *Original Blessing: A Primer in Creation Spirituality Presented in Four Paths, Twenty-Six Themes, and Two Questions*. Santa Fe, NM: Bear & Co., 1983.

_____. *The Coming of the Cosmic Christ: The Healing of Mother Earth and the Birth of a Global Renaissance*. New York: HarperCollins, 1988.

_____. *Sins of the Spirit, Blessings of the Flesh*. New York: Harmony Books, 1999.

Funk, Robert W., Roy W. Hoover, and The Jesus Seminar. *The Five Gospels*. San Francisco: HarperSanFrancisco, 1993.

Kazantzakis, Nikos. *The Last Temptation of Christ*. New York: Simon and Schuster, 1960.

Levine, Amy-Jill. *The Misunderstood Jew: The Church and the Scandal of the Jewish Jesus*. San Francisco: HarperOne, 2006.

_____, and Mark Zvi Brettler, eds. *The Jewish Annotated New Testament*. New York: Oxford University Press, 2011.

Loney, James. "118 Days: How I survived captivity in Iraq." *Sojourners Magazine* (December 2006).

McFerrin, Bobby. "The 23rd Psalm Dedicated to My Mother." New York: Original Artists, 2003.

Miller, Robert J., ed. *The Apocalyptic Jesus: A Debate*. Santa Rosa, CA: Polebridge Press, 2001.

_____. *The Complete Gospels* (4th Edition). Salem, OR: Polebridge Press, 2010.

Moore, Robert, and Douglas Gillette. *King Warrior Magician Lover*. San Francisco: HarperSanFrancisco, 1990.

National Council of Churches of Christ in the United States of America. *The Harper Collins Study Bible, New Revised Standard Version*. San Francisco: HarperCollins, 1989.

Priests for Equality. *The Inclusive Psalms*. Lanham, MD: Altamira Press, 1999.

Raven, Sea. *Theology from Exile: Commentary on the Revised Common Lectionary Vol. I, The Year of Luke*. Amazon.com, CreateSpace, 2013.

Scott, Bernard Brandon. *The Trouble With Resurrection: From Paul to the Fourth Gospel*. Salem, OR: Polebridge Press, 2010.

Smith, Dennis R. "Report on the Acts Seminar." *The 4th R* (January-February 2008).

Spong, John Shelby. *Rescuing the Bible from Fundamentalism*. San Francisco: HarperCollins, 1991.

_____. *Liberating the Gospels: Reading the Bible with Jewish Eyes*. New York: HarperCollins, 1996.

_____. *Why Christianity Must Change or Die: A Bishop Speaks to Believers In Exile* New York: HarperCollins, 1999.

Taylor, Jeremy. *Dream Work: Techniques for Discovering the Creative Power in Dreams*. New York, Paulist Press, 1983.

_____. *Where People Fly and Water Runs Uphill*. New York, Warner Books, 1992.

_____. *The Living Labyrinth: Exploring Universal Themes in Myths, Dreams, and the Symbolism of Waking Life*. New York: Paulist Press, 1998.

United Synagogue of Conservative Judaism. "Avoth, Chapter 1." http://www.uscj.org/Learning andTeaching/ DailyStudy Materials/ Mishnah Yomit/

Made in the USA
Lexington, KY
06 January 2014